W9-ABL-988

THE
HERETIC
PHARAOH

THE
HERETIC
PHARAOH

JOY COLLIER

THE JOHN DAY COMPANY / NEW YORK

*To the memory of my very dear parents
and of John Pendlebury, who together
kindled my enthusiasm for archaeology.*

Library of Congress Cataloging in Publication Data
Collier, Joy.
    The heretic pharaoh.
    First published in 1970 in London under title: King Sun.
    1. Amenhetep IV, King of Egypt, 1388–1358 B.C.
I. Title.
DT87.4.C63 1972   932'.01'0924   71–143407

The John Day Company, 257 Park Avenue South, New York, N.Y. 10010
An Intext Publisher

Printed in the United States of America
Designed by The Etheredges

CONTENTS

ACKNOWLEDGMENTS

I would like to express my sincere thanks for their assistance to Dr. Mohammed Abd-ur-Rahman, curator of the Cairo Museum and the Tutankhamen treasures; to Dr. Ramadan, who is in charge of the antiquities of Upper Egypt; and to the staff of the department of Egyptology at the British Museum. I am especially grateful for the help given me by the Egypt Exploration Society, of which I am proud to be a member. A series of most important articles in the society's annual publication, *Journal of Egyptian Archaeology,* proved invaluable. In particular, I must thank the editors and Professor R. G. Harrison for permission to use the reconstruction of Smenkhare's face from No. 52 of the journal. Finally, I must express my deep gratitude to my husband for his unfailing patience while the book was being written and his invaluable assistance in its preparation. Throughout I have used the new dating given by Professor Cyril Aldred in his scholarly study of Akhenaten, being gratified to find that in my independent researches I had reached many of his conclusions. His strong belief (which I share) in the coregency of many of the eighteenth-dynasty kings led him to allow an overlapping of reigns and a subsequent telescoping of time.

JOY COLLIER

THE
HERETIC
PHARAOH

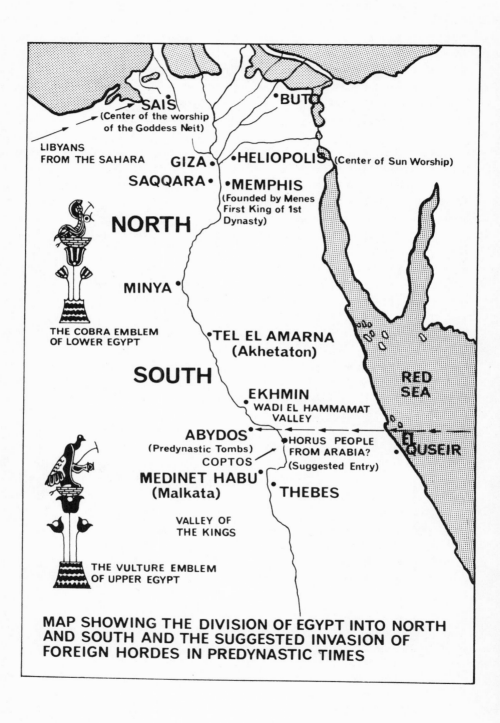

SAIS
(Center of the worship
of the Goddess Neit)

•BUTO

LIBYANS
FROM THE SAHARA

GIZA •   •HELIOPOLIS (Center of Sun Worship)

SAQQARA •   •MEMPHIS
(Founded by Menes
First King of 1st
Dynasty)

NORTH

THE COBRA EMBLEM
OF LOWER EGYPT

MINYA •

•TEL EL AMARNA
(Akhetaton)

SOUTH

EKHMIN
•   WADI EL HAMMAMAT
VALLEY

RED
SEA

ABYDOS •
(Predynastic Tombs)
COPTOS

•HORUS PEOPLE
FROM ARABIA?
(Suggested Entry)

EL
QUSEIR

MEDINET HABU •
(Malkata)   •THEBES

VALLEY OF
THE KINGS

THE VULTURE EMBLEM
OF UPPER EGYPT

MAP SHOWING THE DIVISION OF EGYPT INTO NORTH
AND SOUTH AND THE SUGGESTED INVASION OF
FOREIGN HORDES IN PREDYNASTIC TIMES

1.
FIRST PERSON PROLOGUE

A TRAVELER TO TEL EL AMARNA

I met a traveller from an antique land,
Who said: Two vast and trunkless legs of stone
Stand in the desert. Near them, on the sand,
Half sunk, a shattered visage lies, whose frown
And wrinkled lip, and sneer of cold command,
Tell that its sculptor well those passions read,
Which yet survive, stamped on those lifeless things
The hand that mocked them, and the heart that fed:
And on the pedestal these words appear:
"My name is Ozymandias, King of Kings:
Look on my works ye mighty and despair!"
Nothing beside remains. Round the decay
Of that colossal wreck, boundless and bare
The lone and level sands stretch far away.
SHELLEY

I

Shelley's immortal poem was inspired by a fallen colossus in the Theban Ramasseum. But the lines always brought to my mind's eye the curious visage carved in stone of the eighteenth-dynasty pharaoh, Akhenaten.

For Akhenaten had been a name to conjure with, a name of power since the far-off time when I had listened, surreptitiously and entranced, to my father discussing this heretic pharaoh with archaeologist John Pendlebury, son of one of his oldest friends. Then words half comprehended passed over my head adumbrating a mysterious adult world, postulating values beyond the simple tenets of childhood, probing, exploring, and leaving the central figure—the man-god with the mask-like face, slanting eyes, and secret smile—shrouded in shadow. Saint or sinner, Akhenaten hovered on the horizon of my mind, an enigma. For even as a child I had found a strange fascination in the past and what had been salvaged from the gigantic rubbish heap of history. Those treasures of remote ages rescued from the soil of the long-forgotten tomb were, to me, charged with mystery. Like the dagger of Meskalam-dug that Sir Leonard Woolley had once allowed me to handle they seemed to my childish mind to possess esoteric power— the answer to the *then* and the *now*—even to life itself. And the objects Pendlebury had retrieved from Akhenaten's ancient city at Tel el Amarna were no exception. Shown in a fund-raising exhibition in a hall at the far end of Wimpole Street, they comprised a collection that is now scattered all over the world, and engaged so much of my interest that Pendlebury promised that I might one day join his expedition and myself assist in the excavations he was conducting in Akhenaten's City of the Sun.

This never happened. When I was grown and visited Egypt for the first time, the site was deserted and Pendlebury had moved to Knossos, while the elderly Mr. A. Lucas, whom I was enabled to meet, had more interest in Tutankhamen than in his supposed brother Akhenaten. As director of the chemical department of the Egyptian government, Lucas had been responsible for the exacting task of transporting the Tutankhamen treasures from Luxor to the Cairo museum. These he showed me himself, brooding lovingly over them like a benign and ancient spirit. The marvelous treasure, today more than ever considered a wonder of the world, added fuel to my enthusiasm. For as Mariette, the renowned French antiquarian, once wrote, "One peck of the Egyptian decoy duck, it injects its venom, and there you are, an Egyptologist for the rest of your life."

But whatever our ambitions, mice and men, we are in the hands of fate. Many years later, decades after John Pendlebury's tragic and heroic death in Crete, the opportunity came at last to revisit Egypt and seek to piece together the story of one of the most interesting and controversial figures in all Egyptian history.

II

My first aim after arrival in Egypt and a return visit to the Cairo museum was to reach Tel el Amarna. For this small village on the eastern bank of the Nile is built on the site of Akhetaton—a name that means the Horizon of the Sun's Disk or City of the Dawn. It is a site unique in ancient and modern times. Approximately three thousand three hundred years ago (1373 B.C.) when the pharaoh Amenhotep IV ruled over what was then the richest and most powerful state in the world, a revolution occurred, led not by the people but by the king himself. As I then saw it, he changed the time-honored worship of Amen-Ra at Thebes, altered his name from Amenhotep IV to Akhenaten, and abandoned his capital city to build a new center of sun worship on virgin ground. Pitting his frail mortality against the immensities of time and space, he established it—as he wrote on the commemorative stelae set up at the boundaries of the town—"eternally, forever." It lasted barely eighteen years, a gift to historians who can study there a particular moment of time, a brief but enthralling period of Egyptian history. I had been warned by Dr. Mohammed Abd-ur-Rahman, the director of the Cairo Museum, that little of real interest remained at Tel el Amarna, but the shade of John Pendlebury beckoned me. My mind was made up, and by journeying to Minya, a large town sixty miles from the village, I hoped eventually to reach my goal.

Setting off by train into the unknown seemed the start of an adventure, and the carriage was equipped with all the most modern gadgets to alleviate discomfort. Unfortunately the air conditioning was out of order; the tap marked ICED WATER dried up, and the electric light failed. By the time the train pulled into the station at Minya at the inconvenient hour of four in the morning my adventurous spirit was at a low ebb and all one solitary traveler craved was the boon of a bed.

It was summer. The platforms were feebly lit and deserted; the air smelled stale and still seemed to carry the burden of yesterday's heat, but the ancient porter in turban and galabia had the charming manners of most southern Egyptians and did his best to be helpful. As far as I could understand from our conversation in broken English and Arabic, he undertook to guide me to the only hotel in town where a vacant bedroom might still be found. He shouldered my suitcase and we set off, his long pale gown flapping to the movement of his stride. It acted as a beacon through the dark and dirty streets that grew narrower as we approached the hotel, which was heralded only by a naked electric light bulb above the door. Looking at the facade, I wondered if ever before it had been entered by foreign visitors. Inside the lights had been extinguished for the night. A frowzy watchman, furious at being woken, came down the stairs with a candle and told me to wait until morning. But as the sun rose and daylight filtered in, I was not prepared to wait. There was something macabre about the dark stains on the faded red velvet curtains, festooned with frayed pompons, the mangy cat noisily chewing a fish bone under the cane chair, the glass chandelier clouded with dead flies, and the viscous dirt coating the wall.

No one was about. The watchman had again retired to bed. It was simple to rescue my suitcase and issue forth once again into the comparatively untainted air of the streets. In a few minutes I had overtaken a fiacre or cabriolet de place, one of those quaint horsedrawn carriages of the Victorian age still common in Egypt. Both horse and driver were old, tired, and underfed, but the driver at least was sympathetic when I described my situation. He promised that there was a good hotel —"very big, very rich, very fine, very new"—to which he would immediately convey me. The carriage smelled of straw and sweat. The bright printed cotton of the lining, muted by moonlight, was torn and the slow clip-clop of the horse's hooves reverberated like a sadly beaten drum through the shadowy, deserted streets until we came to the boulevard facing the Nile. Here were the largest and most imposing of the town's buildings. Beyond the farthest of them was the hotel. It was everything the driver had said, particularly the last; in fact it was so new that it had not yet officially been opened and the wall plaster was still wet. But I was not prepared to cavil at this or the fact that the flush system was not in operation. At least the hotel was clean and modern, the manager warm-hearted and welcoming—even in the small hours—and Tel el Amarna within striking distance.

Later, when the town was up, I visited the Bureau of Tourism established by General Fouad, then governor of Minya Province. Because the director of tourism, Mr. Adly Mikhail, undertook to arrange everything just as I wished, I tried not to find fault with the familiar way he patted my shoulder, purred with self-satisfaction through his words, or waved his hands over his paunch, smiling like a slave of the lamp who could conjure Cadillacs out of the air. A car, he promised, would wait for me next morning to drive me to the ferry opposite the village, sixty kilometers away. On the farther bank a jeep, together with protective escort, would be waiting to bear me in comfort to the rock tombs and sites I wished to see.

It sounded simple, but in Egypt promise does not always match performance. Dawn came but not the taxi. Being May it was already 120 degrees Fahrenheit in the sun when the transport, no Cadillac but a 1938 vintage car, finally arrived, and we set off on one of those long straight roads, dusty with passing cavalcades of donkeys and camels, so common in modern Egypt. Every few miles or so was a military checkpoint manned by a garrulous and friendly official. Questioned about these, my driver informed me that each official was in charge of a section of the road and was supposed to deal with all accidents and breakdowns in his sector, and I saw the point of the arrangement when our own vehicle ground to a halt. A boy on a bicycle was sent back to the checkpoint to fetch some wire that lasted as a repair until the next breakdown a few miles farther on. This time the driver disappeared bodily under the car and I sat beside the road and grilled, not so gently, in the sun. It was midday and hot even by Egyptian standards before we reached the river bank opposite Tel el

Amarna. Here we were again delayed by a violent altercation between the owners of a felucca and a motor ferry, who both claimed the right to transport us across the river. I preferred the felucca, but heard afterward that the two handsome young banditti who owned it—cousins in looks of Omar Sharif—were in the habit of anchoring in midstream and holding their passengers up to ransom. My driver, rightly, favored the ferry. It was for passengers only and as we left its awning and walked up the ramp leading to the village on the farther shore the sun beat down with a palpable steady force that made me view the cavalcade of donkeys lined up in readiness for us without enthusiasm. In Egypt jeeps are relatively few and donkeys plentiful. As I had half feared, the jeep turned out to be a chimera and the heat was enough to depress the spirits of even the most experienced donkey rider. Not being one of these, or geared for the occasion, I mounted the largest animal with some distaste, trying to remind myself of an earlier traveler's praise of the Egyptian ass. "They have elegance in their attitudes," wrote the Frenchman Sonnini in 1790, "gracefulness in their movements, nobleness and almost haughtiness in their carriage. Their foot is sure, their paces quick, brisk and easy. In short, they are very pleasing to ride." My own donkey, looking perhaps, unlike its rider, noble, graceful, and haughty, stepped out. The protective escort overstrode their mounts with the nonchalance born of long custom; the donkey boys shouted and resoundingly thwacked the poor animals' rumps. We set off in a cloud of dust for the distant amphitheater of the mountains. We seemed a veritable army. The arrangements had been made and it was too late to question why four able-bodied men, one undersized policeman with a rifle, an immense dragoman with keys, my own taxi driver plus grandson, and five donkey boys were needed for a solitary traveler.

It was very quiet in Tel el Amarna. Understandably nobody stirred but ourselves. The village slept in the sun. Those Amarnans not engaged in escorting me to the tombs had wisely sought the shade of their own mud houses. The pigeons had also taken cover in their curious, conical castellated cotes. Two oxen lay ruminating in the shade of a knot of palms and

Donkeys. Tel el Amarna

a tethered camel, looking disdainful, knelt by a water furrow. Even the cement kiosk for tourists was locked up and a detachment of soldiers under canvas lounged on their stretcher beds. They were engaged, when active, in building a row of brick houses for the Amarnans who some months previously had experienced a sudden catastrophe when torrents of rainwater poured from the mountains and swept the central portion of the village away.

The cultivation extended along this part of the river only in a narrow strip of bright green. The division between the "desert and the sown" was as exact as a ruled line. Dotted palm trees threw brief patches of shadow and the distant heavens were pale with the sun's warmth as we left the cultivation, and the patter of our donkeys' hooves came muffled on the soft sand. It was a dead terrain stirred to uneven humps and hillocks by the hand of man. For between the village and the mountain, on this infertile-looking crescent of land, Akhenaten built his virgin city in opposition to the Theban priesthood. As Norman de Garies Davies wrote in 1903, "Long ages before an insignificant Bedouin occupation gave the name of Tel el Amarna to the site, the level area, guarded on all sides by the mountains and the river front, had attracted a settlement of the utmost historic importance. It was to this spot that King Amenhotep IV (Akhenaten) retired to give unhindered expression to his overmastering ideals.''

The stirred-up look of the land was not only due to Akhenaten's workmen. Generations of excavators looking for treasure, or knowledge, or both, had also been active. For this site—''a chance bivouac in the march of history filled for a moment with all the movement and color of life and then abandoned to deeper silence''—proved for more than a century a magnet to the archaeologist. Napoleon's conquest of Egypt first opened the eyes of the western world to the fascination of Egyptology and the beauty of its ancient arts and monuments. Champollion, by deciphering the Rosetta Stone, laid the foundations of the knowledge of Egypt's past, and in 1824 an Englishman, Sir George Wilkinson, identified some of the Amarnan tombs. He was the first explorer of many. May and the Frenchman Nestor L'Hote also copied scenes from the tomb walls, and the exponent of hieroglyphs, Alexander von Humbolt, noticed the detritus of human occupation scattered over the Amarnan site. Moved to curiosity, he persuaded William IV of Prussia to send there an expedition under Richard Lespius. After three years' work, Lespius uncovered portions of a large city and learned something of its architect.

So gradually the story of Akhenaten, the heretic pharaoh, as he came to be called, began to be pieced together and immediately attracted attention.

For, by an irony of fate, the king, whom his Ramesside successors viewed with such horror that they sought to obliterate his name entirely, became famous three thousand years after his death. Then his monuments had been shattered, his temples broken up, his name expunged, his city razed to the ground and abandoned. As for the vast religious structures he erected at Tel el Amarna and elsewhere to the sun disk, it was not thought sufficient by his posterity to throw these down. The razed sites, doubly defiled in their eyes, were cleansed by being covered by layers of pure sand as if to seal them forever from sight. Even the historians of Egypt's greatness consigned Akhenaten to oblivion. His name was dropped from the king lists, as were the names of two younger brothers who followed him, and the usurper, Horemheb, was placed by Manetho, the Egyptian scribe and historian, directly after Akhenaten's father, Amenhotep III.

In modern times these efforts have had the effect least desired and the period the ancient Egyptians sought to bury out of sight has become a focus of particular interest.

A chance discovery made in 1888 gave new impetus to the search. A village woman, seeking for *sebakh* (mud brick) manure at the foot of the Amarnan mountains, found a cache of three hundred and twenty cuneiform tablets of baked brick. Cuneiform was the lingua franca of the ancient world; the woman had stumbled on the archives of Akhenaten's foreign office and the correspondence filed by his clerks between Egypt and her friendly allies or dependents in Syria and Asia Minor. Nothing like it had been found before and the importance of the find and the interest it aroused equaled the discovery of the Linear B tablets at Pylos in our own times.

It led to a fresh expedition being mounted in 1891 to explore the site. Under Sir Flinders Petrie the center of the city was excavated and the beautiful painted pavement, now in the Cairo museum, discovered.

But undoubtedly the best-known single item unearthed at Tel el Amarna was found in 1912 by a German expedition. On the afternoon of December 12 when their leader, Professor Ludwig Borchardt, was taking his customary nap, he was woken by an excited workman. The reis, Mohammed Ahmes Es-Senussi, had sent to tell the professor of a spectacular find. It was near a part of the excavations the Germans had named The House of the Sculptor Thutmose. There, Borchardt first saw the painted limestone bust, only half exposed, of Akhenaten's queen, Nefertiti, which is now in the Berlin museum. Later the right of the Germans to the bust was questioned. There was much correspondence and recrimination, which gained the queen's portrait head an unusual amount of publicity. By the time the archaeologists, the art lovers, and the press had praised its astonishing and modern-seeming beauty, the name of Nefertiti had passed into common parlance. For the delicate features of the queen were declared by many to be the quintessence of female beauty and the artist was thought to have succeeded in deifying the ideal woman. Leonard Cottrell, in a recent book, has written enthusiastically, ''The face immortalised is the perfect equipoise between what we long for and what we know to be possible. . . . The portrait of Nefertiti, one mere mortal creature out of billions, born over 3,000 years ago, seems to bridge the canyon between man and God.''* No wonder, perhaps, that although so little is known of her history it might be said her claim to fame rests solely on this (and one other) sculpture; she has become, with Cleopatra, the most celebrated of Egypt's queens. There can be few tourists not familiar with her name and few south Egyptian villages that do not boast a Nefertiti Cafe—sometimes owing to a rudimentary knowledge of English misspelled Nevertitti. But a complete study of the Amarna site had yet to be undertaken and it was the Egyptian Exploration Society, aided by generous funds from America and led by such giants of the archaeological world as Woolley, Peet, and Pendlebury, who followed up the work of the German expedition by planning and carrying out the colossal task of an overall excavation of the main areas of Akhetaton. Many seasons were spent in digging, sifting, measuring, and in the painstaking work of drawing accurate plans of buildings, palaces, temples, private houses, wharves, and streets.

These enthusiasts were still engaged on their work in 1922 when the interest stirred by their finds became overshadowed. For in that year Howard Carter, working for Lord Carnarvon, discovered the tomb of Tutankhamen in the Biban el Moluk at Thebes.

This discovery had in it all the elements—drama, mystery, buried treasure—of popular appeal. The finds beggared description. No adjective—and all the superlatives were used —quite caught the romance of it: the dazzle of so much gold; the human interest of the boy king coffined in such unimagined wealth; the splendid workmanship of the objects, their number, and the miracle of their preservation during three

*Queens of the Pharaohs by Leonard Cottrell

thousand years, hermetically sealed in the forgotten tomb. It was indeed "the most incredible burial treasure in the world today."*

Yet in time the treasures of Tutankhamen intensified interest in Akhenaten, for the history of the one was bound up in the history of the other. Tutankhamen, Akhenaten's successor and almost certainly his younger brother, brought the wheel of destiny to full circle. Akhenaten defying, perhaps, the priests of Amen had moved his capital from Thebes to a fresh site, creating a new form of sun worship and a new way of life at Tel el Amarna. Tutankhamen, reverting to the old faith, returned to the older capitals of Thebes and Memphis. Part of his childhood was spent in Akhetaton before his triumphant coronation in the Theban temple of Karnak, and it was in the Valley of the Kings that the beautiful youth was laid to rest after his brief reign. Akhenaten grew up in Thebes; but the drama of his life, spectacular and mysterious in its end, was played out against the backdrop of the Amarnan mountains.

III

The semicircular range of cliffs we were approaching did indeed look like the backdrop to some gigantic stage—but not to any play with an urban theme. We had ridden over an area of Akhetaton marked on Pendlebury's map as the North Suburb. But no one, however vivid his imagination, could have mentally reconstructed a thickly populated town from the scene before us. Most of Akhetaton had been built of mud brick. It had been pillaged by its own inhabitants before abandonment and subsequently very thoroughly destroyed. When the irrigation channels silted up, the trees and bushes dried up and turned, like the bricks, to dust, and of this part of the town nothing visible remained. Not even a blade of grass grew on the uneven ground.

But halfway up the mountain, like a row of foxholes,

* *Tutankhamen* by C. Desroches Noblecourt

gaped the dark entrances to the tombs. To visit them we were forced to leave our donkeys and struggle up the slope against a heat that seemed to glue our feet to the rock. Each entrance was protected by a massive iron grill and we were thankful to hear the key grate in the lock and enter the shelter of the sepulcher. In its gloom our pupils, pinpointed by the brilliant sunlight, could at first see nothing but blackness until the dragoman spread out the skirts of his white galabia as a light reflector and illumined the darker corners.

Mohammed Abd-ur-Rahman had been specific about the carvings on the walls of the tombs, which are of supreme historical value, constituting as they do one of the chief records of Akhenaten's reign. They could, he said, be very much better studied in reproduction between the pages of a book. In this he was correct, as in his other comments on Tel el Amarna. Norman de Garies Davies spent years (fourteen weeks on one tomb alone) accurately copying the inscriptions and drawings on the walls of the sepulchers. Printed in six large volumes, they can be studied at leisure without the disadvantages of heat, dust, and darkness.

Carved on the tomb walls, the inscriptions have to be sought out and peered at through the dim light. In each case the central panel, which depicts Akhenaten, Nefertiti, and their daughters beamed on by the benevolent rays of the sun's disk, has been defaced in antiquity. Silica has coated some of the surfaces, which are further blurred and blackened by the smoke of torches lit for generations of interested travelers. Although much of the carving is crude, repetitive, and roughly drawn, the information that can be deciphered from it is of absorbing interest. The tombs were hollowed out of the living rock and carved in the pharaoh's lifetime by the principal nobles and officials of his court. But few actual burials are thought to have taken place. The inscriptions and carvings must have been made therefore as much with the object of pleasing and flattering the live king as insuring the dead man's happiness in the hereafter. They show the pharaoh's courtiers engaged on their several duties. Aahmes, fan bearer on the right hand of the king and steward of the palace, waves a long-handled spray of ostrich feathers; the high

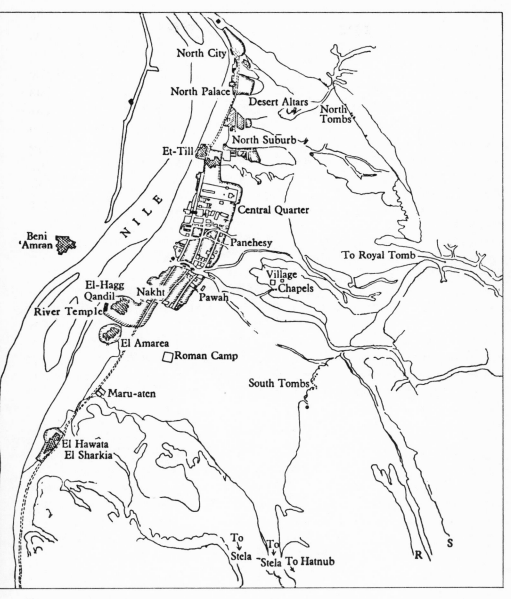

Map of Akhetaton (City of the Horizon) from Pendlebury's City of Akhenaten. *The area of the tombs can be seen on the right-hand side of the map.*

priest Mery-Ra sacrifices a bull to Aten; Panehesy, the Nubian, leads the king's horses; the spies of Mahu, head of the police, bring two robbers to book; and Auta, the sculptor, puts a finishing touch to a statue of one of the princesses. Artist, scribe, general, courtier, priest, steward surround the image of their larger than life-sized master with obsequious homage and adulation. For the great pharaoh—living for ever and ever—was more than the apex of their world, the head of the bureaucratic pyramid. He was also the living representative of the God, the being from whom all benefits, secular and spiritual, flowed. Without his goodwill his followers could neither enjoy the blessings of this world nor hope to attain them in the hereafter.

When the last sepulcher had been visited, we left the tombs with reluctance. Akhenaten and all his works had long since been swept away, but the power and strength of the solar disk he worshiped seemed, in that cloudless climate, undiminished. We emerged from the shade to shoulder the weight of heat and, sluggish under the pall of sunlight, remounted our donkeys to ride to the northern limits of the ancient city. There in 1926 the Egyptian Exploration Society unearthed the ruins of the North Palace.

This was certainly one of the most interesting of all the buildings excavated, both on account of the discoveries made and in relation to the piecing together of Akhenaten's history. From evidence found both here, in the central city, and in the southern temple of Maru-Aten, Pendlebury concluded that toward the end of Akhenaten's reign his apparently ideal family life with the queen and their six daughters came to a sudden end, and that Nefertiti parted from her husband. Removing from him as far as possible, she retired, according to Pendlebury, to, or behind the North Palace on the extreme boundary of the town. Little Prince Tutankhamen seems to have been with her, since several fragments of his ring bezels and tiles were found, with hers, in the excavations.

But, in the first place, the building seems to have been designed less for living in than as a combined temple and zoological gardens, an extraordinary combination to us but not, perhaps, to the sunworshiping Atenists. When T. Whittmore

excavated the rectangular block, whose walls were still standing to the height of two meters, he found the entrance close
to the Nile led into a large forecourt, which must have been an
impressive approach to a massive architectural feature—
possibly one of those "windows of appearance" from which
the pharaoh and his queen distributed gold necklaces to the
fortunate. The whole structure had been carefully designed
on a preconceived plan. It centered on a water court with a
large pool behind the window of appearance, which led in
turn to a raised, pillared throne room and dais so that all
who approached could see the golden glitter of royal pomp
duplicated in the mirrored surface of the still water. There
was also a bathroom in which a stone basin had been placed
to catch waste water, while the bath itself, a replica of the
one discovered in the palace of Akhenaten's father, Amenhotep III, at Thebes, was made of limestone flags. A dado of
white plaster protected the walls from the splashings. But
how can one reconcile the noble altar, the great throne room,
and the pillared water court with a zoological garden that
opened from the water court and housed bulls, ibex, and
gazelle whose images decorated a series of stone and cement

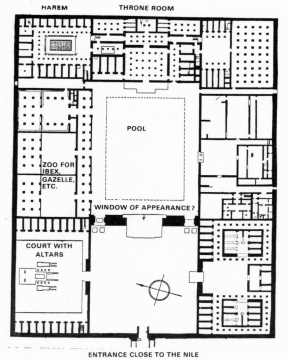

*Plan of
the North Palace.*

mangers? And what of the northeastern corner of the palace, called by Whittmore the harem? Here twenty-one small rooms —mere cubicles—opened onto an ambulatory shaded by a colonnade of sculptured and painted columns. They surrounded a small sunken garden divided into flower beds, around which flowed a little gurgling watercourse. The walls of the cubicles were cut into by niches and decorated by wonderful paintings of bird life and a frieze of a papyrus thicket teeming with wild birds. Could this have been an aviary? On the other hand, Whittmore found fragments of gold leaf, delicate gilded furniture, and necklace beads that seemed to mark these quarters indubitably as the abode of women. According to him the whole palace was "a highly adorned if gloomy edifice." The prevailing color of the walls was sun yellow, and all the ceilings were painted and molded throughout realistically to represent a trellis on which a grapevine was trained to carry its full leaves and hanging clusters, plaster molded in the round, to give the verisimilitude of an arbor.

This remarkable building, in which, according to W. Stevenson-Smith (but not to Whittmore, the archaeologist who excavated it), there were no identifiable living quarters, may first have been conceived and built as an Atenic form of solar temple. Taken over by Nefertiti after her rift with the king, it could have served later as a palace. This suggestion has the merit of reconciling opposing views and is discussed in a later chapter.

Only the skeleton of the structure remains today. The pools and watercourses are depressions in the sand. The flowers and trees are dust. Only the stone bases of some of the pillars can be seen. The three-foot-high walls, stripped of their plaster and paint, show only the repetitive dun of ageless and crumbling mud brick.

Mercifully, by the time we had thoroughly explored the palace, the sun had begun to decline. A cooler air drifted from the river and the whole landscape became suddenly transformed. The mountains lost their harsh outlines and looked mysterious and inviting; the pale sky flooded with the brilliant colors of the sunset; and cubist shadows broke up the dull reality of the desert landscape. The donkeys pricked their ears and quickened their paces, the donkey boys ran to keep up with them, and soon the whole cavalcade—moving faster and faster—was racing through the dusk, the riders blinking as the barred shadows of the palm trees struck their faces.

Even hampered by the need to hold onto my hat with one hand and securely clutch my purse (bulging with precious pens, pencils, notebooks, passport, and wallet) with the other, I enjoyed that evening rush back to the rest camp. Afterward, lapped in the soft colors of the setting sun, we sipped ambrosial cups of mint tea. The noise and hurry of the space age seemed far away. The moment was prolonged: the moving hands of the mechanical clock no longer oppressed us and we were in a timeless eastern world of courtesy and hyperbole.

IV

Intending again to visit Tel el Amarna the following day and sore, in more senses than one, after so many hours of donkey riding, I reproached Mr. Adly Mikhail that evening when he called to be complimented on the excellence of his arrangements. Why had the taxi arrived so late, I asked, and what had happened to the jeep? But about this chimerical combustion engine he was offhand. There had been a fault in its works, a screw loose in the mechanism. It was fate; it was kismet, something no organizer, however excellent, could control. As for the taxi, it had taken me where I wished to go and brought me back again and what more could be asked of any vehicle? Finally in a manner that Jane Austen would have described as everything that was affable and insincere he promised that not only would the taxi call for me early next morning, but also the jeep, recovered from its indisposition, would be ready and waiting on the eastern bank.

Foolishly sanguine, I rose next day at dawn. The taxi driver, it seemed, did not. And that sun-soaked Egyptian world was already in the grip of its deadening daily summer heat before he made his appearance. Again his vehicle broke down; again we had a prolonged altercation with the two handsome young men who owned the Nile felucca at the crossing. Again, alas, as the ferry in which we embarked moved over the turbid water to draw in at the landing stage at Tel el Amarna we saw no jeep but the same cavalcade of donkeys, the small policeman, the large dragoman, the posse, and the donkey boys. Remembering yesterday's baksheesh they greeted me with an enthusiasm I could not, looking at my mount, entirely reciprocate.

It was with a sigh that I climbed on to the hard, if beautifully decorated, saddle and we set off southward for the center of Akhetaton where the main complex of buildings— the temple, palace, and administrative offices—had once stood.

A broad road like an artery running through the heart of the city and once swept for the wheels of Akhenaten's golden chariot is still called Sikket es Sultan, or the King's Highway. It is bordered on both sides by the remains of the great palace: on the one side the private, on the other the official quarters. The two were connected by a covered way, almost Venetian in style, so that the king could move unseen between the official quarters, the harem, and his private apartments. Here also, it is thought, in the center of the gateway, was a window of appearance. Nothing is left of the structure now, alas, but two mounds of mud brick. The remains of palace and temple sites are equally disappointing. We wandered, it seemed for hours, through courts where a few stone bases were all that remained of pillared porticoes; past mazes of mud-brick wall; up shallow steps, all baked by the sun and flattened by time, empty of life. Akhetaton certainly seemed "abandoned to deeper silence" for no one in that vast landscape stirred but ourselves. Some ancient Muslim tombs where the former sheikhs and hadjis of the village had been laid to rest dotted the foreground. Fragments of stone, glittering like mica, and over much of the site a scattering of potsherds were all that showed it had once been a capital city, teeming with people, full of the "movement and color of life."

Seven miles away, up a narrow canyon, or wadi, that broke the mountain range, was Akhenaten's royal tomb. His first boundary stela set up at Akhetaton in the sixth year of his reign promised that "there shall be made for me a sepulcher in the eastern hills; my burial shall be made therein . . . and the burial of the Great Wife of the King, Nefertiti, and the burial of the king's daughter Meritaten . . ." In these arrangements Akhenaten followed the pattern set by his father Amenhotep III who had prepared his tomb in the Biban el Moluk at Thebes and, intending to be buried with his Great Wife Tyi and his daughter Sitamen, included chambers for their coffins.

The entrance to the royal tomb, on the floor of the valley, has a main passage that descends until it reaches a level chamber formerly supported by four pillars. Flinders Petrie claimed that this chamber had once been carved and painted throughout on a superimposed coat of stucco, which had long ago dropped off or been deliberately destroyed. Professor Gaston Maspero, on the other hand, referred to "a mere commencement of decoration" and described the funeral chamber and passages as "scarcely roughhewn." What seems certain is that whatever calamity overwhelmed the king in the eighteenth year of his reign was sudden and complete. His tomb was never finished; his great red granite sarcophagus was found, viciously smashed to pieces, on the floor of the tomb; and his canopic chest, unearthed by Pendlebury, had never been used. So it is possible that neither the king, Nefertiti, nor Meritaten were laid to rest in the royal mausoleum intended for them. As far as is certainly known it served only to house the catafalque of Princess Meketaten, Akhenaten's second daughter, who predeceased her parents in the twelfth year of the reign. Although empty when discovered, her burial chamber near to the entrance is the only one decorated and shows scenes of her death that, in their intimate detail, are unique in Egyptian history. They depict the king and queen and the court lamenting over the body of the princess and convey the intensity of parental grief. While the mourners keen and the royal pair bend in sorrow over the corpse of their dead daughter, a woman leaves the room holding a newborn child to her breast, suggesting that Princess Meketaten died in childbirth, having married her father as her sister Ankhesenpaaten was to do some years later.

The ride to the tomb seemed a great distance by donkey. The heat was if possible greater than before. The sand, reflecting light and sun, dazzled the retina and doubled our discomfort. Even the policeman wilted. The magnificent dragoman perched a folded copy of *El Ahram* on top of his turban and the donkeys ambled slowly, with lowered heads, and meekly suffered, poor beasts, the buffets of the donkey boys.

After an hour's riding we could perceive the mouth of the valley—a deep cleft in the rocks. The concentration of heat in that natural oven was paralyzing in its intensity.

In earlier days of travel a visitor to Egypt was slowly conditioned to the heat, took no chance, and fully equipped himself for the ordeal of a day in the desert. The modern traveler, flying direct from a cooler clime, no longer prepares himself for discomfort or is burdened with such impedimenta as topees, sunshades, or water bottles. So that to find my lips dry, my tongue swollen, and spots dancing before my eyes was an unforeseen ordeal.

In view of the circumstances it was not strange that, by common consent, our visit to Akhenaten's tomb proved cursory, our return as rapid as possible. And all the long way back thirst created images of water in my mind—rushing streams, fountains, gushing springs. They hovered before my eyes like mirages over the droughty desert and the words I had read only that morning from the Book of the Dead seemed most apposite:

> *O Osiris . . . the Nile, the greatest of the gods,*
> *Comes to fill thy gifts with cool water.*
> *He gives thee water from Elephantine,*
> *The Nile which comes out of the two caves,*
> *The Watery Abyss which comes from the mountains,*
> *The Flood which comes forth from the cavern,*
> *The eddy which comes from the cool flood.*
> *Thou drinkest from them, thou art satisfied,*
> *Thy body fills itself with fresh water . . .*
> *Thy throat overflows . . .*

And I remembered from my childhood the tag of verse that so teased Allan Quartermain on his journey to King Solomon's mines:

A nice little boy held a golden ewer
Embossed and filled with water as pure
As any that flows between Rheims and Namur . . .

Even with the quickened pace of the donkeys it seemed a far ride for a dehydrated and thirst-bedeviled traveler. And when at last the rest camp was reached, it was found to be securely locked. The prospect of cool drinks and mint tea vanished. For the caretaker, we were told, had crossed the Nile to Malawi taking the keys with him. But first he had thoughtfully provided us with a bucket of Nile water. Far from looking "as pure as any that flows," it was tepid, discolored, and clouded with sediment. But with my companions and no thought of modern hygiene—of virus, germs, bacilli, or bilharzia—I swallowed cupfuls of the uninviting-looking fluid that tasted like nectar. We soaked up water like thirsty plants until our bodies indeed filled with fresh water and our throats overflowed.

Later, as the car rattled along the road back to Minya, passing the evening cavalcade of mules, ambling camels, and slow-moving oxen, I reflected that Akhenaten could have chosen no better site for a concentrated worship of the sun's disk than Tel el Amarna. The place was not only remote but primeval, stripped to the bare elements of earth, rock, and sky. Without the life-giving (if murky) waters of the Nile, it was a dead world, as dead as the cratered surface of the moon or that long distant past when, with a flourish of trumpets, Akhenaten had founded his city "eternally, forever."

But, although of powerful interest to me, the visit had done little to lighten the shadows that shrouded so much of Akhenaten's life. Would the darkness ever be penetrated, fresh evidence discovered, or solutions to the many controversial questions found? Or would I ever find a new interpretation to satisfy the questions numbered in my mind since childhood?

Whatever the answer there was no turning back. My curiosity was inflamed and the journey must be continued in search of Akhenaten to the end, even if the expedition just completed was a mere prelude to the laborious if enthralling pilgrimage yet to be undertaken into the remote past.

2.
THE SEARCH BEGINS

We must consider how very little history there is; I mean real authentic history. That certain kings reigned, and certain battles were fought, we can depend on as true; but all the colouring, all the philosophy of history is conjecture.
JOHNSON

Out of monuments, names, words, proberbs, traditions, private records and evidences, fragments of stories and the like, we do save and recover somewhat from the deluge of time.
BACON

I

Egyptologists complain that much written on Akhenaten is "an intolerable deal of conjecture to a quantum of fact." Unfortunately the "quantum of fact" is all the biographer has to go on although popular interest has turned the searchlight of inquiry on a period as quarried for information as the sands of Tel el Amarna for artifacts. But because the written records of the Egyptians date back five thousand years, and because they were a most conservative people, there are many clues from this aptly named First Time World.

The search is vital to the main theme. For if Akhenaten instituted the state worship solely of the sun's orb, Aten, sun worship in other forms had been present in Egypt even before recorded time.

A close study of the thousand and one gods and goddesses of the Egyptian pantheon can be bypassed: Taueret the hippopotamus goddess of childbirth with her swollen belly; the bestial jovial dwarf Bes, grinning above his pendant phallus; Anubis flitting shadowlike, jackallike among the dark tombs of the dead; or Osiris, spiritual god of resurrection. But the origin of sun worship must be sought if only as a background to Akhenaten's reformations.

The cherished beliefs of the Egyptians were passed on from generation to generation, an inheritance from the childhood of mankind. Then the world in which it groped for understanding seemed filled with fearful and unknown divinities. A spirit trembled at the heart of every tree and a god to be propitiated lurked behind every facet of life.

In time the conservative nature of the Egyptians became a thraldom for they seemed unable to discard a belief or custom once it had been hallowed by antiquity. After many centuries in the isolated and fertile Nile Valley, this accumulation of revered and sacred superstition produced a clutter of gods, an endless and untidy polytheism. An enormous pantheon of strange creatures, ibis-beaked, crocodile-tailed, jackal-headed, came into being; deities derived largely from primitive nature cults and totemic symbols of the original tribes living along the Nile. They were locally worshiped, but the worship of the sungod had a general appeal. His holy place was at Heliopolis, or On, near modern Cairo, on the primeval hill that, so it was said, rose out of chaos.

The first rulers of historic Egypt were also sun worshipers, but their god was the horus, or hawk. It was their symbol of royalty, the totem of their clan, the lord of the sky. And so the hawk must have seemed to desert or steppe dwellers. They saw it appear suddenly, out of nowhere, planeing, wing tips spread like the fingers of a human hand. Then sweeping high over the immeasurable heavens it became pinpointed in space and vanished into the empyrean—back to the sun god of which it was an emanation.

It is of great interest to the writer on Akhenaten with Syrian leanings that the first rulers of Egypt, those once mythical kings who set it on the path to greatness, were newcomers to the banks of the Nile. A measurement of skulls from dynastic and predynastic tombs conducted by experts showed so marked a difference that the conclusion that the dynasts came from outside Egypt seemed inevitable. Because these long-headed leaders of the south worshiped Heru the falcon, and the Arabic word for falcon is *huru,* their provenance can be deduced. The climatic conditions in the eastern desert were different in those times. It was steppe country, supporting a pastoral people who herded cattle. As the land began to dry into desert, the dynastic race reached Egypt as a horde, perhaps after a considerable amount of peaceful penetration.

The Falcon tribe was first settled at Hierakonpolis, later at Thinis near Abydos in Upper Egypt not far from Thebes where the Nile curves widely toward the Red Sea, at this point no more than one hundred and fifty miles away.

Their celestial hawk deity represented the entire empyrean—his right eye the sun and his left eye the moon. But Horus was very soon confused with Ra, the Sun god worshiped from ancient days at Heliopolis.

Ra, sovereign lord of the sky, was the beautiful youth born in a lotus flower from Nun, the waters of chaos. He had produced, it was said, all living creatures from his own sweat and tears. He created a First Universe, a golden age where men and gods lived together in a paradise free from want, sorrow, or fear. The legend ran that Ra governed this First Time World from his "Prince's Palace" (or temple) in Heliopolis. And from thence every day he was rowed in his boat through the twelve provinces of his kingdom, which corresponded to the hours of daylight. In time he grew old and his subjects murmured against him. Deeply wounded by their ingratitude, he determined to withdraw himself beyond their reach, and with the assistance of Nut, the sky goddess, he was raised high into the vault of heaven. There he continued his existence as the sun, sailing his golden bark across the heavens by day. At night he battled with Apophis the serpent and other evil creatures of the underworld and rose again with the dawn. The boat graves recently found in the tombs of the archaic kings at Abydos and Saqqara show how sincerely they believed in the legend of the sun god. They too piously hoped in a future existence when they would sail with Ra across the sky, eternally.

These remote ancestors of Akhenaten's, although as far removed from him in time as the Roman epoch from today, are not unimportant to this story. Certainly they came from the east, from Asia Minor, Syria, or Arabia.

They were settled in southern Egypt not far from the eighteenth-dynasty capital of Thebes. And it was their special god—a fusion of the Horus sky god with the solar deity, bearing the sun's orb on his hawk's head and named Ra-Harahkte—to whom Akhenaten first turned in his attempt to reform the religion of Thebes.

II

One of the many controversial issues relating to Akhenaten's reign is the relationship and descent of his family. Who were Yuaa and Tuaa, the parents of his mother, Queen Tyi? Who was his wife, the beautiful Nefertiti? Here again the era of the early Egyptian kings can be searched for the origin of the curious custom of royal inheritance from mother as well as father, which resulted in the marriage of royal brother with royal sister.

As Gaston Maspero, one of the greatest of early Egyptologists wrote, ''The peculiarity of Egyptian manners which seems to us a refinement of incest was regarded as an institution of divine origin, most fitting to preserve the purity of race.'' But in Maspero's day the archaic tombs had not yet been explored. Since then, Petrie at Abydos, de Morgan at Nagadah, Quibell at Hierankonpolis, and Emery at Saqqara have added to the scanty knowledge of the epoch and thrown new light on the possible origin and sanctity of the royal marriage customs. As they are of great importance in the difficult task of unraveling the genealogy of Akhenaten and his family, they are worth examining at some length.

Manetho, a native of Sebennytus in Lower Egypt, was a scribe who lived in the third century B.C. and wrote a history of his native country. Compiling his information from the ancient temple records at Heliopolis, where he served as priest, he divided the rulers of Egypt into dynasties. He wrote that "in succession to the spirits of the dead came the demi-gods." These were the kings of the first dynasty led by the great Menes, who unified the country and moved from Thinis, the town of his birth in southern Egypt, to found the central city of Memphis near present-day Cairo.

Menes and his successors were long considered legendary until, to the astonishment and delight of the Egyptologists, their huge mastaba tombs were unearthed.

One by one these embryonic pyramids were uncovered, each surrounded by a formal rectangle of graves—servants who had died to accompany their master to another world.

Information derived from these excavations proves that the unification of Egypt was the work of not one but several generations. A picture emerges of this First Time World of 3200 B.C., over a millennium before Abraham left Ur. It shows a cattle-herding warrior race entering Upper Egypt possibly across the Red Sea and by the ancient trade route that runs from El Quseir down the Wadi el Hammamat to Coptos. Settling a few miles down the Nile at Thinis (Abydos) they proved their superior strength and fighting power, being soon acknowledged as overlords by the tribes of Upper Egypt. They identified their Horus sky god with the sun god of Heliopolis and moved by the powerful propellants of ambition and fear led a coalition against the rich lands of the north.

The great authority on this early period, Professor W. B. Emery, suggests that the Horus people may have entered Egypt, not from El Quseir on the Red Sea, but via the Wadi el Tumilat on the eastern side of the delta and that a section of horde penetrated and controlled the delta itself from Buto. But the civilization in the north remained predominantly Libyan-Syrian and both the late Professor Newbury and G. K. Sethe have established that Egyptian writing was born in the delta.

So at the dawn of history there were two independent states in Egypt, Lower Egypt being richer, more advanced, and much influenced by Mediterranean and matriarchal culture. To the Falcon people the northern delta must have appeared a land of esoteric knowledge, power, and wealth as well as a threat. For there may even have been a time when all Egypt was ruled from the delta and it was perhaps a Libyan ruler, deified after death, who was worshiped by the original tribes of Upper Egypt as Seth, the wild, red-haired, white-faced god, whose sacred animal was the hippopotamus. Seth was the most popular god in predynastic Upper Egypt, but when the Horus kings made war on the delta his worship became involved with politics. To the new rulers he came to represent those hostile to Horus and Ra and so in time to embody in legend Satan, the prototype of civil strife and evil. (Seth however remained a powerful god until late in Egyptian history.)

In attributing the unification of Egypt to Menes, Manetho was simplifying a confused period. Not one but at least three consecutive Horus rulers—kings Scorpion, Narmer, and Hor-aha—were involved in the struggle for unification of the country. In the end it seems to have come about not by conquest alone but through a significant dynastic marriage.

One of the principal towns of the delta at this prehistoric period was Sais, whose people, like those of Crete and Babylon, worshiped a mother goddess. A most ancient divinity called Neit, she was the female principle personified. She was single, supreme, self-producing, mother of the sun. Above her celebrated temple, of which nothing remains today, an inscription read:

I am all that has been, that is, that will be.
No mortal has yet lifted the veil from my face.

Her religion was very much more than a fertility cult. Like Athena, with whom she was later identified, she led her people into battle hurling thunderbolts at their enemies. She was the great weaver of the world who taught the arts to mankind; she was the celestial cow who fed them; she was the First Principle—and she was Libyan. Because she is depicted wearing the red crown of the north, it is possible to think that, like the rain queen of Central Africa, a flesh and blood priestess-queen ruled at Sais who was recognized throughout the delta. And it is no romance but a fact accepted by such an eminent authority as Professor W. B. Emery that this lady of Sais married the early dynastic King Narmer. The attraction that a priestess-queen, who called herself mother of the sun, would have for a sun king is evident, apart from any political power she might wield. There are signs that an alliance already existed between the Horus kings and Sais. On his ceremonial mace-head, recovered from Hierakonpolis, Narmer is shown enthroned wearing the usurped crown of Lower Egypt. Opposite in a shrine attended by Libyans sits a woman—almost certainly the Queen Neit-hotep. For Neit-hotep was a real person and her tomb, a magnificent monument prepared for her by her son Hor-aha, has been found. King Hor-aha (Fighting Hawk) succeeded Narmer and, because his *nebti** name was Men, Professor Emery has identified him as the Menes of Manetho, founder of a united Egypt and possibly by inheritance as well as conquest ruler of the two lands. Significantly one of his first acts was to build a temple to the goddess Neit at Sais.

Mary Renault in her novel *The King Must Die* has skillfully portrayed the clash of two civilizations—matriarchal and militant—and the marriage of queen-priestess and warriorprince. A millennium and a half before the time of Theseus it seems such a marriage took place and resulted in the spectacular and splendid flowering of Egyptian civilization.

The curious royal marriage customs of the Egyptians can surely be also traced to this marriage. For if, as in most warrior castes, the Horus king passed on his power from father to son and believed in his solar divinity, by marrying a queen divine in her own right a situation was reached where only the son and daughter of such a pair, united, could claim the throne. Also as mother of the sun the queen must have held divine precedence. Hence brother-sister marriage became

---

Nebti: The *nebti* name was the second title of the king and celebrated the union of Upper and Lower Egypt by combining the names of the ''Two Ladies'': the vulture goddess Nekhbet of Upper Egypt and the cobra goddess Wadjet of Lower Egypt. According to Professor Emery, the *nebti* name goes back at least to the commencement of the first dynasty.

inevitable. Hor-aha's son Zer seems to have married his sister Her-Neit and the next ruler was Queen Mery-Neit, who reigned in her own right.

But to return to the age of Akhenaten, it can be said with certainty that at no time in Egypt's long history was royal descent from a princess of the pure solar blood considered of greater importance than among the kings of the eighteenth dynasty.

III

From this brief outline of the dawn of Egyptian history emerges the natural geographical and political division of north and south, a division that has been largely ignored in the study of Akhenaten's epoch. It is true that the reign of Menes was followed by nearly a thousand years of unity. But when the break came, the country divided once more into the ancient northern and southern spheres of influence, the south more conservative, more militant; the north open to foreign influence and more easily conquered.

The forebears of Akhenaten originally came to the throne through a breakdown of government at Memphis. This produced a decentralization of power. A vizier was appointed nomarch of the Theban nome, keeper of the door of the south. His descendants, consolidating their position, seized the throne about 2133 B.C. and founded the eleventh and twelveth dynasties of the Middle Kingdom. So after a thousand years power returned to that region whence the Falcon people had set out at the dawn of history to conquer the Nile Valley. When, about 1684 B.C., the foreign Hyksos secured control of Egypt, they administered it for over a hundred years from Memphis and their new capital of Avaris in the far eastern delta. At first they were content to require only token fealty from the south. The Theban rulers continued to hold power, and when the revolt against the Asiatic overlords came, it originated in Thebes.

There was almost a return to the prehistoric wars of north and south—of Libyan against Egyptian. Even the clash of religions recurred for the Hyksos adopted Seth as one of their deities and the first exchange of shots was a verbal arrow fired at the sun god of the south—Amen-Ra. King Apophis of Avaris sent a messenger to the court of the Theban king, Sekenenre Tao II "The Brave," three hundred miles away. He brought word from his master that

There is a hippopotamus pool in the Southern City (Thebes), and the hippopotamus do not allow sleep to come to us either by day or by night, but noise is in our ears. Let the Prince therefore cause to be abandoned the hippopotamus pool which is in the flowing spring of the city.

The hippopotamus was the sacred animal of Seth. It appears that some ritual hunt or killing of the hippopotamus took place in Thebes to signify the triumph of the Theban sun god Amen-Ra over the powers of evil. In modern terms, King Apophis, sheltering behind the power of Seth, sought a confrontation with Sekenenre and his protector Amen-Ra. We are told that

The Prince of the Southern City on hearing the message remained silent and wept a long time nor did he know how to return an answer good or bad . . .

Here the papyrus that allows us to glimpse a dramatic moment of Egyptian history breaks off. We know that Amen-Ra, light of the heavens, triumphed over his satanic enemy, but not at once nor easily did the Hyksos give up the gold, the might, and the fertility of Egypt.

Finally Ramose, son of Sekenenre, rose as leader of the south. Over the centuries the prosperous and peace-loving Egyptians had almost forgotten how to make war. Ramose, the legendary freedom fighter of ancient Egypt, inspired them with a new militant spirit, forged an army that included chariots, the revolutionary new fighting weapon introduced by the foreigners, and attacked the Hyksos. His end is not known but as can be seen from his mummy, recovered from a cache at Deir el-Bahri, he died in battle. A blow from an ax had fractured his skull and must have sent him senseless to the ground. And a dagger or javelin opened the forehead above the left eye where there was a flattened patch of exuded brain.

He was followed to the Theban throne by his brother Amosis who by driving the Hyksos out of Egypt* reunited the country and is considered the first king of the eighteenth dynasty. Amosis was determined to prevent further foreign domination of Egypt. He pursued the Hyksos into Palestine and by so doing showed the way to his successors and laid the foundation of that empire that was to see Egypt at the climacteric of her power and prosperity and over which Akhenaten was to reign.

Amosis gave thanks not to the sun god of Heliopolis but to Amen-Ra for his victories. Amen was the god of Thebes and yet another aspect of the sun god. His similarity in almost every respect to Atum-Ra does not say much for the originality of the Theban priesthood, but there was one supreme difference—he was southern and Theban. As Thebes rose to power with its kings and became the wealthiest city in the world, so Amen-Ra rose also in divine status until he dominated the Egyptian cosmology.

Amosis, as every successive Theban king was to do, gave thanks to his god by dedicating a temple in Thebes. He also endowed the sanctuary with a magnificent service of sacred vessels in precious metals and built a new temple barge upon the river from cedar extracted from the princes of the Lebanon. But, in the words of the historian James Henry Breasted, "His greatest work remains the eighteenth dynasty itself for whose brilliant career his own achievements laid so firm a foundation." His mummy, still bearing the mourners' funeral wreaths, was found in a cache at Deir el-Bahri. It was in such perfect condition that Gaston Maspero was moved to write, "Long garlands of faded flowers still decked it from head to foot and a wasp, attracted by their scent, must have settled upon them at the moment of burial and become imprisoned by the lid; the insect had become completely preserved from corruption by the balsams of the

*The question whether Amosis did succeed in driving out the Hyksos entirely is discussed in the Appendix.

embalmer, and its gauzy wings have passed uncrumpled through the long centuries.''

IV

If the kings who followed Amosis laid stress on their descent through the solar princess, it may be that, as Maspero stated, ''the part which the princesses of older times played in the transmission of power had, from the 12th Dynasty downwards, considerably increased in importance, and threatened to overshadow that of the princes. The question presents itself whether, during these centuries of perpetual warfare, there had not been a moment when all the males of the family having perished, the women alone were left to perpetuate the solar race on the earth and to keep the succession unbroken.''

There is also the distinct possibility that some of the invaders from Syria, inclined to the worship of a mother goddess, left more than a trace of their culture and goddess worship on the country they dominated for so many decades.

But however much the canons of Egyptian religion dictated the marriage of royal brother and sister, the system repeatedly broke down against the rock of hard reality. The divine solar king and queen were as much at the mercy of the uncertainties of childbirth, the quirks of fate, the limited pool of genes, and the heavy incidence of infant mortality in those days as the ordinary man and woman. And if there was no son born to the royal pair who survived infancy, no god to sit on the Horus throne, what then?

As might have been expected this occurred not once but several times. But the harem system had dynastic as well as other advantages. And the crisis could be overcome by the priests of Amen choosing a prince, son of one of the king's lesser wives, to succeed. The young king then married the solar princess and legitmized his position. That the line might break at its strongest link and that there might be no solar princess for the succeeding king to marry was an eventuality not to be thought of. Indeed for many generations the Great

Wife of the King did not fail to do her duty. She passed on, diluted perhaps, but intact, the blood of the Horus kings, precious elixir of divine inspiration, that legacy from the long-distant past—a tenuous link between god and man.

V

No assessment of Akhenaten or of the eighteenth dynasty would be complete without some account of the empire founded by its kings (see Genealogical Table). It had a profound effect on the insular Egyptians and the admixture of blood that resulted was not confined to the rank and file but could be seen in the royal palace and in the faces of the royal offspring.

Amosis, father of the dynasty, had set a pattern to his successors. He stood out as a warrior-prince, a true Horus king, who personally led his troops into battle. Driving a chariot of wood plated with gold and electrum, he seemed, in the words of a contemporary, "Like a flame of fire showing the way." So led, the Egyptians penetrated south through Nubia to the borders of modern Abyssinia. And each king pushed farther through the Lebanon and Syria into the mysterious east until they reached a great river that, unaccountably to them, flowed not north but south. This was the Euphrates. Thutmose I was the first Egyptian monarch to reach its waters where he set up a commemorative stela on its west bank to mark the boundary of his empire. He was also the first to come into personal contact with, and defeat, the armies of Babylonia and the Mitanni.

These most interesting people represented one of the earliest and most westerly outposts of the Indo-Aryan race yet disclosed. E. D. Phillips wrote, "During the second millennium the long process began by which the Indo-European peoples from the northern steppes beyond the Caucasus established themselves about western Asia, Iran and northern India."

They overran Anatolia—a name that means The Land Toward the Rising Sun—and formed the powerful Hittite empire. As Kassites they threatened Babylon and by the end of the sixteenth century B.C. established their own dynasty on the ancient Babylon throne. A third group, the Mitannians, were a people small in numbers but great in energy and achievement. They ruled as an Indo-European aristocracy from their capital at Wassuganni on the Khabour River, and in Akhenaten's time their empire stretched from the Tigris to the shores of the Mediterranean.

The Indo-Europeans were the first to use the horse in war to draw a light chariot with spoked wheels. Their conquest of Asia Minor and Mesopotamia, by chain reaction, helped to propel the Hyksos into Egypt, so that Thutmose I's defeat of Mitanni and Babylonia two hundred years later can be considered a kind of rough justice.

Thutmose III also invaded them, and because they were being threatened at the same time by the powerful Hittites from the north, it was natural they should seek to make what terms they could with the Egyptian pharaoh. When Amenhotep II came in turn to the Euphrates with his chariots, bowmen, spearmen, and all his military might, the chiefs of the Mitanni hastened to pay him homage and woo him with gifts. As a contemporary historian wrote:

They came with their tribute upon their backs to beseech his majesty that they may be given the sweet breath of life; a mighty occurrence it has never been heard since the time of the gods. This country which knew not Egypt, beseeches the Good God [the pharoah].

Amenhotep II was graciously pleased to accept the tribute and his son Thutmose IV went further, so much further that some historians have wondered whether this young king could have been the result of an alliance between Amenhotep II and a Mitannian princess. Such an alliance could have occurred and would explain a great deal that is obscure, but evidence is lacking. Little more is known than the queen's name, Tia, inscribed in a black granite statue where she is shown with her arm thrown protectively around her son, Thutmose. The pair's statue was found buried below ground in the temple of Amen at Thebes and is now in the Cairo museum.

Whether Thutmose IV was motivated by ties of blood or political considerations he concluded close treaties of friendship with Mitanni and Babylonia that were sealed by marriage—a pattern followed by his son Amenhotep III and his grandson Akhenaten.

Such intimate association with foreigners was bound to affect the outlook of the Egyptian royal house, and it is worth while studying what little is known of the most powerful of the two groups, the Mitannians.

The Mitannians had established their capital on the Khabour River in the center of a well-watered plain. They had much in common with the Egyptian hierarchy being a warrior aristocracy whose passion was the breeding and management of horses.

During the excavations in the Hittite capital of Hattusas, archaeologists found a text on the breeding and training of horses—certainly the oldest handbook of horsemanship in the world. And although the Hittites prided themselves on being expert horsemen the treatise was written not by a Hittite but by Kikkuli of Mittanni.

The kings of Mittanni had more in common with the pharaohs than a love of horses. Both worshiped sky gods, and the cosmology of the Indo-Aryan Mitannians centered on the Vedic gods—Mitra, Varuna, and Indra. Mitra was, like Horus, a sun god; Varuna his dark counterpart of the night; Indra the swashbuckling warrior god who swilled ambrosia to get drunk, rode in the sun chariot, and clove demons asunder with his mighty sword. The symbol of Mitra was the winged sun's disk. He was the intermediary between god and man who presided over the day. The wind was in his hair and the stars in his eyes. Golden-headed, golden-tongued, he drove his four immortal white steeds daily across the sky in a chariot whose rays dazzled mankind. Even the hooves of his horses were shod with the precious metal. His worship has been so confused with that of the Roman Mithras, who derived from him, that it is difficult to discover exactly how he appeared originally to the Mittanians. But it is interesting to find his image recurring late in Egyptian Coptic art, on horseback with the god Horus (identified in Christian iconography as Saint George) crushing the crocodile. Whatever Thutmose IV's provenance on his mother's side, there can be no doubt that he, his court, and indeed the whole of Egypt were profoundly affected by their glittering Indo-European and Syrian-Semitic neighbors. Egyptian conquest of the Near East meant that not only the wealth of spoils but also new ideas entered the country and mixing loam with the heavy soil of south Egyptian conservatism acted as humus.* Thebes became a hub of the universe, sharing with ancient Memphis the position of administrative and religious capital. Like Memphis it was a universal trading center. Commerce throve and goods were insufficient to meet demands so that every route, whether by land or water, to both capitals became thronged with traders. Their merchandise included foreign slaves for workshop or harem, herds of Hittite bulls and Mitannian stallions, horses from Singaar, oxen from Alashia, rare and curious animals such as elephants from the land of Nihi, brown bears from the Lebanon, smoked and salted fish, live birds of bright plumage, goldsmiths' work, precious stones and rare woods, musical instruments, weapons, chariots, embroidered cloths, oils, wine, and perfume. The new cosmopolitanism of the Egyptian capitals could be seen in the foreigners who thronged the cities: Mycenaeans, their outlandish ships anchored at the wharves, seeking to trade amphora and oil; Asiatic lords and Nubian princes, housed in a special building called Castle in Thebes, being educated in the southern capital before returning as loyal Egyptian vassals to their own lands; and, everywhere from the four corners of the empire, slaves. Thousands of these, some of whom became Egyptian tax-paying serfs, crowded the streets. There were artisans and laborers, handsome Nubians with crimped

---

*Since the Hyksos ruled all Egypt for over a century from their base on the delta it is impossible to overestimate their influence on the country. It is evident from the stela of Khamose that they were not unpopular. This contradicts of course the legend assiduously fostered by the eighteenth-dynasty kings. We know that the Hyksos were expelled by Khamose and his son Amosis and we can assume from the Biblical story that large numbers of their immediate followers were enslaved. But were there no intermarriages between Hyksos and northern Egyptians? Did no Hyksos foreigners take service with the new regime? Was Yuaa perhaps of Hyksos-Semitic origin and could not Akhenaten perhaps have inherited Semitic blood through his grandfather?

hair, Syrians, Mitannians, Kassites, Libyans. To show how great the influx of foreigners must have been, Amenhotep II brought with him from one eastern campaign alone five hundred subjected north Syrian lords and two hundred and forty of their women, some of whom must have entered his harem.

If Winckler is correct in saying that civilized peoples are never racially pure but always the product of a number of different strains, then the acceleration of civilization that occurred in Egypt at this period was a natural process.

Thebes with its enormous wealth, splendid palaces, and solemn temples became celebrated throughout the civilized world. Even the distant minstrels of Minos and Mycenae sang of the treasure of its citizens and the power of its armies. And centuries later when its glories had already faded, Homer remembered the legend and wrote:

Thebes of Egypt where the greatest possessions lie up in the houses.
Thebes of the hundred gates,
Where through each of the gates two hundred fighting men
Come forth to war with horses and chariots.

VI

In attempting to fit together the jigsaw puzzle of Akhenaten's family tree, the question of caste in ancient Egypt must also be considered. Who exactly was termed *royal,* who *noble,* and who a *commoner?* For instance, are those historians who have designated Akhenaten's mother, the Great Wife Tyi, as a commoner correct or are they seeking to impose too modern a pattern of thought on those ancient times?

The French Egyptologist Pierre Montet has distinguished three orders of Egyptian society: the *rekhetu,* or lower orders, who may originally have been those indigenous dwellers conquered by the Horus people; the *iry-pat,* or nobles; and the *henemmet,* or sun people. These divisions of society were still in force in Akhenaten's day as an inscription from a contemporary tomb wall makes clear—"The king [Akhenaten] seated himself upon the throne . . . and the sun folk, the patricians, and the common people . . . brought gifts of homage . . .''

At the same time one of the great advantages of eighteenth-dynasty life was the fluidity of its social distinctions. Education was the key to advancement, and a man could rise from comparative obscurity to such a position of power and distinction as vizier of Thebes, and an *iry-pat*.

But who were the sun people? Could these have been a group emerging from the harem system that has no analogy in western history? Ramses II of the nineteenth-dynasty produced two hundred children, of whom one hundred and eleven sons and fifty-nine daughters are known by name. Was this army of descendants all considered royal, as in European kingly houses, and thereafter their children and children's children?

Because the ancient Egyptians were a practical people, it seems unlikely. What can be deduced from the inscriptions suggests that perhaps only the sons and daughters of the Solar Princess were designated as royal. The subject bristles with question marks. Why was no precise indication of Tutankhamen's parentage inscribed in his tomb? Was it that in the house of the dead he was considered a simple son of Osiris, the god of resurrection? Was a queen's title of daughter, wife, and mother of a king a greater or lesser one than great hereditary heiress of the north and south? Did father of the god (king) mean in fact father-in-law? The answers are arbitrary and interpreted by different Egyptologists to suit their own theories. But the sun people* may well have been the children of the king's wives and concubines.

A failure of the direct male line resulted in a sun person or son of the king by a lesser wife or concubine being chosen— possibly by the priests. Married to the solar princess, he was brought up from childhood to fulfill his function as the new pharaoh.

This was certainly the case with Thutmose III, who in-

---

*Pierre Montet believes the term to indicate the priesthood, but surely these would be named specifically—priests of Atum or Aten or Amen?

scribed the story on a wall of the temple. It seems that on a feast day when the open court of the temple of Amen was thronged with worshipers, the priests bore out an image of the god and, among the acclamations of the people, carried it on their shoulders around the colonnade. The young Thutmose, aged according to modern chronology only eight, was already a temple novitiate. When the statue of the god stopped and inclined before him, the priests interpreted it as a divine sign. The child, who had prostrated himself, was raised and placed immediately in the station of the king, the ceremonial place where only the king might stand to celebrate the temple ritual. It was an unparalleled honor and thereafter he was duly crowned and given his royal names by the god himself. The mother of Thutmose was a minor wife or concubine of no position, named Isis, possibly of Nubian extraction. At least she gave her son health and strength, although his appearance did not answer to Maspero's idea of a conqueror.

When Maspero examined the Great King's mummy, he found the body squat and thickset, the face with a forehead abnormally low, the eyes deeply sunk, jaw heavy, lips thick, and cheekbones extremely prominent.

So, in spite of the insistence on solar, divine, and royal blood, owing to the plurality of royal marriages and the frequent failure of the royal male line, the purity of that blood had been much diluted.

But until the sudden death of Akhenaten's grandfather in the prime of youth, the pious myth had been maintained. Each king could imagine that the sacred ichor flowed in his veins and that he was in flesh and blood as well as spirit heir to Ra-Horus of the Horizon.

3.
GREAT WIFE TYI

She begins to speak
And her words are as drops of honey.
She is charming, her bower is green,
Greener than the papyrus.
She is laden with fruit,
Redder than the ruby.
The color of her is as glass,
Her body is as the color of the opal . . . .
It is cool in her shadow.
TURIN PAPYRUS

My father and my mother told me my name,
And it has remained hidden in my heart
since my birth.
EGYPTIAN TEXT

I

The popular adjective most often associated with Queen Tyi, the mother of Akhenaten, is mysterious. And the legend suggests a woman of character, making up for her lack of direct royal blood by a masterful personality.

Her mother and father can be designated as court officials, although they both held priestly offices at Akhmîm, where they must have spent much of their time away from the royal entourage.

The mystery is, of course, why Tyi was chosen from all others for the supreme position of wealth and dignity that being the Great Wife of the King entailed.

Tyi's parents were Yuaa and Tuaa, whose tomb was discovered in 1905 at the entrance to the Valley of the King. Yuaa held the sacerdotal office of priest or prophet of the god Min. At the same time he was master of the horse and chariot captain to the king and bore the title Divine Father (of the pharaoh).

His wife Tuaa was Superior of the Harem of Min.

However influential they may have been there is little in their titles or tomb furniture to explain why their daughter was accorded such signal honor. Love can be ruled out as an explanation. Tyi was most likely twelve or thirteen at the time of the marriage, her husband Amenhotep III possibly a year older. The marriage must have been arranged by the queen mother, and any girl the king desired would, without loss of honor, have entered his harem.

But, as has been suggested, the king's marriage with his Great Wife, the wife whose children were to inherit the throne, was not a matter of choice in the eighteenth dynasty. The princess was heiress. The prince achieved the throne only through marriage with her. Our western ideas of romance, love, and suitability must be discarded to realize the rigid legal and religious requirements that probably directed the king in his search for a Great Wife.

Why then did the young Amenhotep not marry his sister on his early accession to the throne? The answer can only be that Mutemwaya, his mother, had no daughters living. Nor do there appear to have been any daughters of his father to fill the vacant role of sun princess. To understand the predicament in which Amenhotep III must have been placed on the death of his father that king's own youth can be recalled during the last months of his predecessor, the warrior king Amenhotep II.

Amenhotep's end was darkened, as Maspero wrote, "by the open or secret rivalries which the succession usually stirred up among the king's sons. The king had a daughter only by his marriage with one of his full sisters who, like himself, possesed all the rights of sovereignty; those of his sons who did not die young were the children of princesses of inferior rank or of concubines, and it was a subject of anxiety which of them would be chosen to inherit the crown and be united in marriage with the king's heiress . . . One of his sons named Thutmose, who resided at the White Wall (Memphis), was in the habit of betaking himself frequently to the Libyan desert to practise with the javelin or to pursue the hunt of lions and gazelles in his chariot. On these occasions it was his pleasure to preserve the strictest incognito, and he was accompanied by two discreet servants only. One day, when chance brought him into the neighborhood of the Great Pyramid, he lay down for his accustomed siesta in the shade cast by the Sphinx . . .''

The actual inscription, translated by Brugsch, carved on the base of the Sphinx describes the occasion. The young prince (who became Thutmose IV) ''held a spear-throwing for his pleasure on the territory of the Memphite nomes in a southerly and northerly direction and darted brazen darts at the target and hunted lions in the valley of the gazelles. He went there with his chariot with two horses and his horses were quicker than the wind; with him were two of his followers. No man knew them. It was the hour in which he granted rest to his servants.'' And before falling asleep the prince is said to have ''prayed to the lady of Sais.''

At that time the Sphinx, built half a millennium earlier by Cheops, was silted up with sand. As he lay alseep the young prince dreamed that the man-headed monster spoke to him and promised the throne should be given him on condition he swore to clear the silt of the desert from the gigantic statue. That there was a political reality behind this charming story is evident and will be discussed later.

Maspero continues, ''Thutmose was in fact chosen to be the husband of the Queen Mutemwaya and immediately after his succession fulfilled his oath; he removed the sand, built a chapel between the paws, and erected against the breast of the statue a stela of red granite on which he related his adventure.''

Thutmose's brief reign of nine years began in 1414 B.C. Like his forefathers he led his troops up to the land of Naharin (Mitanni) in what was probably a token show of force. He concluded friendly alliances with the Mitannian and Babylonian monarchs and on his return to Egypt wrote asking

Artamata for the Mittanian king's daughter in marriage. After exhibiting the reluctance demanded by royal etiquette, Artamata consented and the princess was dispatched to Egypt under escort. It was the first of several political marriages between the Indo-European and Egyptian kings.

Some Egyptologists have postulated that this Mitannian princess was renamed Mutemwaya and became the mother of Amenhotep III.

The custom of royal inheritance through the mother makes this impossible. Because Thutmose IV was evidently a minor prince he must have based his principal claim to the throne on his marriage to the solar princess. Mutemwaya's styling on the model of a sacred boat of black granite in the British Museum is Great Hereditary Princess of the North and South. This sounds conclusive, but some Egyptologists query her pure royal descent. They point out that she does not state that she is the daughter of the king, and that her son Amenhotep III may have deliberately exaggerated his mother's regal status.

But if Amenhotep invented no spurious titles for his wife, Queen Tyi, would he have done so for Mutemwaya? Or would her true royal Egyptian descent be so boldly proclaimed on the walls of the temple at Luxor?

Maspero, at least, had no doubts of Mutemwaya's origins ". . . the heiress, daughter, sister and wife of a king had at least one son (Amenhotep III)," he wrote. "In this case again the noble birth of the mother atoned for the defects of the paternal origin. Moreover, according to tradition, Amen-Ra himself had intervened to renew the blood of his descendants; he appeared in the person of Thutmose IV, and *under this guise* [author's italics] he became the father of the heir of the pharaohs. Like Queen Ahmose [the mother of Hatshepsut] in the bas-reliefs of Deir el-Bahri, Mutemwaya is shown on those of Luxor in the arms of her divine lover and subsequently greeted by him with the title of Mother . . . her son Amenhotep, on coming into the world, is placed in the hands of the two Niles to receive nourishment and the education meet for the Children of the Gods. He profited fully by them, for he remained in power forty years and his reign was one of the most prosperous ever witnessed by Egypt during the Theban dynasties.''

In this carefully worded passage Maspero, acknowledged the greatest authority of his day on Egyptology, almost sounded as if he had doubts as to whether Amenhotep was or was not the son of his supposed father Thutmose IV. An account of the examination of the mummy of Thutmose explains perhaps why, for the king was declared to be a young man of twenty-five at the time of his death. But his son Amenhotep is considered by most historians to have been not less than twelve or fourteen—sixteen at his accession according to Petrie. If so, Thutmose must have experienced his dream of the Sphinx as a mere child and successfully consummated his marriage at the tender age of eleven! Cyril Aldred surmounts the difficulty by suggesting that Amenhotep III was only seven or eight at his father's death. But the year after he came to the throne there was a public proclamation of his marriage to Queen Tyi and of a wild cattle hunt when the king personally slew fifty-six great bulls in one day. The exploits seem more suited to a youth of fifteen than a child of eight or nine. Can there by any other explanation for the discrepancy in the ages of Amenhotep and his father?

Thutmose had six sons (at least one, Prince Amenenhet, died in early childhood, his mummy being discovered in his father's sepulcher). They are depicted on a wall of the tomb of the king's tutor, Hekreshu. In a curious scene Hekreshu is shown seated with King Thutmose IV upon hs knee. The young prince, looking about ten years of age, bears on his forehead the royal uraeus, in his right hand is the scepter, in his left the ankh, and he wears a pectoral inscribed with his praenomen. Hekreshu is described as ''Tutor of the king's son, eldest of his body Thutmose Khakhawa.'' Before him stands Amenhotep, already half his father's size and aged (apparently) five or six. He wears the royal sidelock and holds in one hand a bouquet of flowers and in the other a sprig of green leaves. Suspended from his neck was once a pectoral with the praenomen of Thutmose IV and he is accompanied by his own tutor Hekerneheh.

Thutmose IV and Amenhotep III with their tutors were depicted in a wall painting from the vestible of Tomb 64 at Thebes. If the ages of the two royal princes are shown correctly vis à vis one another, then Thutmose (sitting on his tutor's knee) could hardly have been the father of Amenhotep (standing). The painting must pre-date Thutmose IV's accession (at the age of sixteen) since he is styled "Prince." Six infant males depicted on the same wall suggest, if Amenhotep III really was his son, precocious virility.

Strangely enough, the lady most concerned—Queen Mutemwaya—openly stated on the walls of the temple at Luxor that not Thutmose but the great god Amen-Ra was the father of her child. There was a precedent for this.

Queen Hatshepsut had depicted her own divine origin on the shrine of her mortuary temple at Deir el-Bahri, and the marriage of her mother, the Solar Queen Ahmose, to Amen-Ra. Hatshepsut's purpose was probably twofold. Because her father Thutmose I was not of the direct royal line she wished to reestablish the purity. of her descent; and she wished to prove her superiority over her husband and half brother Thutmose II.

Did Mutemwaya also need to overcome the awkwardness of her husband's semiroyal birth? Because the dawn of Atenism can be traced to that husband's reign, might the queen, a Theban, also have felt Amen's ascendancy threatened and the need to invoke the special protection of the god. Or could there have been some other reason for the insistence (which technically was always claimed by the king) on Amenhotep's divine origin?

This is to return to Tyi and the mysterious choice of the Great Wife. When as a young man still in his twenties Thutmose IV died, leaving apparently no living daughter to carry on the line, it must have appeared as a disaster to those who sincerely believed only a sun princess could legitimize the new king. In the circumstances all that Mutemwaya and her advisers might do was to find the nearest possible equivalent of a sun princess, a girl of royal blood, a substitute sister, as nearly related to Amenhotep as possible.

Can Tyi be fitted into this category?

Arthur Weigall was one of the first to discuss Tyi's father and mother and from an examination of the two mummies to suggest that Yuaa was a foreigner, possibly of Mitannian origin, while the visage of Tuaa so strongly resembled the mummied physiognomy of Thutmose III as to suggest a relationship. This seemed to be borne out by one of Tuaa's titles, Royal Mother of the Great Wife of the King. More recently, Cyril Aldred has discussed further the provenance and family of Tyi's parents. He discovered a reference to a mid-eighteenth dynasty official called Yey who was, like Yuaa, father of the god and master of the horse.

Many high offices at this period seem to have been hereditary, and Yey could well have been the father of Yuaa; and of Hittite, Syrian, or Mitannian ancestry. From the time of the introduction of horses and chariots into Egypt, such foreigners had taken appointments in the Egyptian army. That Yuaa was the son of one of these foreigners can be adduced from the several ways in which his name was spelt— such as Aay, Yaa, and Aya—suggesting, wrote Aldred, ''an outlandish-sounding word not established sufficiently long to receive the sanction of uniform orthography.''

If Yuaa, a young master of horse with a high position at court, married Tuaa, a daughter of Amenhotep II or Thutmose III by a harem woman, their relationship to the Egyptian royal family would be explained.

This hypothesis and several others are possible. What is unlikely is that Amenhotep was breaking with tradtion in marrying Tyi. He was as concerned as all the other kings of the eighteenth dynasty with the ancient marriage rites, and as soon as he was able, married his own daughter Sitamen. With a paternal injection of divine blood she approximated most nearly to a sun princess.

It is surely logical to believe that the choice of Tyi as Great Wife was determined by one consideration alone, her consanguinity to the king. Without any distortion of the known facts, she could very well have been a cousin. Could there have been a closer relationship? Could Tyi have been the king's half sister?

Because it is evident she was the child of her parents and not of either Mutemwaya or Thutmose, there is only one way in which such a relationship can be traced and that is by believing that the pious myth of Amenhotep's divine origin was based on reality. We know too little of the period to be certain that the public announcement of the queen's marriage to the god was not accomapnied also by a ceremony—and an official visit to the god's sanctuary. There, as described on Hatshepsut's temple at Deir el-Bahri, the god Amen-Ra, dressed in all the regalia of a pharaoh, visited the queen, heralded, in the words of the scribe, with a brilliant light and a strong smell of perfume and incense.

On such ceremonial occasions it has been considered that the king acted as proxy for the god, but could it not have been at certain times the other way about? Could not the god, in the person of his chief priest, have acted as proxy for the king, especially if the latter then was too youthful to ensure an heir?

The ithyphallic aspect of Amen-Ra was the god Min, to whom the people turned in matters to do with progeniture. He was, wrote Weigall, "a god of the sun whose fertilizing rays made pregnant the whole earth . . . . and he represented the pristine desires of lawful reproduction . . ." He was the pre-dynastic deity from whom Amen was almost certainly derived. If Yuaa was of foreign extraction, as Weigall and Aldred both suggest, there would have been no Egyptian god to whose service he would have attached himself so readily as to that of Min, and he was in fact prophet of Min.

The very tentative suggestion that Yuaa might have deputized for Amen-Ra on an important occasion is one that can, of its nature, never be proved or disproved. But it would clearly explain Tyi's marriage to Amenhotep and the consideration accorded her as coequal of her husband. And it would also explain the very close association of Yuaa and his family with three generations of royal pharaohs. The Egyptians were used to mental gymnastics in divine matters and were perfectly capable of accepting Amenhotep III as the true son of Thutmose IV as well as of the god and at the same time acknowledging (if this was indeed the case) that Yuaa, the priest of Min, had a special claim on the royal family. (Against this theory is the fact, cited by Aldred, that Amenhotep closely resembled Thutmose, both kings having similar facial structures and cephalic indexes. But Thutmose was, if not the father, at least the uncle of Amenhotep III.) On the public espousal of Amenhotep and Tyi—boy king and girl queen—marriage scarabs were distributed with an inscription that was tantalizingly brief, merely stating the names of Tyi's parents and that ". . . she is the great wife of a mighty king whose southern boundary is as far as Karoy

and whose northern boundary stretches to Naharin [Mi-
tanni]."

According to protocol, a sculptor was commissioned after·
this auspicious occasion to produce a larger than life-sized
group of the young couple, which is now in the Cairo Museum.
Whatever their real relationship or facial similarity the sculptor followed the pious tradition of marriage of brother and
sister and carved them alike, replicas each of the other.

Another little-known likeness of the queen in her youth
is on a relief found in the tomb of Userhat at Thebes and now
in the Brussels museum. It also portrays the very close likeness to the young king.

II

Because the contents of the tomb of Yuaa and Tuaa are
of such importance to the history of the time, and the most
valuable collection of treasure (with the single exception of
Tutankhamen's) found in the Theban necropolis, the story of
the discovery is worth retelling.

Maspero had induced a wealthy American, interested in
archaeology, Theodore Davis, to advance money for the purpose of scientific investigation. A site had been chosen in the
Valley of the Kings, where the eighteenth- and nineteenth-
dynasty kings were known to have been buried, and in fact
not far from the as yet undiscovered tomb of Tutankhamen.

The work was under the supervision of Arthur Weigall,
acting for the Egyptian government, and many tons of rubbish had already been removed by the workmen before the
top of a stairway was uncovered on February 5, 1905. To
those reading of the discovery today, the drama of the
moment seems as a curtain raiser for the great find of Tutankhamen's tomb in 1922.

By February 11 the stairway had been laboriously cleared
and the lintel of a doorway exposed. It was the threshold both
to a tomb door and a dramatic discovery that brought a number of experts hurrying to the scene—as much from the
perennial excitement of finding buried treasure as for the

These two reliefs, which were not originally together, clearly show the resemblance between Amenhotep III and Great Wife Tyi. The young king is shown after his accession. The beautiful carving of Tyi as a young girl comes from the tomb of Userhat at Thebes. It is now in the Brussels Museum.

interest of scientific investigation. This was the golden age of Egyptology. Each season the rich, the interested, and the famous flocked to Luxor to enjoy the perfect winter climate, the romance of the Egyptian past, and the picturesque view of the Egyptian present. Maspero, head of the Antiquities Service since 1881, left his steamer and hastened to investigate. Professor A. M. Sayce of Oxford, who was living in the luxury of the *Ishtar,* one of the largest sailing boats on the Nile, hurried up, clad as usual in the long black skirts of his clerical garments. Weigall and the American artist Joseph Lindon Smith and his wife waited impatiently for the signal to pentrate into the tomb and an official visit by the Duke of Connaught and the Duke of Devonshire was expected. It was a moment of tension. The dignitaries were

This colossal statue of Amenhotep III and Great Wife Tyi and their first daughter is in the Cairo Museum.

late, Davis fainted from sheer excitement, and Weigall and Lindon Smith, overcome by curiosity, crept surreptitiously into the tomb for a preview. But at length the official investigation got under way. Professor Sayce observed that "the door was closed with a slab of stone and sealed with a royal seal. The dried up clay used for the sealings and the stick with which it had been laid on the stone were still in the bowl that rested on a step on a level with the middle of the door."

But the seal had been broken. Thieves had already penetrated the tomb and tunneled through the debris concealing the outer blocked-up doorway. Beyond this was a passage cut out of the rock and descending into the bowels of the earth. It led to a second walled-up doorway, pierced like the first by robbers. A human touch was the bunch of onions and dried herbs thrown onto a bench on the left of the passage and abandoned by one of the last visitants to the tomb, three thousand years before. At last the second doorway was penetrated and the archaeologists' dream realized, an intact—or almost intact—burial. Like Tutankhamen's, the tomb had been entered by robbers in remote antiquity who had left everything "in a kind of orderly disorder." According to Maspero, the tomb had been ". . . violated with discretion by persons who almost possessed respect for the dead and who were in too great a hurry to despoil it thoroughly; if they broke open the coffins and took the jewels from the mummies, they did not touch the equipment . . . it seemed the thieves, after despoiling the mummy, felt some qualms of conscience at carrying off . . . any more."

Perhaps it was less qualms of conscience than the approach of the necropolis guard that deterred the depredators. But they left enough to make the burial of Yuaa and Tuaa in size, wealth, and interest second only to that of Tutankhamen.

Everywhere was the gleam of gold, the blaze of blue lapis lazuli: boxes, furniture, pottery, a chariot, and two anthropoid coffins. Sayce described the scene as ". . . one that can never be forgotten. From floor to ceiling the tomb was filled with objects of all kinds—the broken gilded shroud, the inlaid cases in which soft muslin garments were kept, carved and gilded chairs, alabaster vases and the like—all piled promiscuously one upon the other. Wherever we stepped we trod upon fragments of gold foil. In the light of our electric lamp, the whole place seemed to blaze with gold. . .''

The foil had fallen from what were described as "two great wooden boxes or crates" that had been broken open. As will now be realized, these were the remnants of the gold-plated shrines originally placed over the coffins but which, until they were found in position and in situ among Tutankhamen's burial furniture, were not recognized as such. It is interesting to remember that in 1905 the elaborate ritual of royal or semiroyal burial was as yet unknown.

The dead dignitaries lay each in a nest of coffins whose covers had been neatly tilted off by the thieves. In their search for jewels they had even torn the wrapping from the faces of the mummies, leaving their features exposed. Joseph Lindon Smith described Yuaa as white-haired—"an old man of striking appearance and dignity. His splendid head and fine features bore a marked resemblance to Lincoln." Tuaa's face he considered "serene and interesting, a low brow and eyes wide apart and a curiously expressive mouth." Looking almost as though they had been brought into the tomb yesterday, the parents of Tyi lay with closed eyes and the calm mask of death in the midst of their half-looted splendor.

Weigall wrote as an eyewitness: "Imagine entering a town house which had been closed for the summer: imagine the stuffy room, the stiff silent appearance of the furniture, the feeling that some ghostly occupants of the vacant chairs have just been disturbed, the desire to throw open the windows to let life into the room once more. That was perhaps the first sensation as we stood, really dumbfounded, and stared around at the relics of the life of over three thousand years ago . . . [There were] three beautiful armchairs, decorated with gold, and a pillow made of down and covered with linen. It was so perfectly preserved that one might have sat upon it . . . without doing it an injury. Here were fine alabaster vases, in one . . . a liquid like honey or syrup still unsolidified by time. Boxes of exquisite workmanship stood in various parts of the room, some resting on delicately wrought legs . . . wicker trunks fitted with trays and partitions . . . beds with springy string mattresses . . . and the light chariot which Yuaa had owned in his lifetime. In all directions stood objects gleaming with gold undulled by a speck of dust and one felt that the entire human conception of time was wrong. These were the things of yesterday, of a year or so ago. Why, here were meats prepared for the feasts in the Underworld . . . Yuaa's favourite joints, each neatly placed in a wooden box as though for a journey. Here was his staff, here his sandals—a new pair and an old—and . . . the magical figures by the power of which he was to make his way through Hades . . . But though the eyes passed from object to object they ever returned to the two lidless coffins in which the owners of this room of the dead lay as though peacefully sleeping . . .''

Of a special interest to historians were those objects in the tomb inscribed with the names of Amenhotep III, Queen Tyi, and their daughter Sitamen, the princess who had been selected by her father to perform for him the role of solar queen. Two of the chairs bore her name. Of wood, inlaid with gold, they showed the young Sitamen paying homage to her enthroned mother. In one, Tyi is surmounted with the sacred plumes of Atum. Like the goddess Sekhmet, whom she is impersonating, she holds the crux ansata or ankh—symbol of generation—in her hand and shelters the sacred cat of Sekhmet under her chair. One would like to think that the cat was not only symbolic but the queen's special pet.

With so much of interest it is perhaps ungrateful to cavil at what was missing from the tomb and the absence of much desired and vital information, but all the personal jewelry, solid gold ornaments, and rings on which names and attributes might have been written had been lifted by the thieves. Although it was discovered what these two ancient Egyptian dignitaries, grandparents to Akhenaten, looked like, what they wore, what they ate, and how they furnished their rooms, there was no clue as to their parentage. Even more strange was the absence of all reference to their grandchild, the great Pharaoh Akhenaten, or to Ay, the man who was most likely their youngest and most illustrious son.

Aldred has suggested that Ay, Akhenaten's right-hand man

and master of horse, was the son of Yuaa and Tuaa. Ay lasted into Tutankhamen's reign, was one of the boy king's chief counselors, and came to the throne on his premature death. Most Egyptologists now agree in supposing him the brother of Queen Tyi. Another brother was Aanen, whose titles were Second Prophet of Amen, Greatest of Seers in the temple of Ra-Atum and *Setem*-priest belonging to Karnak. He is mentioned on his mother's sarcophagus and, wrote

Ay as Nile god.

Aldred, ''his intimate relationship to the royal family has to be divined from such expressions as 'He may approach near his lord', 'Greatly beloved in the palace', 'He whose favours endure in the palace'.''

Aldred bases his arguments on the likeness of name—Ay to Aya, one form in which Yuaa's name was sometimes written. Also he believes that certain court positions were hereditary. Like Yuaa, Ay was Master of the Horse, Father of the God, and referred to himself with the similar honorific titles of ''one trusted by the good god in the entire land,'' ''foremost of the companions of the king,'' and ''praised of the good god.'' The circumstantial evidence is so great that, although final proof is missing, it is impossible not to agree with Aldred that Ay was the more powerful and influential of the two sons of Yuaa and Tuaa. Yet Aanen but not Ay was mentioned on his mother's sarcophagus, and there was no reference whatever to Akhenaten throughout the tomb, nor was any gift or token found from the pharaoh to his deceased grandparents.

Setting aside the possibility that all objects referring to Ay and Akhenaten were rifled by thieves, the omission of the two names can be deliberate and for the same reason. Yuaa and Tuaa died, it is thought, at the beginning of Akhenaten's reign. Ay was Akhenaten's man and a strong supporter of the new religion.

If the elderly and conservative prophet of Min and his wife, mistress of the harem of Min, a god who was an aspect of Amen, had shown themselves antagonistic to the heretical views of their son and grandson, then the absence of reference to these close royal relatives in their tomb is explained.

4.
THEBES
BY MOONLIGHT

The tradition of the country people says that this was once the dwelling of a king; it has certainly that appearance, for one sees there the great and beautiful remains of a castle with avenues having Sphinxes on either side. The gates are monumental and rear up beyond all measure and belief, covered with the most beautiful stones it is possible to see.

FATHER CHARLES FRANCOIS, 1668

At Luxor it would be difficult to describe the sensations which the sight of objects so grand, so majestic, raised within me. It was not a simple admiration merely, but an ecstasy which suspended the use of all my faculties. I remained for some time immovable with rapture, and I felt inclined more than once to prostrate myself in token of veneration before monuments, the rearing of which appeared to transcend the strength and genius of man . . . Let the so much boasted fabrics of Greece and Rome come and bow down before the temples and palaces of Thebes of Egypt. Its lofty ruins are more striking, its gigantic wrecks more majestic in their perfect preservation. The glory of the most celebrated fabrics vanished before the prodigies of Egyptian architecture and to describe them justly a man must possess the genius of those who conceived and executed them . . .

C. S. SONNINI, 1799

I

Although, from the middle of the eighteenth dynasty, Thebes remained the religious center for the worship of Amen-Ra, as an administrative capital it acknowledged the ascendancy of ancient Memphis.

Just as the Thinite kings had moved north to found a centrally situated capital, so Thutmose I founded a Memphite palace after his northern conquests. From the time of Thutmose III onward Memphis seems to have been the real seat of government. It is more than probable that the Theban kings spent at least half the year in their northern, half in their southern, capitals. Yet it is difficult to avoid the conclusion that Thebes was the town beloved by Tyi and Amenhotep III and that it was here they passed the major part of their lives.

Amenhotep was in a special sense under the divine protection of the god of Thebes, Amen-Ra, and because Amen-Ra was also the god singled out for Akhenaten's most vicious attacks, it is necessary to know something about this Theban deity.

He was almost certainly derived from the prehistoric deity Min, whose shrine was at nearby Coptos. Amen's name meant "hidden" and he dwelt in his home in Ipet-esut, or Karnak. The great temple and its adjuncts came into being through a period of more than two thousand years, and there were constant replacements, alterations, and additions to the existing fabric. Ipet-esut, pronounced i-*Taype*-sut, sounded like, and became, Thebes to the ancient Greeks.

Amen and Min wear tall plumes above their heads, a sign of some connection with the Libyans. For the latest concept is that these wild cattle herders, who entered Egypt in predynastic times when the savannas of the Sahara were drying into desert, greatly influenced early Egyptian thought and religion. The Libyan symbol of chieftainship was the double head plume. This became an attribute of some of the predynastic gods, such as Min and Amen, and later the royal Egyptian kings.

The religion of Egypt showed a love of family life and reflected perhaps that marriage of matriarchal and patriarchal civilizations that took place at the dawn of history. In consequence the major gods were all married, members of a trinity, father, mother, son. Amen-Ra's wife was Mut, whose name signifies "mother." As Amen rose to become king of the Gods, Mut usurped the functions of several other goddesses, and was identified with Bast, the cat goddess, and Sekhmet, the powerful goddess of war, from whom she borrowed the head of a lioness. At first childless, she adopted the god Mont. Later, during the great period of Amen's ascendancy, she produced the child Khons, and the triad of Thebes was complete.

Like the pharaoh, with his palaces at Memphis and Malkata, Amen also was worshiped in two temple complexes—the largest and most revered at Ipet-esut, the second known as Southern Opet, at Luxor. Here Amenhotep III built a magnificent court with a double row of cluster columns and at the same time set up the sanctuary to his mother. On its walls was inscribed the story of his miraculous birth.

Later when the houses of the living masked the temples of the dead, this sanctuary was part of a house and roofed in. In the nineteenth century a visitor found it difficult to decipher the wall engravings "by the light of a candle tied to the end of a stick." Today they are open to the sky and are still difficult to decipher. Akhenaten's erasures everywhere of Amen and the lesser gods, added to generations of use as the walls of an eastern living room, make their survival something of a miracle.

The sanctuary is reached by a doorway in the east wall of Amenhotep III's hypostyle hall. The chamber contains three clustered columns and is roofless, and the story, told in strip-cartoon style, begins at the lower right hand corner of the west wall. It begins with Amen, king of the gods, presiding at a council of twelve deities—Osiris, Horus, Nephthys, Seth, and Hathor in the top row; Mont, Atum, Shu, Tefnut, Geb, and Nut below. (These gods defaced by Akhenaten were again restored after his death. It is significant that Atum-Ra, god of Heliopolis, was the only carving not mutilated by Akhenaten.) Amen has, it seems, summoned the gods to announce his intention of visiting the queen and impersonating her husband. The hieroglyphics show the words, "I will join for her the two lands in peace . . . I will give to her all lands and all countries."

The next scene shows an ancient Egyptian annunciation. The cow goddess Hathor, an aspect of Nut, wearing the horned disk of the moon, embraces Mutemwaya and tells her of her approaching happiness and the glory awaiting her. The queen is styled Great Royal Wife, Mutemwaya, living like Ra. There is apparently no parallel in Hatshepsut's temple of Deir el Bahri to this scene, or to the following one in which Thutmose IV appears opposite Amen-Ra, to be told of the subordinate role he will play as father of his son. Amen then interviews Thoth, called in the Pyramid texts the Son of Ra. Sometimes, as here, he is Ibis-headed or, as elsewhere, represented as a dog-headed baboon bearing the moon's disk. Thoth was a god of the Delta, in Egyptian mythology the embodiment of knowledge and wisdom, the patron of art, music, magic, medicine, and mathematics. He was also the inventor of writing, without which humanity might, from generation to generation, forget its knowledge. Aptly, the Egyptians made Thoth the messenger between god and man, and in his interview with Amen this is his role. It is he who arranges the divine assignation and leads Amen-Ra to the queen.

The carvings of the divine nuptials are among the least disfigured of the series. Amen-Ra and the queen sit closely confronting one another on the couch of the sky. Both wear the lofty plumes of royal divinity. The god is holding the emblem of life to the nostrils of the queen who, responding with an affectionate gesture, touches his left hand and supports his right elbow. The queen wears the vulture headdress, symbol of maternity. She and her divine lover are born aloft on the hands of the two sky goddesses Neit and Serquet, while, above, the horned sun disk spreads vulture wings as if beaming the light of divine approval.

The text, which is here in a fair state of preservation, reads, "Amen-Ra, King of the Gods, Lord of the Thrones of the Two Lands . . . hath made his appearance like the majesty of this husband, king of Upper and Lower Egypt, Menkheprure (Thutmose IV) Giver of Life. Amen-Ra found the queen reclining on her couch in the beauty of her palace; she waked at the odor of the god; she was glad before his majesty; he advanced towards her . . . he made her behold him in his godlike form when he came upon her; she exulted on beholding his beauty; his love went into her members and the sweet odors of the god filled the palace; all his fragrance seemed from the land of Punt."

The queen's speech has been preserved. "Sayeth Mutemwaya, before the majesty of this august god Amen, Lord of the Thrones of the Two Lands: Twofold deity, what is thy will? . . . pleased art thou with my womanly majesty; thy dew pervades my every member. Then . . . did the majesty of this god all which he desired with her.''

Amen-Ra in reply predicted the birth of his son. ''Sayeth Amen-Ra before her majesty: Amenhotep Prince of Thebes will be the name of this son which is in thy womb; this is the saying that came forth from the mouth. He shall wield excellent sovereignty in this land to its farthest horizon. My soul is his; my bounty is his; he shall rule the Two Lands like Ra forever.''

The story continues with Amen-Ra's directions to Khnum, the potter god, who was the molder of mankind and who was represented with the head and twisted horns of the wild goat. Obeying Amen-Ra's instructions, Khnum is seen at his potter's wheel forming the bodies of the child and his ka (soul). Khnum promises that they shall be formed with unique members.

The birth follows. Mutemwaya is led by two goddesses to the birthstool placed on a long couch. A whole pantheon of gods and spirits surround her protectively. These include the two Niles and the deities associated with the four cardinal points, while Bes, the cheerful, libidinous household god, and Taueret, hippopotamus goddess of childbirth, lend their sanction.

Thus divinely inspired and encompassed, Amenhotep III is brought into the world, preceded by his ka, or soul, and is immediately presented to his father Amen-Ra, who acknowledges paternity, taking him in his arms and crying, ''Come, come in peace, son of Ra, of my loins, Nebmaetra, giving life.'' It can be seen from these words and the subsequent phrase, ''son of my body, made of one flesh with me,'' that Amen-Ra's paternity was looked on as a physical reality.

The scene is completed by the arrival of the goddess Mut, patron of the queen and heavenly consort of Amen-Ra. She wears the two crowns of Egypt and holds the palm branch of years in her right hand, where can be seen the restored Ra name of Amenhotep III with the words ''son, beloved.'' The child has his left arm around the god's neck and Amen-Ra says again, "Come in peace, son of my loins, Nebmaetra. I have given thee to live millions of years like Ra." Handed on to his divine foster nurse, the cow goddess Hathor, he is given his Horus name of Horus-Ra, Strong Bull, appearing in Truth.

The final scene shows Safekh (or Seshat), the female counterpart of Thoth, inscribing the young prince's numerous titles for posterity, while Ptah, priest god of Memphis, looks on.

The scenes described take place on the east wall of the sanctuary; on the north is shown the adoration of Mut; on the south the coronation of Amenhotep III, and, to bring the story full cycle, the west wall depicts the death and Osirification of the king.

In the coronation scenes the young king appears to be about twelve years old. Another point of interest is that the figure of the ithyphallic Min appears under the title of Amen-Ra here and everywhere in this part of the temple, his phallus erect and his arm raised beneath the flail.

II

Such divine blessings as those promised on the sanctuary wall of Luxor seem to presage greatness. Amenhotep III is often compared to Louis XIV of France and has, perhaps, a more genuine claim to the title of Sun King than the Roi Soleil. Like Louis he has also been called The Magnificent. If not great, he was at least fortunate—fortunate in his wealth, in the prosperity of Egypt during his reign, in the ability and loyalty of the men who served him, and in his wife Tyi. There was no demand for him to be a general or play the hero on the battlefield. Egypt at the height of her power was able to dispense with a warrior-king and Amenhotep, with a clear conscience, could enjoy in peace the spoils accumulated by his forebears through generations of war.

The mummy of Thutmose IV shows the emaciation likely from a wasting disease such as tuberculosis. Whether he died unexpectedly or after a prolonged illness, it must have caused consternation in court circles. Although the Egyptians prepared early in life for their departure from it, the death of the militant young king at twenty-five would have come as a shock. The procedure of choosing a young heir, designated as coregent, and marrying him to the heiress solar princess insured a peaceful succession. It worked so successfully that there is no example at this period of a younger king taking up arms against his father.

Amenhotep, as can be seen from the tomb of Hekreshu (see page 45), had been designated crown prince from his earliest years, although the vital matter of a wife for him was lacking. In the event his mother, Queen Mutemwaya, stood up for him at the coronation ceremonies when Amenhotep, with his own hands, loosed four birds to carry his name as supreme king, pharaoh, and emperor to the four corners of the earth.

Many have commented sympathetically on the tender age of Tutankhamen at his accession—a child king placed in supreme authority on the throne. But Amenhotep III, only a year or two older, also succeeded as a mere lad to the wealth and dignity of a pharaoh. Under the dominance of the powerful queen mother, married at puberty, what must the boy have thought of the endless pomp and pageantry of his existence? Brought up to believe in his divine origin, surrounded by the greatest luxury the world had then to offer, what sort of king did this scion of the sun god prove to be? The major events of the early part of his reign can be followed in a series of commemorative scarabs. The first, of year 2,* announced his marriage to Tyi. In that same year he took part in a cattle hunt in the land bordering the delta, when a herd of one hundred and seventy wild cows and bulls was driven into an enclosure. Entering it in his chariot, the king personally slew fifty-six of the savage beasts in one day and twenty more at a second onslaught.

*All dates in ancient Egypt were regnal dates, and dated from year 1 of the current king's reign. This is most confusing when the date is found but the king's name is missing!

The king is unlikely to have performed this feat under the age of fifteen or sixteen, which would make him fourteen at the time of his accession. That he was fond of hunting is evident since in the year 10 he claimed to have brought down with his own arrows one hundred and two fierce lions. This was also commemorated by the issue of a scarab, but it is possible that the hunts were some sort of ritual act, in which the young king proved his strength in overcoming the bulls of Atum-Ra and Memphis in the north and the lions of Sekhmet in the south.

Again in the year 10 he celebrated a second marriage: "A miracle brought to his majesty, Gilukhipa, daughter of Suttarna, prince of Naharin (Mitanni); and persons of her suite, three hundred and seventeen women."

The king had by now exhibited his physical virility and proved his manhood on the field as well as in the marriage bed. Syria and the east were pacified. Nubia, after a minor campaign of year 5, in which the young king may have taken part, gave no further trouble. And Amenhotep was free to devote himself to the planning of noble architecture, colossal statuary, and the erection of those buildings that have made him justly famous.

III

Amenhotep III was a compulsive builder. Not only was he responsible for the hypostyle hall of Luxor, but also for an even more magnificent forecourt, left unfinished at his death. He raised a massive pylon at Karnak, richly inlaid with gold, silver, and no less than twelve hundred pounds of malachite; before it his architect, the king's namesake, Amenhotep, erected a mighty portrait colossus, hewn from a single block of tough gritstone sixty-seven feet long, which had been brought up the river from Memphis by an army of men. The king also built a temple to Mut, south of Karnak, and excavated a crescent-shaped lake beside it. On the mile and a half that separates Karnak from Luxor he laid out a beautiful garden and connected the two temple complexes by an avenue of ram-headed sphinxes each bearing a statue of the pharaoh between the forepaws.

"The general effect," wrote Breasted, "must have been imposing in the extreme; the brilliant hues of the polychrome architecture, with columns and gates overwrought in gold and floors overlaid in silver, the whole dominated by towering obelisks clothed in glittering metal, rising high above the rich green of the nodding palms and tropical foliage which framed the mass—all this must have produced an impression both of gorgeous detail and overwhelming grandeur."

This was the east bank. On the west he built for himself a magnificent funerary temple, of which, in the words of Madame Desroches Noblecourt, "only the famous colossi of Memnon remain—huge, dramatic witnesses of a vanished world . . ."

It was connected by a causeway with his palace. Earlier palaces had been constructed on the west bank by his forebears at Deir el-Ballas. Amenhotep chose a new site, south of the funerary temple, and many jar labels show that the palace must have been in occupation as early as the eighth year of the reign. In all it covered eighty-two acres and is now known as Malkata—in Arabic "the place where things have been gathered," an allusion to the finds made there by villagers before the site was officially discovered.

Excavations in the palace began through a chance discovery of floor paintings made by the French Egyptologist George Daressy in 1888. They continued in desultory fashion over the decades and were completed in 1917 although much was left unexplored. The most extensive excavation of the remains was undertaken by Professor Percy Newberry in 1903, and a vertitable labyrinth of courtyards, pillared halls, and small chambers uncovered for which it was difficult to find a cohesive plan.

These excavations, of which a full account was never published, must be of the greatest possible interest to students and enthusiasts of the period. The temples were priestly and impersonal, but the palace contained the king's private apartments where he lived not only as a god in the public eye but as a man, a husband, and a father. And the painted pavements and decorated walls uncovered by the archaeologists have such an immediate link with the past that the imagination is stimulated. Over the pavements (now, alas, seen only in photographs) must have walked all the notabilities of the age. Akhenaten may have leaned, bored, against the huge picture of a rampant bull; Tyi's fine linen garments may have brushed against the painting of water birds in full flight; and, if the reconstruction is accurate, the king woke in his golden bed to look at an ornate psychedelically checkered ceiling that bore his titles in a frieze of royal vultures in flight. It was not a ceiling any man suffering from a hangover could have regarded with pleasure.

This was the palace complex, which, in the king's words, Tyi "filled with her beauty."

From notes left by the excavators the mud-brick walls had been originally eighteen feet high. They had then been covered with a rough coat of plaster and painted. The floors, of beaten earth, were also painted. Cedarwood roofed the larger rooms while the smaller made do with beams of palm or acacia thrown from wall to wall, over which were laid heavy fiber mats covered with beaten earth.

The basic construction was as simple as the modern houses of the fellahin. It was the artists who, by painting floor, walls, and ceiling, transformed the labyrinth of rooms into a palace and carved the elegant tapering wooden columns with lotus capitals that supported the ceilings.

The complex, comprising in all four loosely connected palaces, a private chapel to Amen, a walled village for the palace servants, and a military parade ground, was built on a north-south axis. It was approached by a causeway from the mortuary temple and the river, and entered through a gateway.

The largest of the four palaces centered on a huge pavilion where the king gave audience and where, as Maspero wrote, "Persons admitted to the honour of the royal presence suddenly saw before them, framed by columns of painted wood, the dais on which the *Majesty of the Living Horus* deigned to reveal himself to them and set off against the semi-darkness the luminous figure of the Pharaoh. Blinded by his glory they were forced to cover their eyes, throw themselves flat, and *smell at the earth.*''

This pavilion was a pillared court, one hundred and twenty by sixty feet. On either side were four identical suites for the women of the harem, and at one end opening from it was the throne room with raised dais. Behind the throne room, three small rooms were conveniently placed for the king—robing room, bedroom, bathroom. The bathroom water pipes were found still in place as was a hip-high platform, paved with slabs of stone, on which the king had lain to be massaged with scented oil.

The harem suites were identical, two being more spacious than the others. A narrow door admitted the visitor to a small room with two columns and a raised dais; behind was a living room also with a raised dais, and to the rear two smaller rooms—a bedroom with a raised and recessed platform for the bed and a robing room. These were backed by convenient cupboards of stone with wooden shelves for pottery.

Every surface—wall, floor, ceiling, and column—was covered with paintings. Some were found in place. Most lay where they had fallen in the dust and their motifs had to be pieced together like a puzzle.

The harem suites were decorated appropriately with rampant bulls and friezes of food tables. On the robing room ceiling were exquisite paintings of birds such as doves seen from below flying freely against the sky. Other harem motifs were ducks swimming and trellises of grapes—the fruitful vine of the Bible.

The king's audience hall was paved with a floor painted to represent a pool in the marshes with a wider border of growing plants and water birds. High overhead on the ceiling was a repetitive design of flying vultures, the most popular ceiling motif in the palace. On partition walls leading to the throne room were huge representations of the king enthroned, flanked by the traditional captives of the north and south, so that from the dais the king's majesty was framed by paintings of himself seated in state, and the partition walls gave privacy while maintaining the magnificence of the king's presence. They lent a private character to the throne room, at the same time allowing suppliants and ambassadors, assembled in the hall, to glimpse the royal majesty through the open central portals.

There was no shortage of audience halls. An additional small hall for private audience had a flight of steps, four columns, and a second dais. "This room had also preserved a large part of its rich decoration. The gaily painted brick dais had painted figures of bound captives on the floor and on the treads of the steps and was surmounted by a wooden canopy. The gorgeous effect of these canopied thrones can easily be imagined," wrote W. Stevenson-Smith.

The king's private apartments were of special interest. His bedroom, twenty-five feet long by fifteen feet wide, could be approached only through the robing room. It contained a raised platform in a recess for the bed, which, like Tutankhamen's, would have been of ebony overlaid with sheet gold, with legs of feline type and an engraved foot panel. Above the bed a kind of wind vent opened onto the roof to catch the cooler air in summer.

Lying in bed, the king looked up at an ornate ceiling of vultures and rosettes inside a checkered border, with his own names and titles inscribed in hieroglyphs, while on the bedroom wall, above the amuletic signs of life and protection, Ankh and Sa, was a frieze of paired naked figures of the god Bes, male sex symbol of ancient Egypt.

The ceiling of the robing room illustrated one of the king's names—Strong Bull. It was covered with a repetitive pattern of bulls' heads showing Cretan influence.

In addition to the dadoes, floral borders, and designs

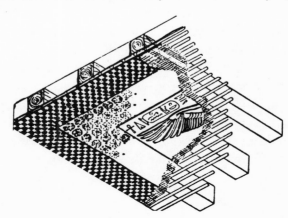

A frieze of figures of the god Bes in the king's private apartments.

around every door and window, there were large paintings in
some of the more important rooms. Only fragments of those
remain. The figure of a court lady with an elaborate headdress resembled the one found at Mycenaean Tyrens. And the
king-size painting of a black and white bull, described by
Daressy, showed a background of undulating bands of mountains painted blue, yellow, and red, and scattered with
rosettes.

It was noted to be the work of two artists with different
styles; one careful and exact, the other impressionistic. Exactly this duality of technique was noticed in some of the Tel
el Amarna paintings. Both artists seem to have accompanied
Akhenaten to his new capital. Men was the name of Amenhotep's principal painter and he was assisted in his work by
his son, Bak. Perhaps these two showed the duality of style,
traditional and impressionist, noticed at Malkata.

Today cultivation covers the site of Malkata. All that
strikes the eye are the earthen mounds, like sand hills,
thrown up by Amenhotep when he constructed a pleasure lake
for his queen, Tyi. This was at the end of year 2 when a commemorative stela and scarab were issued to mark the event.
The lake, two miles long, was stated to have been built for
the king in fifteen days during the "third month of inundation." On its completion Amenhotep and his Great Royal

Wife entered their golden barge *Splendor of Aten* and set sail ceremoniously over the waters. Between the official phrases of eastern hyperbole it is possible to perceive Amenhotep's genuine love for the queen. It was blazoned to the world in the words of a text in which she was descrbed as

The Princess, the most praised, the lady of grace, sweet in her love, who fills the palace with her beauties, the Regent of the North and South, the Great Wife of the King who loves her, the lady of both lands, Tyi.

IV

Amenhotep's palace, in use for the brief span of an earthly life, was built of mud. It was a case of dust to dust. Only the temple, abode of the gods, was considered worthy to be carved of everlasting stone. So that although there is nothing now to see of the site where possibly Akhenaten was born, the beauty of Amenhotep's temple court, an architectural wonder, still draws crowds of tourists from all parts of the world.

They have been coming to Luxor for over a century to lose their hearts to the romance of its long history, to enjoy the freshness of the winter air and the picturesque look of the inhabitants. Even today, despite the ugliness of large hotels built to accommodate the enormous influx of visitors, the charm has not wholly departed.

If the Victorian palaces of the pashas fronting the Nile are decayed or demolished, the temples of Karnak and Luxor are being splendidly restored. And, to the pleasure of the sophisticated traveler, the greater part of the inhabitants are still robed in the dignity of the galabia with its long hanging folds. Outside the town the countryside preserves the life of a premechanical age. Groups of camels can be seen, men riding their donkeys with their farm produce bulging behind them, or in the field using the ancient methods of husbandry: hand winnowing, plowing with oxen, herding goats. In the evening the air from the broad expanse of the Nile comes sweet and sharp. The muezzin intones to the setting sun. Women sway along the dikes in their dark robes balancing water pots on their heads, and the wheels of a sakieh creak as the patient ox turns the shaft, ruminating while the hay-scented saliva flecks from its mouth. Rich fields glisten with moisture, buffalo splash into the shallows of the river, and the exquisite fronded leaves of the dom and date palms, etched against a luminous sky, tremble in the still evening air.

Those with the good fortune to arrive in Luxor at the cycle of the full moon and with an introduction to the authorities, may even be allowed behind locked gates to see the spectacle of Karnak by moonlight, free of the tourist hordes. Then, if ever, the ghosts rise and the great temple stones seem dissolved in the moon's radiance until only the shadows appear solid. The colonnades become mysterious avenues, half draped with sable. Beyond, in an open expanse, is the sacred lake. The surface of its turbid water shines like pewter. An observer can stand on the brink and gaze mesmerized at the flat, still, unrippled surface, expecting something from the past to break the solemn silence, some strange god to emerge from the water and enjoy the feeling that he is lost in time, poised between the *Then* and the *What Is to Come*. Maspero quoted one of his most trusted Theban workman as telling him that at night, "once or twice a year the old sacred lake of the temple of Amen is illuminated and a golden dahabeah sails round it. The rowers are statues of gold and the cabins are filled with golden furniture. Whoever likes to go aboard and seize the treasure can return to land without hindrance, provided that during the adventure he does not utter a word. There is no example of a fellah being able to restrain himself from crying 'Ah!' or invoking Allah at the sight of so much treasure set out before him; then everything vanishes and the foolish fellow, falling into the water, has to swim ashore."

Maspero thought that folk memory would explain this story. In southern Egypt it is possible that some of the inhabitants go back, father and son, to the time of the eighteenth dynasty, and that the workman was "inspired by the remembrance of the ancient Theban rites . . . The golden dahabeah is the ark of Amon . . . On certain days and nights it was sent into the lake to perform certain mysteries . . . and then returned to the sanctuary."

5.
THE RISE OF ATENISM

AKHENATEN'S ACCESSION

*With your light purifying and protecting god, you cover
the earth which bears men, you flood the sky, the vast air,
and gaze down on all that is.*

Arise! Come onwards! You shine as the sole king.
FROM THE RIG-VEDA

I

If one of the many scribes employed in the palace of Amenhotep III had listed the names and regnal birth dates of Queen Tyi's children and if such a document had been preserved, how much would be made clear that is at present confused! It is known neither when Akhenaten was born nor where. And apart from the prince only two of Tyi's children are authenticated—Sitamen, who married her father, and the little Princess Beketaten, child of Tyi's middle age. Were these three the only offspring of the queen?

It seems most likely that there were several others. Dr. Karl Heinrich Brugsch, the eminent nineteenth-century Egyptologist, stated that the queen bore in all sixteen children. He derived this number from the walls of the tomb of the royal scribe, Prince Kheruef, personal steward to Queen Tyi. The relief on which he based his surmise, dating from the year 36 of Amenhotep III, showed eight princes and eight princesses paying homage to the royal pair. Since Brugsch's day the tomb of Kheruef has suffered at the hands of time and

Smenkhare

the tomb robbers. The relief of the princes has entirely disappeared and that of the princesses (now in the museum of the University of Pennsylvania) is described simply as "eight royal princesses making libations to Amenhotep III and Queen Tyi." If they do represent the queen's own children, excessive childbearing would be enough to account for the contrast between the radiant, smiling girl of the marriage portrait and the power-conscious, worldly-wise, worn, and weary woman of the famous ebony head. But the equal size and number of the royal progeny, walking two by two like acolytes, make it most unlikely that they could all have been Tyi's children. Yet their appearance in a tomb devoted to the magnification of the queen (and so of her steward) is certainly significant. And because the queen cohabited with the king during the length of his long reign and bore him children both at the beginning and the end of his adult life, it is certain that some must have been born in the intermediate years. Most Egyptologists agree that Smenkhare, the beautiful and delicate prince who became coregent with Akhenaten, was his full brother. Tutankhamen was also almost certainly a son of the queen, but the parentage of Nefertiti, considered by Pendlebury to be her daughter, is more controversial.

There is some evidence in Tomb Number 226 that the queen bore a number of sons. It belonged to a royal scribe and palace steward whose name is obliterated. This scribe, who lived earlier in the reign of Amenhotep III, is depicted on the walls of the tomb sitting with four boys of varying ages in his lap.* The royal sidelocks they all wear show them to be sons of the king. The eldest is designated by the title "the king's true son, beloved of him, Akheprure."

A pharaoh is known to history by his Son of Ra title. But in addition he bore a Horus title, a Two Ladies title, a golden Horus, and King of Upper and Lower Egypt, or coronation, title. The coronation title of Amenhotep III was Nebmaetra; Akhenaten was named Neferkheprure; Tutankhamen was Nebkeprure, and Smenkhare was Neferneferuaten, a name first bestowed on Nefertiti. Who then was Akheprure? Was he Smenkhare or another older prince?

There is some evidence suggesting that Akhenaten may not have been the eldest son of his parents. Carter found a whip in Tutankhamen's tomb that bore the problematic inscription: "The son of the king, captain of the troops, Thutmose." Madame Desroches Noblecourt suggests that this unknown prince, who is also mentioned on a monument found at Memphis, was "probably the king's eldest son who died prematurely." And certainly the concept of Akhenaten succeeding suddenly and unexpectedly to the throne seems to fit the known facts.

These are tantalizingly few. To imagine him walking hand in hand with Nefertiti through the water courts and gardens of the Theban palace is entirely fanciful. He may not have been born in Thebes, and very likely did not grow up there, so that to reconstruct his youth and formative years is like building a house without bricks. When he does at last

---

*It has been suggested that these princes may have been the surviving sons of Thutmose IV.

emerge from the shadows of his childhood to step into the light of history, his biographer must at once face the controversial issue of whether there was, or was not, a long period of coregency with his father, Amenhotep III.

One thing at least is certain. From the beginning of his reign Akhenaten, who came to the throne as Amenhotep IV, was a dedicated follower of the new dogma of Atenism; indeed it would hardly be straining the truth to call his approach to religion fanatical.

II

Akhenaten became king at the age of about twenty-six. There is one slight indication of how he may have passed his childhood. He claimed to be a prophet of Ra-Harakhte and, according to one authority, held this office before his accession.

Ra-Harakhte, or Ra Horus of the Horizon, was the principal deity of Heliopolis near Memphis, the Greek name for On of the Bible. The earliest god worshiped at On was Atum, who was the unknown essence behind the reality of the sun god, Ra. Atum, it was said, had existed before the creation and was a "spirit still formless, who bore within him the sum of all existence." His name meant "to be complete." In his temple precincts, besides the sacred tree was a holy well in which, as the sun god Atum-Ra, he had bathed his face for the first time. The tree grew in the great hall of the temple on the very place where the sun cat had once slain Apophis, serpent of evil. The tree was sacred to the sky goddess Nut of Hathor. It was a sycamore and its leaves possessed the power, when inscribed with the pharaoh's name, of endowing him with immortality. It was rendered doubly sacred by that fabulous bird, the phoenix, who roosted nightly among its branches. The bird seems to have been a double-crested gray heron. The Egyptians, with a marvelous sense of poetry, seeing it fly at dawn with such grace and dignity over the waters of the inundation, had endowed it with magic properties. Like the sun of which it became an image, it appeared shining in the glory of the morning light and seemed to have created itself from the gray mist of the primeval waters. The appearance of the phoenix on the temple tree was eagerly looked for and greeted as a sign of joy and hope.

The priests taught that Heliopolis was founded on the first land exposed after chaos. Ipet-esut (Karnak) made the same claim and the legends may reflect both the yearly miracle of the inundation and the actual geographical shrinking of the Nile bed in Paleolithic times. At On, possibly a sacred site from those prehistoric times, Atum manifested himself in a natural rock formation, a huge conical stone resembling an obelisk. This was another object of special sancity in the temple precincts. It was called the Benben and the temple that surrounded it Het Benben, or palace of the sacred stone.

Nothing remains of ancient Heliopolis today but a battered obelisk set up beside the vanished temple four thousand years ago by Senusert, a pharaoh of the twelfth dynasty. Two other obelisks from Heliopolis survive. Called, wrongly, Cleopatra's needles, they were brought to Alexandria by the Roman Emperor Augustus. The larger of the two was presented by Muhammed Ali, pasha of Egypt, to the British nation and was transported in 1877 to the Thames embankment where it stands today. The smaller is in New York City. (The inscriptions on them establish the veneration in which the Theban kings held the primary religious center of Egypt. On the London obelisk is written, "Thutmose III made this monument for his father Ra-Harakhte . . . because he so much loved his father . . ." The text of the obelisk in New York proclaims the king as "Horus, mighty bull, shining in Thebes . . . Born of Atum, lord of Heliopolis, son of his body whom Thoth fashions.")

Modern Heliopolis is a suburb of Cairo. Even in the early years of this century all that remained of a temple complex at least as magnificent as Karnak were a few deeply buried fragments of fallen columns. As it was near the city, the site was for centuries quarried for stone. A visitor, Mrs. Lorimer, remarked on the "absolute nothingness of this most celebrated, venerable spot."

In her day (1909) it was among fields in a peaceful

countryside intersected by canals and rich in vegetation. Ancient customs die hard. There was then standing a huge sycamore, perhaps a seedling descendant of the sacred tree of Heliopolis. It was still venerated by the Christian Copts as the tree under which the Virgin Mary rested on her flight to Egypt, and she was said to have washed her Child in the waters of that spring, once sacred to the sun god, and re-named the Virgin's Well.

Apart from the sacred and magic objects venerated by the common people, On was a great center of learning, the parent of all the universities of the world. Medicine and mathematics were taught, astronomy and the secret science of magic, as well as the principal subject, theology. Priests, instructed in the seventy-five separate names of Ra, learned the story of the creation and the Ennead or nine gods of On. The novitiates were told that the First One of All, Atum-Ra, came out of chaos. Without recourse to woman, he produced the atmosphere, Shu and Tefnut (Shu's wife), the dew; then Geb, the earth, and Nut, the sky; then Osiris and Isis, Seth, and Nepthys.

The predynastic kings adopted some of this sun worship. Grafting it on to their own sky deity, they created a new aspect of Ra, Ra-Harakhte. He was depicted as the god with the head of a falcon bearing the sun's disk, and became special protector of the kings of Egypt.

Strangely enough, Ra-Harakhte was also the proper name of the Great Sphinx of Giza who cried to Thutmose IV, "Oh, my son, it is I, thy father, Ra-Harakhte-Khepre-Atum. The throne will be thine . . . so that thou do what my heart desires."

Such unrelated facts—that the Falcon people came to Egypt from the East, and that the sphinx was a symbol of Asiatic origin—make it possible that Ra-Harakhte had eastern connotations. And as Atum-Harakhte he was the principal deity of Heliopolis, which had been a cosmopolitan university from the first.

When Thebes became powerful and began to dominate the Egyptian pantheon, Amen's ascendancy was demonstrated not only in religious but in material and practical terms. The priests of Amen became rich as the priests of Atum lost in wealth. This is clearly shown in a list of the temple revenues of Thebes placed side by side with those of Heliopolis. Thebes is listed as having 569 gold articles, Heliopolis none; Thebes 10,964 articles of silver, Heliopolis 586; Thebes 25,405 jars of wine, Heliopolis 2,385; Thebes 849 oxen from Egyptian herds, Heliopolis 98.

It must have been galling for the priests of On, whose repute was known throughout the world, to watch their precedence, power, wealth, and revenue diminish year by year. They would have been less than human had they not hoped for a change in the tide of events and sought to bring about such a change wherever possible.

The founding of the empire made the Theban king look north and led to the reestablishment of government at Memphis. Can the rise of Atenism also be traced to this moment of reorientation?

It seems so. There were universalist ideas in the orthodox cult even before Amenhotep II. Brief invocations to the sun have been found on private monuments as early as the Second Intermediate Period (1786–1570 B.C.) And Amenhotep I, second king of the eighteenth dynasty, was hymned at death in these poetic words:

> *His Majesty passed through life in happiness,*
> *through the years in peace,*
> *He ascended into the sky and became one with*
> *the Disk,*
> *He became blended with him out of whom he had come.*

The disk, or Aten, was the impersonal orb of the sun borne on the head of the Falcon god, and the first evidence of Atenism as a cult comes from the reign of Amenhotep II's son, Thutmose IV.

There is definite proof on a scarab in the possession of the Reverend G. D. Nash that Aten was worshiped as a separate deity by Thutmose. The text of the scarab, the age and authenticity of which was carefully checked by the British

Museum, is, "Thutmose arouses himself to fight with Aten before him; he destroys mountains . . . in order to bring the inhabitants of foreign lands like subjects to the rule of Aten forever."

The chain of circumstance cannot be fortuitous. When the Memphite upbringing of Thutmose IV is considered—his sponsorship of Ra-Harakhte (vide the Sphinx), his mention of Aten on a scarab, and the worship of Atum-Ra-Harakhte as the principal god of Heliopolis—the conclusion that Atenism at least partly originated in the north and at Heliopolis is hard to avoid. The total destruction of the Heliopolitan temples has been a factor in confusing the issue. But when Akhenaten defaced the images of all the gods except Atum on the walls of his grandmother's sanctuary, he showed the unmistakable northern and Heliopolitan orientation of Atenism.

How great a part did these strangers from Syria—Mitannian, Babylonian, Amorite, Semite, and Habiru (Hebrew)—play in the rise of the new doctrine? They worshiped (among other deities) Mitra, the sun, whose symbol was the winged disk supported by the column of the atmosphere (Shu, to the Egyptians). Yet another aspect of the sun god worshiped by the Asians was called Aden, or lord, a beautiful youth who became the Adonis of the Greeks. The similarity of the name to Aten is striking.*

But when Amenhotep II, in the second year of his reign, returned from the land of Naharin (as his father Thutmose III had done) and entered Memphis in the triumphal procession that included the five hundred northern Syrian lords and two hundred and forty of their women, he did more than import a useful body of slaves. By the law of averages, some of these aristocratic lords and ladies must have entered the royal court, the royal harem, and the temple precincts, and affected the Egyptian mores. Even if the mother of Thutmose IV was not a Mitannian, an exchange of ideas was bound to occur. Heliopolis, whose emblem was also the sun's disk, and

*There is also the possibility that the prophet Moses influenced Egyptian religious thought. See Appendix.

whose worship of Atum-Ra-Harakhte resembled that of Mitra, would have attracted the interest and faith of the newcomers.

The large-hearted polytheism of the Egyptians made the advent of a new faith and a new god as normal as the birth of a child in a large family. And would not the priests of Heliopolis have welcomed any new aspect of Ra-Harakhte that challenged the supremacy of Amen-Ra of Thebes? Or would not the king have lent tacit approval to a cult that appealed not only to the sun-worshiping Egyptians but to many of the influential inhabitants of the lands over which Egypt had established suzerainty?

The situation examined at this point shows that the Theban king, pledged to be loyal to Amen-Ra, may have found himself in a quandary. Thutmose IV was a Memphite but he was married to the Theban princess Mutemwaya. Named after Mut, the wife of Amen, Mutemwaya was most likely a staunch adherent of Amen-Ra. If she considered her husband's leanings disloyal to the Theban god, there was a special reason for her to seek out the priest of Min and claim for her child, Amenhotep III, the care and protection of Amen as a father. And when Thutmose died young, Mutemwaya chose as a substitute for the solar princess a girl from the ranks of Amen's supporters.

If this interpretation is correct, the first years of Amenhotep's reign must have turned out as the queen mother wished. The king built her a sanctuary glorifying Amen and his divine birth. He began the magnificent multipillared court in the Luxor temple, the pylon at Karnak, the temple of Mut, and all the other grandiose projects designed to lend luster to Thebes and its great god.

All this was consistent, natural, expected. Then in the year 11 a stela was erected and scarabs issued. They announced that the king had built a great palace far from the Theban temples on the left bank of the Nile. He had also constructed a pleasure lake for his queen. The palace was named the House of Nebmaetra Is Aten's Splendor, and the barge that spilled its golden reflection on the lake was called Splendor of Aten. One of Amenhotep's regiments was given the same name and a temple, Gem-Aten, built in Nubia. Be-

cause Amenhotep, called after Amen, claimed to be the actual
son of the god, he was pledged, surely, to give all allegiance
to his divine father.

How can his apparent volte-face be accounted for?

In the first place, although there is only negative evidence,
it is likely that Mutemwaya vanished from the scene before
the move to Malkata took place, and it was under new influence that Amenhotep named his house, his sacred barge,
and his regiment in honor of Aten.

But before discussing Amenhotep III's Atenist inclina-
tions, it is useful to examine a stela set up in his reign by the
two architects of the temple of Amen. Their names were Suti
and Hor (Seth and Horus, both gods of Heliopolis) and they
inscribed a psalm to the sun in which the official line vis-à-vis
Aten and Amen is made clear. The gods were not two but one!
The hymn begins with the words, "Praise to Amen when he
rises as Horus of the Horizon (Ra-Harakhte)." It continues
by hailing the "beautiful Ra of every day who rises at dawn
without ceasing" and "the disk of Ra of the day, creator of
all and maker of their living . . . Horus the first born in the
midst of the sky goddess . . . the fashioner and Amen of mankind." To Suti and Hor, Aten the disk and Amen-Ra were one
supreme being.

This fitted in with Egyptian theological thought. In their
attempt to define God, the priests had envisaged Him as Aten,
the visible light of the sun that gave birth to all living things.
At the same time He was also Ra, the mysterious and invisible
source of power behind the disk. But these dogmas, which
originated in Heliopolis, made no mention of Amen, either in
the famous *Book of What Is in the Underworld* or the *Book
of Gates*. Both were written at Heliopolis. In spite of this
omission, theoretically Amen, being invisible, mysterious, and
one with Ra, was not threatened by the worship of the disk
and its rays, which could be considered merely as an aspect
of his powers. And Alexandre Piankoff, the great expounder
of Egyptian religious thought, considered that both gods were
but "two different manifestations, two different aspects of the
solar divinity."

This may have been so, but the wealth of the Theban

Amen and his priests, the northern orientation of Ra-Harakhte, the jealousy of men, and the ever-present human failing of sectarianism, made Atenism a creed that could easily become dangerous to the unity of the country.

It is not known who introduced it to Amenhotep and fostered it at court, but after the possible death and departure of his mother Mutemwaya, Tyi and the pharaoh's counselor and namesake Amenhotep wielded the most powerful influence over the king.

The innate greatness of kings whose reigns are considered outstanding and who are served by men of talent and genius has frequently been questioned. Yet a small-minded and foolish king seldom tolerates a wise counselor.

Amenhotep III must finally be given credit for the peace and prosperity of his long reign, for the splendor of his monuments, and the quality of its art. Yet by heaping honors and tribute on his right-hand man, Amenhotep, son of Hapu, the king seemed to acknowledge the magnitude of his debt to another. Amenhotep of Hapu's family came from Arthribis in the delta, a town where Akhenaten early built a temple to Ra-Harakhte-Aten. Some of the Hapu family had married Theban wives, so counselor Amenhotep was in a position to keep the balance of power between Memphis and Thebes and between the northern and southern aspects of the sun god. But in the inscription engraved upon his statue, he showed his northern sympathies by referring to Amenhotep III as "heir of Atum" and "firstborn of Ra-Harakhte"—both Heliopolitan gods.

A genuinely wise and good man, Amenhotep the sage* did much to promote civilizing influences at court and looked the part of a venerable philosopher, disdaining to wear the fashionable wig and keeping his hair long. He held no doubt such sage tenets as these from a contemporary text:

> *Laugh not at a blind man nor tease a dwarf.*
> *Keep thy tongue from unkind words.*
> *Be not greedy . . .*

*Could the sage have been a disciple or follower of Moses? See Appendix.

*Remove not the landmarks from the boundaries
of the sown
Far better bread with a happy heart than
riches with vexation,
And a bushel that god giveth thee is worth
five thousand obtained by force.*

His beliefs may have been that

*The passionate man in the temple
Is like a tree grown in a forest.
In a moment comes its loss of foliage;
Its end is reached in the dockyard.
It is floated from its place.
The flame is its winding-sheet*

*But the tranquil man
Is like a garden tree.
Its fruit is sweet.
Pleasant its shade in the sun,
And it lives on in the garden.*

He was reputed by James Breasted to have lived to a ripe age—a hundred and ten—the age of the just. He had by then, Breasted wrote, "gained such a wide reputation for his wisdom that his sayings circulated in Greek some twelve hundred years later among the 'Proverbs of the Seven Wise Men,' and in Ptolemaic times he was finally worshipped as a god and took his place among the innumerable deities of Egypt."

There is a confusion of names at this period for it is now known that the king had two namesakes, both outstanding men. One was the sage, the son of Hapu; the other the architect.

It was Amenhotep the builder who began his career as a royal scribe in the king's service and obtained the key position of royal chief of works, a role that combined architect and master builder. He was given the honor and responsibility of quarrying the "miracle" sandstone that, like the red stone of the Easter Islanders, was supposed to have magic properties. It was believed to be under the sepcial protection of Atum.

Amenhotep directed, and evidence points to him as being the mastermind behind, the construction of the Luxor temple, the mortuary temple, and the colossi of Memnon.

Of the two Amenhoteps the sage was by far the greater man. It was he who was chosen as master of ceremonies to act at the feast of Amen. As the reign progressed, rewards were heaped upon him.

The sage was appointed steward to the Princess Sitamen, who had been given vast estates on the Theban left bank by her father. But his chief work was as Administrator of North and South Egypt—a title later taken over by his brother or cousin Ramose, vizier of Thebes. He was also First of the King's Companions and Chief Counselor.

His work in all spheres was well done. For thirty years the ship of state moved forward steadily and smoothly. Overseas trade with Asia Minor, Crete, and Cyprus flourished and, to control pirates infesting the sea routes, a marine police was developed that patrolled the coast of the delta. The trade routes were similarly policed and business enterprises encouraged, protected, and taxed. Slaves were distributed throughout the land and enrolled as tax-paying serfs, and justice to all was maintained; while the affairs of diplomacy in relation to neighboring states were so well conducted that Egypt kept free from war. Internally, except for the minor revolt in Nubia in year 5, there was a thirty-year period of unprecedented prosperity. And there was even a compromise peace between new and old ideas in the sphere of religion.

No wonder that in a barbaric period this age of peace and plenty must have seemed to many little short of a miracle. How much conditions were due to the royal Amenhotep and how much to the son of Hapu there is no means of knowing. But the quite extraordinary marks of approval heaped upon the sage seem to show that Amenhotep III was giving honor where he considered it due. The old counselor was made hereditary prince and even allowed to erect colossal statues of himself in the temple of Amen, where, as herald of the god, he heard the prayers of the people. By these, who had enjoyed with him the greatest prosperity the country had ever known, he must have been deeply loved. The inscription on one of the statues reads:

You people of the South and North, whose eyes can see the Sun and have come to Thebes to pray to the lord of all the Gods, all of you come to me! I carry what you say to Amen of Karnak at the moment you pray . . . for I am the herald, named by the king to hear your prayers . . .

Both as a sage and a northerner, Amenhotep, son of Hapu, would have inclined toward the new universalist ideas emanating from Heliopolis, and we can surely see in him, as W. Stevenson-Smith suggests, the main influence that caused the king to veer toward Ra-Harakhte. In the first place the sage may have counseled Akhenaten's training as a priest. He may have formed his mind to the more spiritual tenets of Atenism and he may have welcomed the young king's accession as prelude to a new age of enlightenment. Whether the sage, the king, Tyi, or the court, when they whistled for the wind, expected the whirlwind of Akhenaten's brand of Atenism or a prince so strong-willed, ardent, and fanatical, is doubtful.

III

There is no subject on which the experts are more divided than the provenance of Nefertiti. Petrie believed her to be the Mitannian Princess Tadukhipa; Pendlebury and Maspero were convinced she was the daughter of Amenhotep III and Tyi, while Cyril Aldred argues that she was the child of Ay, Queen Tyi's supposed brother. Facts and dates unknown to Petrie make it impossible for Nefertiti to have been the Mitannian princess. But was she the daughter or the niece of Queen Tyi or neither?

Aldred bases his conclusions on Ay's title Father of the God, also borne by Yuaa. Aldred suggests that this should be read as Father-in-law of the King. Yuaa was certainly (if not father) father-in-law to Amenhotep III. Was not Ay, honored with the same title, possibly the father-in-law of Akhenaten? But Ramose, vizier and mayor of Thebes, was also Father of the God and he is thought to have been childless. There is a further argument against the concept that Nefertiti was Ay's daughter. Ay inscribed a greater number of resplendent titles on the walls of his tomb at Tel el Amarna than any other courtier.

He was Father of the God; Fan bearer on the right hand of the King; Master of the King's Horses in the Two Lands; Acting King's scribe; Chief of the Bowmen; Leader in the Festival of the Cycle of the Gods; Hereditary Prince; Mayor; Chancellor; Vizier; Doer of Right; and Priest of Maet. One must conclude that Ay believed in the value of self-exaltation and inscribed every distinction he could muster. Would he not then have claimed to be Father of the Great Wife of the King if such was the case? In addition, Ay's wife, Tyi, is specifically referred to as Nurse of the Great King's wife Nefertiti.

The evidence is confusing and contradictory. Aldred points out that Nefertiti nowhere claims to be the child of Tyi and Amenhotep and that her full titles give her no higher position than heiress, a phrase more resplendently translated by Pendlebury as hereditary princess. Unfortunately the nuances of royal relationships and attributes are imperfectly known. The nub of the question is whether the daughters of Tyi did or did not bear royal titles and were considered true solar princesses. By marrying Sitamen, Amenhotep seemed to indicate his belief that she, at least, was able to confer the necessary divine sanction on his kingship.

When Thutmose III, the son of the king by a minor concubine, married a solar princess he made no attempt to wed one of his own daughters. The same applies both to his son, and his grandson Thutmose IV. This suggests that Mutemwaya was of the true blood. But Amenhotep III, by marrying Tyi, was forced to reaffirm his claim to godhead by publicly allying himself with Sitamen and including her in his funerary chamber.

If Nefertiti was Akhenaten's full sister, would she not also have conferred the blessing of the sun on him? By marrying two of his own daughters he seemed to imply that Nefertiti was not a true solar princess.

Yet because of the many innovations he made in religious doctrines, Akhenaten is unpredictable. The divine status he accorded himself makes it likely that he married his full sister, Nefertiti. But at the best she was of the solar blood only through her father. Akhenaten might then have considered it necessary to marry one of his daughters.*

Nefertiti's name means "The beautiful woman cometh." If the titles given her by the king are an indication, he seemed deeply enamored of her beauty. She was "Mistress of Happiness," he wrote, the "Beloved Wife of the King." In a country where royal daughters were at a premium, she gave birth to six princesses, in steady succession, and there would be a poetic justice in being able to write that she and Akhenaten lived happily ever after. But life in Egypt in 1379 b.c. (the year Akhenaten came to the throne) was no more of a fairy tale than it is in the modern world, and the married ideal of the young royal couple, hymned by the court poets and sculptured ad infinitum on the temple and tomb walls of the Amarnan period, seems to have ended in darkness.

IV

While the origin of Nefertiti does not affect the history of Akhenaten's reign to any significant extent, the question of whether there was or was not a coregency of Akhenaten with his father Amenhotep is vital to the biographer. Here again opinion is divided with a majority of the experts in favor of a coregency. But because the two points of view require quite different interpretations of events, the biographer must settle the matter in his own mind at the outset.

H. W. Fairman has reviewed the documentary evidence

---

* In the tomb of Panehesy, Nefertiti is titled: "The Heiress, Great of Favor, mistress of all women, when she saith anything it is done, the Great Wife of the King whom he loveth, Neffertiti living for ever and ever." N. de G. Davies gave his opinion that the queen's rights as an heiress imply a royal Egyptian descent on both sides.

Akhenaten, Nefertiti and the four princesses.

on all the dockets, ostraca, and inscriptions of Amarna with the caution and balance of a fine scholar. The sum of his findings was that, from dockets on wine shards found in Tel el Amarna bearing Amenhotep's name; from several reliefs in which Akhenaten and his father are shown together; from the fragment of a coffin showing the names of both kings; and from a scene in the tomb of Kheruef, in which Akhenaten is depicted making offering to his living, deified father, Fairman deduces that "a coregency is the only satisfactory explanation." Later Fairman found further evidence in records preserved in the museum at Liverpool. These showed two royal cartouches, from the sun temple already mentioned as built by Akhenaten at Athribis in the delta. Akhenaten's name is shown in its early form as Amenhotep IV and immediately behind, enclosed in another royal cartouche, is the name of his father. Fairman pointed out this evidence in Volume 46 of the *Journal of Egyptian Archaeology* and, abandoning his

Amenhotep, Great Wife Tyi, and her youngest daughter.

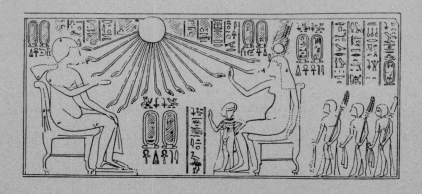

previous caution, stated unequivocally that the appearance of
the two cartouches side by side was unprecedented, extraordinary, and, in his view, proof positive of a coregency.

The modern Egyptians have so little doubt of it that the
story of the coregency of Akhenaten is taught to schoolchil-
dren, and the proof given is the famous carved lintel from the
tomb of Huya at Tel el Amarna. Huya was steward to Queen
Tyi, and the lintel shows the two royal families of Amarna:
on the one side Akhenaten, Nefertiti, and four little princesses
waving plumed fans; on the other Amenhotep, Tyi, and her
youngest daughter, Princess Beketaten. But the final proof
must lie in the question of Tutankhamen's parentage. Because
Akhenaten reigned for seventeen years, and because Tutankhamen was only nine when he came to the throne, then if
Tutankhamen was indeed the son of Tyi and Amenhotep III
the coregency is certain. On the subject of his birth it is surely
churlish to reject the evidence Tutankhamen himself gave of
his paternity. On a stone lion that the young king moved from
Soleb to Gebel Barkal, he wrote a superscription claiming
Amenhotep III as his father. This caused the noted Egyptologist H. R. Hall to write, "I regard the filial relationship
of Tutankhamen to Amenhotep III as proved by this inscription." Finally, there is the mute evidence of the tomb. In a
nest of small anthropoid coffins carefully wrapped in mummy
cloth was found a solid gold statuette of Amenhotep III and a
plaited lock of rusting hair—all that is left of the Great Queen
Tyi. Carter called the objects "heirlooms," but not to accept
as evidence these carefully cherished and pathetic proofs of
royal parentage seemed "futile" to Madame Desroches
Noblecourt.

V

The new king or coregent Amenhotep IV was proclaimed
with the highest titles of kingship. He was called

Mighty Bull, Lofty of Plumes; Favorite of the Two Goddesses, Great
in Kingship in Karnak; Golden Horus, Wearer of Diadems in South-

ern Heliopolis; King of Lower Egypt, Beautiful-Is-the-Beings-of-Ra,
the Only-One-of-Ra; Son of the Sun, Peace of Amen [Amenhotep],
Divine Ruler of Thebes; Great in Duration, Living for Ever and
Ever, Beloved of Amen-Ra, Lord of Heaven.

If he accepted the designation Beloved of Amen-Ra, he began almost at once to promulgate doctrines of the new Atenism that were not then accepted as standard even at the court.

Two questions can be asked. Were his theories derived from his own spiritual conceptions, from Amenhotep, son of Hapu, or were they imbibed at On? And as prophet of Ra-Harakhte did Akhenaten attend this fabled institution?

The vanished temple complex of On, which proved parent of all the schools and universities of the world, was cosmopolitan. To its precincts came men whose names are legendary, and it was twice mentioned in the Bible.

The father-in-law of Joseph, called Potiphar (Pa-ti-pa-ra in Egyptian), was a priest of On. And one authority has suggested that the title given to Joseph by the pharaoh was *Zaphnath Paanesh,* indicating that Joseph himself was elected head of the House of Life or priestly college of On.

Other famous men visited the sacred fane. Piankhi, an Ethiopian priest-king, washed at the Fountain of the Sun and made offering of white bulls, milk, perfume, incense, and all kinds of sweet-scented woods, before entering the temple where he saw his father Ra in the sanctuary. Plato visited Heliopolis in his youth and the Greek writer Strabo came there in 24 B.C. to inquire into the ancient relics and beliefs of the Egyptians.

But most renowned among the priests of On was the great Jewish leader Moses who learned "all the wisdom of the Egyptians." The fact that Moses was a high-grade priest of On with the name of Osarsis (Child of Osiris) is not written in the Bible but suggested in the *History of the Jews* by Josephus. It was believed by Sir Wallis Budge, the great authority on the Egyptian gods, who wrote, "How could Moses have performed all the magical acts related . . . unless he had been instructed in every branch of learning both sacred and profane and had been educated as a priest and magician?"

Expert opinion has placed the time of the Exodus in the reign of the nineteenth-dynasty King Seti I. Akhenaten had then been dead for over fifty years. But new and exciting evidence has come to light that makes it seem probable that Moses lived, not after, but before Akhenaten. This revelation brings a new dimension to the study of the heretic king, for if Moses lived before Akhenaten then there might have been a religious link between them. This thought opens up possibilities of a fascinating and credible historical reconstruction.* That such a link existed is implicit in the statement by Manetho, who attempted to write a coherent account of the religious schism of Akhenaten. But halfway through he confused it with a narrative relating to Moses and the last Hyksos war. What reasons could there have been for Manetho to conjoin the stories of the two men, born more than half a century apart?

Were the records of Moses from which Manetho must have drawn his source material as defaced and indecipherable as those on Akhenaten? Probably the historical chronicles of both were placed together and had suffered at the hands of the iconoclasts and Manetho saw a sufficient relationship between them to believe they referred to one and the same person. Certainly Akhenaten's name and that of his city Akhetaton had been carefully erased. And there were strong similarities between the two men. Both (allowing Moses to have been a Hyksos prince) were heirs to the throne of Egypt. Both were, in their several ways, monotheists, and both, at different epochs, most likely were priests of Heliopolis.

That Moses attended the temple university is almost certain. His collateral ancestor Joseph is supposed not only to have been a priest at Heliopolis but head of the priestly college. The family was settled at Heliopolis, and, as heir apparent to the Memphite Hyksos king, Moses would have been given the best of educations.

The God of the Israelites who had succored and comforted them in their wanderings from the time they had left Haran

---

*See Appendix for the argument for a new dating of the Exodus and the theory that Moses was a Hyksos prince. See also a full version of the story of Amenhotep III and the "polluted people."

was unique, a spirit, formless and faceless. But would an Israelite have had difficulty in worshiping the primeval god of Heliopolis—Atum, the ''Completed One,'' the ''formless spirit who bore within him the sum of all existence?'' Whatever Moses's private beliefs he probably conformed to the sun worship of the Egyptians. Josephus quotes Apion as writing thus: ''I have heard of the ancient men of Egypt, that Moses was of Heliopolis, and that he thought himself obliged to follow the customs of his forefathers, and offered his prayers in the open air, towards the city walls; but that he reduced them all to be directed towards sunrising, which was agreeable to the situation of Heliopolis; that he also set up pillars instead of gnomons, under which was represented a cavity like that of a boat—and the shadow that fell from their tops fell down upon that cavity, that it might go round about the like course as the sun itself goes round the other.'' The sun rising is the sun's disk—Aten. But Moses's personal vision of God was given in Josephus: ''He ordained our government to be what may be termed a theocracy by ascribing the authority and power to God and by persuading all the people to have a regard to Him . . . He informed them that it was impossible to escape God's observation even in any of our outward actions, or any of our inward thoughts. Moreover he represented God as unbegotten, and immutable, through all eternity, superior to all mortal conceptions in pulchritude; and though known to us by his power, yet unknown to us as to his essence.''

Would a man with such noble breadth of vision have failed to make a profound and lasting impression on the priestly college of which he was a member? And when he abandoned Egypt forever would he not have left some devoted followers to cherish his memory and the power of his spiritual insight? And could not one of these have been Amenhotep, son of Hapu, from Athribis in the delta?

By the time that Akhenaten was born at least eighty years had passed since the Exodus. Other foreigners, Mitannians and Babylonians, had entered the country. And other ideas had been infused into Egyptian religion.

The sun-worshiping Egyptians readily absorbed the eastern symbols of sun worship—the winged disk, the mother goddess, the god king, king god concepts. And the young neophite beginning his studies at Heliopolis could have found there many levels of religious thought and countless interpretations of "the thousand and one faces of god."

From whatever source they derived, Akhenaten's ideas were revolutionary, startling, and unprecedented. A new aspect of sun worship or a new deity could have been easily fitted into the overcrowded Egyptian pantheon. But this king dared to face the Egyptian people with a religion that sought to blot out entirely two thousand years of convenient and comfortable polytheism and replace a cheerful and busy cosmic scene with the awful nothingness of the anonymous O, the faceless disk, the everlasting One. An interpretation that seems to fit the facts is that Akhenaten was among those visionaries who arise in the world from time to time. Such men are filled with one overmastering idea. Ignoring the day-to-day demands of practical living, they are willing to ride over everybody and everything to achieve their ambition and establish what they consider "inspired truth" in the minds of men.

Like Icarus, Akhenaten sought to emulate the radiance of the sun's disk he worshiped, and was fated, like Icarus, to fall.

6.

KARNAK
BY SUNLIGHT

Obelisks, colossal and gigantic statues, avenues formed by rows of sphinxes, and which may still be traced although the greater part of the statues are multilated or concealed under the sand, porticoes of prodigious elevation, among which is one of the height of 170 feet by 200 feet breadth; immense colonnades the pillars of which are thirty-one feet in circumference; colours still wonderful on account of their brilliancy; the granite and marble lavished on the buildings, stones of high dimensions supported by capitals forming the roof of these magnificent edifices . . . occupy a space of vast extent.
O. S. SONNINI, 1799

Thou didst establish the earth . . . for thy son
Who came forth from thy limbs . . .
Akenaten, whose life is long. . . .
HYMN OF AKHENATEN

I

Akhenaten may indeed have been a genuine mystic. William James made a special study of mysticism in his book *Varieties of Religious Experience* and discovered that those who claimed such an experience, whatever their age, period, or religion, described similar sensations. In every case the prelude was the onset of light—blinding, brilliant, or white—and the mystical experience was described as an ecstatic feeling of oneness, wholeness, or completeness that transcended the finite body and made ordinary human pleasures seem of no account.

Individuals reacted in different ways to the moment of

revelation. The pure in heart were made humble, the good saintly, and the proud conceited.

It can be seen how Akhenaten, already believing in his divine origin, may have interpreted a mystical experience not so much in terms of an identification with suffering humanity but as a special favor shown to himself and a revelation of his own unique standing. In confirmation of this, without employing the *doubtless* or *possible* terms so often forced on the biographer of Akhenaten, his own words can be quoted from the splendid hymn to Aten, which it is believed he wrote:

> *Thou art in my heart,*
> *None other knoweth thee*
> *Save I, thy son, Splendor of the Sun, Akhenaten*
> *To whom thou hast given understanding of thy designs*
> *And thy might . . .*
> *Thou didst establish the earth . . . for thy son*
> *Who came forth from thy limbs,*
> *The King, Living in Truth, Lord of Diadems,*
> *Akhenaten, whose life is long;*
> *And for the Great Royal Consort, his Beloved,*
> *Mistress of Two Lands, Nefertiti,*
> *Living and flourishing for ever and ever.*

The king, as Davies suggested, "insisted on a very strict acknowledgement of the semi-divine position given him by his special relation to Aten," and underlining this Sir Alan Gardiner added "his cartouches show that he was by no means disinclined to share in his divine father's divinity; indeed one has sometimes the impression that this share approached complete identity."

If the kings of Egypt had always assumed the status of gods, it seems Akhenaten's claim differed in a most personal and immediate sense.

The beautiful disk "glittering high over the earth," which had created all living things, birds, plants and animals, "giving life to the son in the body of his mother, soothing him that he may not weep," even "breath to the chicklet peeping in the eggshell," this emanation of warmth and fecundity was considered by Akhenaten as the source of his being. He was the sun's earthly embodiment. His hymn to the sun bears this interpretation and it was this conviction and belief he must urgently have needed to convey after his accession as king. Lacking radio, television, and modern means of communication, there was only one way to broadcast revolutionary ideas to the people—through art, the popular mass media of the day.

The assumption that Akhenaten enlisted the help of artists to disseminate his new doctrines is borne out by an inscription. It was carved on a rock at Aswan by Bak, the leading court painter, son of Min. The younger man recorded the interesting information that "Bak was the assistant whom his majesty [Akhenaten] himself had taught." If this phrase is pondered over, the naturalistic art of the Amarnan period can be approached from a new angle. For the interest in nature and the greater representational freedom of style was already apparent in the paintings of Amenhotep's palace. A pavement from Malkata showing a central pool surrounded by plants and birds is almost identical to the one discovered at Tel el Amarna by Petrie.

The startling changes in the art style that occurred after Akhenaten's accession were not in the representation of birds, beasts, and plants. It was the human figure that suffered "a sea change," and the forms of the king, the queen, and their immediate circle, which became so curiously distorted. Bak, as first artist in the land, had no need to be instructed in his métier. But Akhenaten must have directed the sculptor to make certain specific changes in the formula for royal representational art.

Some have claimed that the statues and reliefs of Akhenaten showed him as ugly as he really was "in truth." They quote his secondary worship of Maet, goddess of truth, and his claim to be "living in truth." But Maet was not the spirit of truthfulness in a modern sense. She was the cherished daughter and confidante of Ra, a pure abstraction deified, and one of the retinue of Osiris, who sat in judgment on mankind. As dispenser of justice, she represented the truth behind reality. Were the carvings and statues of Akhenaten not attempting to show just such a truth behind reality? Were they not caricatures in the sense that a caricature emphasizes some particular quality in the subject depicted?

Nefertiti, one of the most beautiful of women, is shown in the same exaggerated style as her husband, so that the strange distortions of the royal family and their circle achieved by Bak and his workmen, the prognathous jaws, the elongated faces, the swollen abdomens, must have been specially devised by the king at the same time as the symbol of the sun's disk with its blessed rays.

Surely an esoteric meaning was intended in these same representations of the king, in the vast statues found at Karnak, and those colossi, passed over by many of his admirers, in which Akhenaten is shown naked with no genitals?

W. Stevenson-Smith writes, "The colossi have a compelling force of their own . . . a mixture of harshness and softness . . . we cannot deny the daring vitality of these early works [of the Akhenaten period]." Not all have been so polite about them. The French journalist Pierre Jeannerat, visiting the "hauntingly misshapen" statues of Karnak, described how "I froze in my tracks that day nineteen years ago when M. Henri Chevrier [the archaeologist then in charge] opened the door of his workshop in Karnak and ushered me into the unexpected presence in a confined space of the giant statues of Akhenaten with their pot bellies, wide sneering mouths and puffed lips, cleaving noses, hollow cheeks and cold eyes . . . How are we to reconcile the naturalistic charm of Amarnan art with its contemptuous deformations? The deferential sensitive attitude of the sculptor Thutmose [of Amarna] in whose study the head of Nefertiti was found, and the savagery of the sculptor of the Akhenaten ogres? Not until our times would artists range so freely and deliberately in the gentle meadows of poetic naturalism and the psychopathic jungles of expressionist distortion."

Is not the answer that the "expressionistic distortion" was meant to startle and shock people into recognition of what Akhenaten considered an underlying truth? This may have been that the Aten, creator of life, was impersonal, super-sexual, both *mother* and *father* of mankind, and that Akhenaten, his deputy on earth, manifested these dual sexual characteristics.

If this may explain the physical peculiarities of some of the Karnak colossi, can the curious distortions of Akhenaten's face also be understood in a religious context?

Possibly, if it is remembered that animals had always played a large part in Egyptian cosmology and were not excluded, as will be explained, from the formal services of the new religion. Yet it is strange to find all representation of them banned from the set altarpieces of Atenism. But if Akhenaten had wished to represent himself in revolutionary style, a sun worshiper worshiped, and a being both sub- and superhuman including in himself all life, might he not have exaggerated his own facial characteristics to contain some aspect of those animals sacred to the sun and by tradition most intimately connected with sun worship—the ram, the bull, and the dog-headed baboon?

Whatever the truth, the undertones of hermaphroditism and the simio- and crio-characteristics were faithfully copied by the sycophants of the new king's court. And for the remaining years of the reign the sculptured scenes contain, as Maspero wrote, nothing but "angular profiles, pointed skulls, ample breasts, flowing figures and swelling stomachs."

II

Karnak is a palimpsest of the history of Thebes. Each Theban king added another court, pylon, sanctuary, or obelisk to the glory of Amen. Strange as it may seem, Akhenaten in the early years of his reign proved no exception. For at this stage Aten still bore the title of Ra-Harakhte and could still officially be included in the worship of the established god.

The basic features of Karnak as Akhenaten knew it had been built by Thutmose I and III. It had not yet fallen upon evil times. Gold and electrum tipped the obelisks; the column bases were covered with gold; and the doors between the pylons, also gold-plated, gleamed like the sun. The reliefs on the temple walls were bright with paint and from each of the pylons of this "many-gated Thebes" rose four tall flagstaffs with gaily fluttering pennons.

The large temple consecrated to Aten stood outside the eastern enclosure wall of the Amen precinct and a little north of the gateway at its east-west axis. Its full title was Ra-Harakhte who rejoices on the horizon in his name of Solar light (Shu), which appears in the Solar Globe (Aten).

The latest school of thought believes that Akhenaten took over, or enlarged, or appropriated, a religious edifice already built by his father, which had been dedicated to Ra-Harakhte. Like the Amarnan temples it was totally destroyed in antiquity, but stone in itself is indestructible. Some of the debris was buried and a great deal more was used as filling for later Karnak pylons, so that carved blocks of stone with Amarnan

*The Thebes colossi
of Akhenaten.*

motifs have been turning up regularly for more than a century.

Only a small portion of Akhenaten's temple was excavated when the southwest corner of a great court was exposed. On this site had once stood those huge and disturbing statues of Akhenaten remembered from the author's childhood. The bases for twenty-four colossi were found. They completely surrounded an open court. There, with folded arms bearing crook and flail, satanic eyes, and the secret smile of the initiated, the serried ranks of stone giants stood as if to overawe the worshiper.

On excavation the archaeologists found that Akhenaten's temple had been dismantled to the last stone and only the foundation trenches showed where the walls had stood. In its destruction some of the colossi had been smashed to bits and others dragged from the holy precincts and deeply buried.

Unearthed in the early years of this century, the more complete colossi are now in the Cairo museum. But carved blocks of stone from the Aten temple are at Karnak. Fifteen thousand are stacked in a corner of the temple precincts and await final analysis and classification. More thousands of blocks are known to be concealed in the filling of the second pylon.

Some of these blocks, now laid side by side, can be viewed. Many look as though the carvings and hieroglyphs have been cut yesterday, for, sheltered from the elements since Akhenaten's death, they have retained their sharp edges and bright picture-book colors. Larger stones taken from the ninth and tenth pylons depict scenes that show Amenhotep III offering to Ra-Harakhte—evidently later taken over and reused by Akhenaten. There are also curious carvings of apes praising the sun; and a prostrate figure, possibly Akhenaten, "smelling the earth" in adoration before Aten. He is surrounded by apes and this carving seems to have once surmounted an altar balustrade.

Typical Amarnan themes such as family groups under the disk and the royal progress by chariot show that the new symbolism in representation originated at Thebes. One relief indicated two little princesses. These would be the eldest, Meritaten and Meketaten.

If year 4 was the date Akhenaten planned the move to Tel el Amarna, the inauguration of the Atenist revolution and the building or alteration of the temple at Thebes must have begun as soon as his head bore the double crown.

The swiftness and the suddenness of the change is demonstrated nowhere as dramatically as in the tombs of the period. These were constructed in the owners' lifetimes and record the immediacy of their day in the same way as century-old newspapers. Kheruef, royal scribe and steward to Queen Tyi, has already been mentioned. His tomb, Number 192, was embellished with reliefs in the finest manner of Amenhotep III's reign and showed scenes from the king's two Hebsed festivals. The first, in year 30, may have included coronation celebrations for the new king. The architraves and jambs of the outer court entrance were the last to be finished, and perhaps in anticipation of the coronation ceremonies, Amenhotep IV and his mother, Queen Tyi, are shown worshiping the traditional gods of (be it noted) the Heliopolitan cycle. There is no tendency in these reliefs toward Atenism or the art nouveau of the new regime. Osiris and Anubis still preside as funerary deities and the sun god appears as Ra-Horus of the Horizon or Ra-Harakhte. But in spite of—or, more probably, because of—his traditional approach, Kheruef fell into disfavor and his name was erased from "what had been planned as one of the most magnificent monuments of the old regime."

A different trend of events was shown in the tomb of Parennefer (Number 188). Parennefer was one of the several men of ability who fell in with Akhenaten's ideas and later accompanied him to Tel el Amarna.

Parennefer constructed a second tomb in Aten's city but his Theban sepulcher must have been begun soon after the accession of Akhenaten and shows for the first time the new king and his queen enthroned. The traditional canopy over them has been awkwardly bisected to allow the sacred rays of the sun disk, each ending in a caressing hand, to bless the royal pair. Parennefer styles himself "overseer of all the works in the mansion of Aten Hat Aten," which can have been no other than the new Aten shrine at Karnak, and the speed with which this temple came into being indicates that Akhenaten probably took over and altered an existing temple built by his father.

But the suddenness of the religious revolution can best be seen in the tomb of Ramose, perhaps the most beautiful of the eighteenth dynasty.

Ramose, vizier of Thebes during the last years of Amenhotep, may have risen to his exalted position through nepotism as he was closely related to that extraordinary character Amenhotep, son of Hapu. Ramose became vizier after the death of his famous relative about year 34 of the older king. He was already one of the chief officials of the old regime in which he had held many key positions. Among his personal titles were Greatly Loved Companion, Whom the Lord of Egypt loved for his virtues, and Over the secrets of the house of the King. He was also Priest of Justice and after the death of the son of Hapu, took over the position of Administrator of North and South Egypt, and Regent of the Whole Land. His numerous sacerdotal titles included Overseer of the Temple of All the Gods, High Priest of Maet, and most interesting perhaps, One knowing the mysteries of On.

The tomb was built on a grandiose scale reflecting the increased wealth of the official class at this time. It was never finished and the end of Ramose, as of so many of his royal contemporaries, is unknown. The exquisite reliefs cut in the pale, translucent limestone of the walls have brought him posthumous immortality and vie with the best period of Greek art. As N. de Garies Davies wrote, "The imposing figure cut . . . their good condition, and the technical mastery with which their graceful lines are executed, will incline one to the judgment that they approach the high-water mark of Egyptian sculpture in low relief under the New Kingdom." Most of the tomb, constructed before the advent of Akhenaten, shows the influence of the worship of Ra-Harakhte as it was practiced by Amenhotep III's principal officials. Ramose, making oblation to the gods, stresses the divinities of Heliopolis without offending local opinion. The inscription reads:

To Amen-Ra, King of the gods, to Ra-Harakhte, to Atum . . . to the gods of the south, the north, the west and the east, to all gods and goddesses for the benefit of the King . . . Ramose says—I give praise to Ra-Harakhte when he dawns, that he may cause me to be among my followers and that my soul may rest in the evening boat by day.

If the ancient gods are respected they are excluded from the tomb walls, which bear instead portraits of Ramose, his relatives, friends, colleagues, staff, and servants. (A human touch is an ink memorandum, beside one of the portraits of a member of his household, that this was "Nebmeyet whom the scribe Iry begat.") A feast is in progress; precious oils and embalming ointments are offered to Ramose and his wife; the women mourn and the burial ceremonies are shown. The bier bearing the catafalque drawn by teams of oxen is preceded by a sled with the *teknu* dragged by four men with ropes. In early times a servant had been sacrificed for his master. Civilization brought a regard for human life, but the conservative Egyptians, who abandoned no ancient custom lightly, substituted a mummer. And the mimic *teknu,* wrapped from head to foot, continued to be included in the funeral ceremonies. In their tombs court officials always enshrined a larger than life representation of their master, the king. Bearing out the theory of the coregency, Ramose has depicted both Amenhotep III and Akhenaten. A king-sized representation of Amenhotep III dominates the south side of the west wall.

The goddess Maet, with the features of the young Tyi, guards him protectively under the gorgeous royal baldachin with its frieze of cobras raised to strike, whose circular hoods embody the sun. The king looks young and handsome and in his twenties. The substitution of Maet for Mut shows that the relief was executed after the move to Malkata and the reorientation of the court to the worship of Ra-Harakhte.

Up to this point the tomb, with its tasteful and sophisticated art, and its pious praise of Horus of the Horizon is of one piece. But abruptly there is a change of style and subject

—no gradual transition but a sudden transformation. The north side of the west wall might have been transported from Amarna. There are unmistakably the reliefs of Akhenaten and Nefertiti, caricatured, and inevitably defaced in antiquity, standing at the window of appearance. There are the rows of bent-necked, obese-bellied, and fawning courtiers, and there is the Aten disk whose rays protect and shower blessings on the young couple. Even Ramose is transformed. The sedate, stately official of Amenhotep III has vanished. Instead, wigless, shaven-headed, even the shape of his face subtly altered, Ramose is seen prostrating himself to the ground before the new pharaoh saying, "Thou dawnest, O Neferkheperu-ra, Wa-en-ra! Thou comest forth like thy father the living Aten. May he grant thee eternity and endless life as a happy ruler." For his loyalty he is rewarded with many collars of gold. It is the hour of his triumph as he says to Akhenaten, "Thou art unique . . . The mountains present to thee what they have kept hidden; for thy loud voice gains on their hearts even as thy loud voice gains on the hearts of men; the mountains obey thee even as men obey."

The habit of obedience to the royal authority was strong in the ancient Egyptians, but what Akhenaten with his "loud voice" was saying was certain to have been unacceptable to some of the priests of Amen. Was it also, in some sort, unacceptable to the older king and his advisers?

III

Granted that Amenhotep III appointed his eldest surviving son to rule with him, the king's conduct becomes mysterious. Did this divinely born child of the Theban Amen-Ra stand aside, calm and consenting, while Akhenaten pushed through a fantastic program of religious reform and even desecrated the name and statue of the king and the established god, whose temples Amenhotep III had himself added to and embellished?

This is unlikely. The older king is seen to have veered more and more toward the new religion. That he built a temple to Ra-Harakhte outside the temenos walls shows how altered his attitude had become from his earliest years. But that in addition he should assist in mutilating his own works and Ra-name is hard to believe, and the violence of Akhenaten's attacks on Amen was probably restrained until the coregency had ended and the older king was dead.

The historian is tantalized by lack of information on the behind-the-scene activities of Akhenaten's Theban years. What little is known of the drama is played out on a high level between gods and pharaohs. But what of the other actors and actresses who played important parts? Was Tyi heart and soul behind her son's claim to be Aten's earthly embodiment? And what was the attitude of Amenhotep, son of Hapu? This sage, who may have fostered Atenism at court as a purer and more ideal form of sun worship, once wrote in an inscription, "I was introduced to the knowledge of the Holy Book and beheld the glories of the god . . . I was enlightened in all mysteries." Did the son of Hapu, who was beloved of both king and commoner and held the balance of power at court, welcome the innovations of Akhenaten? Or was he alarmed at the young king's fanatical impetuosity?

Here Manetho's narrative might be of assistance. (The full text of the first part—in the author's opinion the only part that concerns Akhenaten—is in the Appendix.) It relates how Amenhotep was "desirous to become a spectator of the gods." How he asked his namesake, Amenhotep, son of Papis (Hapu), to assist him in this divine enlightenment. Amenhotep's namesake is described as partaking "of a divine nature both as to wisdom and the knowledge of futurities [prophecy]." The sage was from the north and had studied at Heliopolis. At this time he was already an elderly man. It is suggested that he derived his renowned wisdom and spiritual understanding, directly or indirectly, from the great religious thinker Moses. Was it the wisdom of Moses that the king desired to be taught when he asked "to become a spectator of the gods"?

Manetho goes on to relate that the son of Hapu told the king that his wishes could not be granted unless the country was purged of "impure people"—which included "some of

the learned priests." And that these would be assisted by
some who "would conquer Egypt and keep it in their possession thirteen years." At this point Akhenaten's name had
evidently been deleted, but not the thirteen years of the length
of time he reigned at Akhetaton. Amenhotep, the wise man
and prophet, is afraid that the gods would be angry at him
and the king if there should appear to have been violence
offered to them (the impure people). He therefore counsels
that they should be sent to the east side of the Nile, that they
"might be separated from the rest of the Egyptians."

Even if the facts Manetho relates come from a source
biased against Atenism they have the ring of truth. They
suggest that although Akhenaten began his career as an Atenist like his father and grandfather, his version of the new faith
branched from the main stream, being more eccentric, egocentric, and extreme. Where the king and his sage had lived
amicably with the Theban priests of Amen, Akhenaten showed
the ruthless face of fanaticism.

It can only be conjectured what moves the affronted high-
ranking priests of Amen made against their enemies. Even the
might of pharaoh could not have rendered them quiescent in
the face of the growing threat to Amen. Did they come in
embassy to the older king at Malkata, stage obstructive tactics,
or threaten the vengeance of their god? And was partisan
encouragement and support given Akhenaten by those other
priests of the Memphite On? Last but not least, was the beautiful Nefertiti a passive or an active participant in her husband's
delusions of grandeur?

It was written of her that "she sends the Aten to rest
with a sweet voice her two hands bearing the systrum." Many
high-ranking ladies in Thebes bore the title Chantress of
Amen. Apparently it was this role vis-à-vis Aten that Nefertiti
filled during the religious ceremonies of the new religion.

If the historian finds few answers to the questions he
seeks to elucidate, he knows that intrigues, plots, jostling for
wealth and the plums of office, elbowing for position, and
partisan politics are always present at the center of power.
Any student of recent history will believe that, in spite of the

deification of the king and the absence of political parties, this was as true in the Egypt of 1376 B.C. as it is today.

And all these motivations must somehow be allied with the personal elements of love, hate, and genuine religious fervor. The sum total, however apportioned, produced Akhenaten's extraordinary and unprecedented departure to Tel el Amarna.

It was not a wise move for a king whose empire straddled the fertile crescent from the Euphrates to the Sudan. To leave the ancient and established capitals of Memphis and Thebes and resettle the administrative offices in a desert was to hazard the machinery of state. But it is more than possible that this did not happen immediately and that the reins of government were retained by Amenhotep and his established officials.

For an ardent prophet of the Horus of the Horizon there were obvious advantages in removal from a town whose worship of Amen was so entrenched. In spite of Akhenaten's statement on his first stela set up at Tel el Amarna that Aten alone dictated the move, was it sanctioned and even suggested by the older king and prophet? Caught between the violence of the new king's religious extremism and the strong reaction of the Theban priesthood, it is possible that Amenhotep and his advisers hoped that the move might resolve an impasse. Amenhotep over the years had become a devout believer of the new cult. He was an Atenist but not a fanatic and cannot have wished to see the unity of the country threatened. From year 28 he had consistently withdrawn from the center of the stage in favor of his son. Either he was heart and soul behind Akhenaten in his moves to establish the new cult, or the gods had been too good to him and he suffered from a disability that produced lassitude and inertia, made kingship a burden, and the effort of standing up against a younger man's enthusiasm too exhausting. It was in any case the custom for the elder king in a coregency to give way to the younger more virile man. The second hypothesis seems the more likely. Yet if the overabundance of wealth and the maintenance of a large harem sapped his energies, Amenhotep III remained devoted to the Great Wife Tyi. She continued to bear him children.

Smenkhare may have been born in year 27 and Beketaten, the youngest princess, in year 34. But when King Tushratta of Mitanni, yielding to Amenhotep's persistent demands, sent his daughter Tadhukhipa as a bride to the Egyptian monarch, he heard reports that alarmed him. Acting immediately, he dispatched "to his brother, the king" his cherished and miraculous statue of Ishtar, goddess of Love. Addressing his letter to Amenhotep at the Southern Palace (Malkata), he prayed that although Ishtar, mistress of heaven, goddess of the Mitannians, was not worshiped by Amenhotep, yet might she, "The Lady of Fire," bring protection to Amenhotep and give him joy and physical well-being "for a hundred years."

Tushratta's prayers were partially answered if not, perhaps, in the way he intended. His daughter Tadhukhipa bore the king no children, but the Great Wife Tyi, approaching her climacteric, conceived her last and most famous child—Tutankhamen.

IV

Cyril Aldred has postulated a timetable for the Theban years of Akhenaten. He places the young king's accession to the throne in year 28/1. During the next two years, he suggests, the cult developed rapidly from the worship of Ra-Harakhte to the enclosure of the Aten name in royal cartouches and the emergence of the idea of a unique and spiritual god. Year 30, according to Aldred, was a year of great happenings, when Amenhotep III celebrated his first Sed festival, when the royal symbol of the sun's disk appeared with its royal uraeus, and when temples were built to Aten at Karnak, Hierakonopolis, and at Soleb in Nubia. The next four years saw the revolutionary art burst into flower and the iconoclasm of the new religion firmly established. At some time during this period Akhenaten made, or was forced to make, the decision to withdraw from Thebes. A virgin site was chosen on the Nile many miles away from Thebes and work on the new city began.

Two years later, before the final move, Akhenaten visited

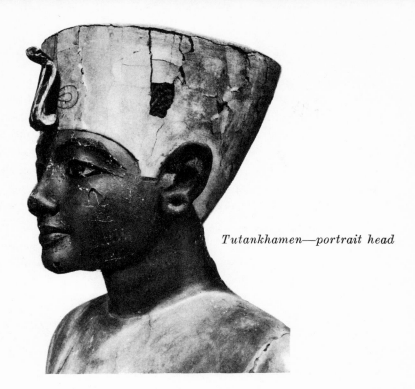

Tutankhamen—portrait head

the site in person. Clad in gold and driving a "great chariot
of electrum," led possibly by white horses with gold trappings
and gold-painted hooves, he deliberately impersonated the
sun. He appeared

*like Aten when he rises from his eastern horizon and fills the land
with his love; and he started a goodly course to the City of the
Horizon . . . Heaven was joyful, earth was glad, and every heart
was happy when they saw him. And his Majesty offered a great
sacrifice to Aten of bread, beer, horned bulls, polled bulls, beasts,
fowl, wine, incense, frankincense and all goodly herbs on this day of
demarcating the City of the Horizon . . .*

*Afterwards . . . (the King returned from) the City and he rested
upon his great throne . . . and the Aten shone upon him in life and
length of days, invigorating his body each day.*

*And his Majesty said, "Bring me the companions of the King, the
great ones and the mighty ones, the captains of soldiers, and the
nobles of the land in its entirety." And they were conducted to him
straightway, and they lay on their bellies before his Majesty, kissing
the ground before his mighty will.*

*And his Majesty said to them, "Behold Akhetaton which the Aten
has desired me to make as a monument for him in my name for ever."*

At this point the king emphasized and reemphasized that only Aten had led him to make the move. "Not a noble directed me . . . not any man in the whole land . . . but the Aten." The stelae set up by the pharaohs are suspect in regard to absolute fact because they stated not the truth but what the king wanted promulgated as the truth, sometimes a very different thing. So Akhenaten's insistence can mean either that he was "in truth" himself inspired to move to Akhetaton, or that circumstances had forced him to leave Thebes and that he was anxious to conceal this.

But in bearing witness to the intensity of the king's religious feelings and their nature, the stela is invaluable. Here the king writes in his own words his inner convictions:

Then his Majesty lifted his hand to heaven unto him that had formed him and said: "As my father Ra-Harakhte liveth, the great and living Aten, ordaining life, vigorous in life, my father, my rampart of a million cubits, my remembrancer of eternity, my witness of that which pertains to eternity, who formeth himself with his own hands, whom no artificer has known, who is established in rising and setting each day without ceasing. Whether he is in heaven or earth, all see him without failing, while he fills the land with his beams and makes every face to live. With seeing whom may my eyes be satisfied daily, when he rises in this temple of Aten in Akhetaton and fills it with his own self by his beams, beauteous in love, and lays them upon me in life and length of days for ever and ever.

Akhenaten next stresses that he will keep to the existing demarcated boundaries of the city and that he does not intend to move it to any other site. At this point in the life of the newly-born community the necessity to establish confidence was imperative.

Neither shall the Queen say to me, "Behold there is a goodly place for Akhetaton in another place" and I hearken to her. Neither shall any noble or other men say "Behold, there is a goodly place for Akhetaton in another place" and I hearken to them.

Akhenaten then enumerates the buildings he will erect. First the temple, then the Sunshade of Ra for the Great Wife of the king, Nefertiti, and subsequently a House of Rejoicing, palace, and sepulcher for himself, Nefertiti, and his eldest daughter, Meritaten. He insists that wherever their death occurs all three must be brought back to Akhetaton for burial, and he allots tombs for the chief priests and officers of the court. There is also a most curious reference that "the sepulcher of Mnevis shall be made in the eastern hills and he shall be buried therein." Mnevis, or Merwer, was the sacred bull of Ra-Atum of Heliopolis. Surely Akhenaten could not have underlined his orientation to the Memphite On more clearly.

Aldred sees Amenhotep III's second jubilee or sed festival in year 34/6 as held to celebrate his son's change of name to Akhenaten (*"Aten is satisfied"*) and his departure to the city of the Horizon of Aten. The move was probably not finally accomplished until year 36/8.

The ancient Heb-sed festival reenacted in pantomime the barbaric ritual murder of the aging king on his approach to senility and his rebirth in his son. It included the passionplay of the good god Osiris, murdered by the wicked Seth, resuscitated by his sister-wife Isis, and revenged by his son Horus.

But at the same time the jubilee could be symbolically adapted to represent the life of the sun, its dawning, setting, and daily rebirth. It also symbolized man, caught in the revolving wheel of fate and time, the everlasting process of evolution, the eternal and mystical cycle of existence.

In the "fourth month of the second season" after the jubilee Akhenaten set sail northward for the city he had designed, contrived, and created. From his boat he could look back and see Thebes, its temples gleaming white, framed by the dark fringes of the palm trees, its obelisks catching the sun on their golden tips, its gardens, avenues, crowded wharves, and houses. But his mind set on the future, he could not know (and perhaps would not have cared) that he was never to inhabit Thebes of the Hundred Gates again.*

---

* One of the Tel el Amarna letters seems to indicate that it was brought to Akhenaten when on a visit to Thebes. This may have been when he accompanied his father's catafalque to the Valley of Kings for burial, or when he attended the burial ceremonies.

7.
THE GREAT EXPERIMENT

Akhetaton, great in loveliness, mistress of pleasant
*   ceremonies,*
rich in possesions,
the offerings of Ra in her midst. At the
sight of her beauty there is rejoicing.
She is lovely and beautiful; when one sees
her it it like a glimpse of heaven. Her
number cannot be calculated. When the Aten
rises in her he fills her with his rays and
embraces his beloved son, Akhenaten, son of eternity,
*   who came*
forth from Aten and
offers the earth to him who placed him on
his throne, causing the earth to belong to
him who made him.

A COURTIER

I

There is confusion between Akhenaten and his god, even grammatically, in the courtier's quotation and the description of Akhetaton sounds like eastern hyperbole. Could this barren and deserted crescent of desert at any time have resembled a "glimpse of heaven" or was the resemblance no more than a figment of imagination in the mind of its creator?

The Egyptian Exploration Society sought to discover the answer to this question. It was established that the city founded with such high hopes by Akhenaten was planned on a most grandiose scale with buildings of vast dimensions and ambitious conception. When selected the place must have looked even more barren and deserted than it does today. A caravan route crossed it from south to north, but—a prerequisite in the choice of sites—it had until then remained uninhabited.

Once the virgin site was chosen, the town could be planned and built as rapidly as possible with, according to Pendlebury, "frantic haste everywhere in the construction of the 'mushroom city.'" The total length was about nine kilometers, the main building sites being crowded into a narrow strip between the "desert," where water was difficult to obtain, and the "sown," land too valuable for farming to be wasted on building acreage.

The workmen—artisans, bricklayers, masons, sculptors, engravers, and painters—must have resembled an army, and clearly an army was needed to create so monumental a city in so short a time. When the total of public and private buildings to be erected simultaneously is considered along with the number of colossal statues and the acreage of wall that needed covering with painting or engraved reliefs, the mind is staggered at the magnificence of the conception and the results that were achieved in the brief time allotted.

The noise of a whole city going up at once—banging, hammering, chipping—must have been deafening. No wonder the workers were housed some distance from the city in a special model village, excavated by Sir Leonard Woolley. It was found to consist of a large walled rectangle packed with three-roomed workers' tenements, as compact and alike as the units of a modern block of apartments. Only a foreman's cottage was larger than the rest. Woolley writes, "Clearly the inhabitants of this walled enclosure were not free workmen but were kept strictly under discipline—there were even patrol roads round it and guard-houses on the main road to the city—and their monotonously ordered quarters out in the desert were very unlike the normal Egyptian village . . . but as an example of ancient townplanning this was a really interesting discovery."

Although not free workmen in today's context, they were neither slaves, foreigners, nor prisoners. They received wages, kept their wives with them, owned goats, donkeys, even horses, and had enough energy after the day's work to paint pictures on the walls of their tenements. Even their religious freedom was not interfered with, and in the very citadel of Atenism they continued their old allegiance to Hathor and Taueret and Bes.

With master builders and stewards directing the thousands of antlike and busy workers, the ideal city rose quickly out of the wilderness. To break the desertlike expanse, pits were dug beside the houses and palaces, filled with Nile mud, and planted with ordered rows of trees whose roots were discovered in situ by the spades of the excavators. Sites, both official and private, were marked by inscribed boulders used as cornerstones and as the wood and imported material arrived by boat it was stacked on the allotted plot. Except for the Sikket es Sultan, road plans were irregular and the final housing arrangements muddled, the estates of the rich jostling the houses of the poor so that—as Sir Leonard Woolley wrote—"High priest rubbed shoulders with leatherworker, and Vizier with glass-maker." But this did not apply to the magnificent buildings set up for the king—the Record Office, the Foreign Affairs Office, the University or House of Life, the Military or Police Headquarters, and the great temple and palace.

First, of all official buildings erected, was the sanctuary of the great temple, confirming the supposition the Akhetaton was founded as a religious center and that national and foreign affairs were at first disregarded. As soon as the sanctuary was finished, Akhenaten visited the new city and made a tour of inspection of its boundaries. It was recorded on his second stela, set up in year 6, that

On this day was the king in Akhetaton in a tent of byssus . . . and the king appeared riding on the golden court-chariot like the disk of the Sun when it rises and sheds over the land its pleasant gifts. And he directed his course to where the beautiful land has its beginning . . . This was the first time since the king devised the plan of founding it as a memorial to the disk of the Sun . . . On that day was offered a complete sacrifice in the temple of the Sun's disk of the living god. Thereupon the king went up the river and mounted his

An aerial photograph of Akhetaton showing the layout of a great city with royal highway, temples, courtyards and offices. This was the city that grew up around the religion of Atenism, built to fulfill the dreams of Akhenaten.

chariot before his father the Sun god going towards the mountain to the south east of the city of Akhetaton the beams of the Sun's disk shining over him with a pure light . . .

When the new Elysium was declared fit for royal occupation, the king set sail from Thebes.

No relief of the flotilla of boats and barges carrying Akhenaten, the queen, the little princesses Meritaten, Meketaten, and Ankhesenpaaten, and their entourage in triumphal procession to their new capital has yet been discovered. Was Akhenaten victor or vanquished in his battle with the priests of Amen, or was he rather forced to a temporary truce? That he seems to have hated them can be seen in a curious reference at the end of his famous first stela: " . . . and more evil are the priests than those things I heard in year 4, more evil than those things which my father heard, more evil than those things my grandfather heard . . . "

The whole episode is made comprehensible by allowing for the coregency and strong government continuing at Thebes. If Ramose remained mayor of Thebes and the older king's counselors, officeholders, and generals maintained law and order, the continued stability of Egypt can be understood. But in any case it is doubtful if Akhenaten would have found time at this moment of his reign for the government of country and empire. On his arrival at Akhetaton he at first assumed the office of high priest and performed all the ritual of the new religion, which he also taught in the priestly college or House of Life and which he had himself devised. He supervised the completion of the half-finished buildings and planned the day-to-day life of the court and community. If at the same time he governed as king, his move to Akhetaton cannot have been in the interests of efficiency. Father and son, cohabiting the same palace complex, might have found no difficulty in joint rule, but what of two kings living two hundred miles apart by river?

The main decision must have lain with one or other of the coregents. Was it Akhenaten, or was his mind so filled with religious matters that he left the mundane affairs of government to his father? The Tel el Amarna tablets do little to help solve this question. One only emanates from Akhena-ten, which may mean no more than that the peasant woman stumbled on the in-box not the out-box of Akhenaten's foreign office.

Among the king's first actions was to set up new founda-tion stelae of Akhetaton to the extreme north and south of the city. On them was inscribed that His Majesty, again "rais-ing his hand to heaven," swore not only that he made the town for his father the Aten "as a dwelling eternally forever" but further that he, himself, would not pass beyond the north-ern, southern, eastern, and western landmarks.

In the first stela he had promised to keep the city within its prescribed boundaries. In the second he seems to be limit-ing his movements. Had something happened between the setting up of the two stelae and could this be taken to mean that the king, joint ruler of half the civilized world, confined himself deliberately "forever and ever" to the small crescent bounded by the inhospitable mountains? Had some promise been exacted from him by Thebes, and the king himself vowed for mystical reasons to remain in Akhetaton, fixed in space, unlike his counterpart the sun, at the center of his empire? Or did he still refer to the boundaries of Akhetaton? Madame Desroches Noblecourt has also suggested that at this stage of his reign Akhenaten was "not free to act" as he chose.

In whatever fashion the Thebans bade farewell to the royal flotilla, it is unlikely on any account to have been celebrated as a moment of rejoicing. But its arrival in Akhetaton would have been eagerly awaited. Nakht, the new vizier, was certain to have arranged suitable ceremonies for the inception of King Sun. By the landing wharves the flags would have been waving, servants and soldiers massed in well-drilled phalanxes, cour-tiers, nobles, and townsfolk huzza-ing a welcome and an impres-sive array of bowed backs. Pendlebury believed that the Nile once flowed east of its present course and that many buildings, including the official palace with the royal wharf, fronted the river.

The present area of cultivation has destroyed the evidence forever, including more than half of this portion of the palace. Added to the wanton destruction of the religious sites and the removal by the citizens of everything of value on returning to Thebes, the Egyptian Exploration Society found a formidable task awaiting it. To complicate matters the site had already been half excavated by Petrie and Borchardt, and it says a great deal for the painstaking thoroughness of the excavators that the whole ground plan for the center of the city was recovered. Even in the temple area where "not one stone was left upon another" the position of the walls was established by the foundation trenches.

This temple, heart and nucleus of the new city, showed several differences of construction from the temples of Amen. Instead of a procession of courts open to the sky and leading to the final darkness and mystery of the sanctuary, the Aten temple had a roofed portico—a prelude to open courts bathed by the rays of the living sun. Instead of an obelisk or benben stone, the symbol of the sun was a huge stela, guarded by a colossus of the king, and a raised central altar, reached by a ramp, surrounded with offering tables crowding as thickly as tree stumps in a ravaged forest. These were found again to the left and right of the temple in orderly rows making a grand total of nine hundred. The adulators of Akhenaten must face the implication of these offering tables. However spiritual the king's worship of the faceless sun's disk might be, he remained a man of his time and the conception of a god who did not require daily offerings of food and drink was beyond him. The ancient Egyptians had always treated their gods as kings, and their kings as god. The logic was simple; both required feeding. And the daily offerings were part of the age-old ritual performed by the priests in the temples. But the proliferation of offering tables in the grand temple at Akhetaton was symbolic of the honoring of the multitudinous rays of the sun. The total nine hundred presumably were used on such special occasions as the Reception of Foreign Tribute. The butchers' yard was within the temple enclosure.

Pierced tethering stones for the sacrificial animals were found, and the mind boggles at the number of cattle needed to supply each offering table with a joint. Who, the modern householder will wonder, ate this mountain of food laid before the insensate god?

Adolf Erman discovered that the Egyptians, practical as ever, offered to the gods in exact ratio to the number of persons attending the religious ceremony. So the daily offerings were presumably absorbed by the king's household and chief priests, while on days of special rejoicing the total nine hundred tables bore their heaped burden of meat, game, bread, wine, and fruit. On such occasions it is to be hoped that the poor of Akhetaton were permitted to join in the general feasting. (Preserved meat, pounded and salted, was one of the delicacies of the City of the Sun. The jars in which it was packed bore the formula " ... pounded meat of the Aten of the kitchen of the house of Aten ... " and may indicate how leftovers were used.)*

A wall relief from an Amarnan tomb illustrates the culminating moment of ceremony in the temple when smoke rose from the bronze incense burners lighted beside the offering tables. And the whole complex, altars, smoking incense burners, pylon, pillared portico, three outer and three inner courts, surrounded, like the many skins of an onion, the central holy of holies where on a stepped altar the king made an ecstatic oblation to the sun, his father.

II

The great palace was built after the sanctuary but at the same time as the temple. Akhenaten, who suffered from no false modesty, had planned it on so gigantic a scale that it was never completed. In size and conception it must have taken precedence of any secular building in the civilized world of that day. Its length extended for seven hundred meters along the Sikket es Sultan and the whole complex was named, perhaps suitably, House of the Rejoicing in Aten. Unlike the palace at Malkata, which developed in an impromptu and haphazard fashion, the new royal residence was carefully planned, and the state apartments, adumbrating the idea of the king as god, were built, like the temple, of stone.

*The word *pounded* may mean *dried* like biltong.

The frontage facing the Nile, which must have been the most impressive approach of all, has entirely vanished, but traces of the Weben-Aten—the principal entrance from the north side—were found. The existing remains suggested two great columned buildings that flanked the doorway and were decorated with reliefs of the royal family on their way to the temple, and the adoration of the Aten. This impressive approach led to the Broad Hall, a vast court completely surrounded by colossal statues of the king and queen. Immediately opposite the entrance was a stepped and pillared portico possibly framing a window of appearance; behind this lay the nucleus of the palace. Three sunken courts, approached by balustraded ramps, led to the majesty of the Central Halls. "The gigantic columns which supported the roof of these halls," wrote Pendlebury, "were of limestone, the shafts like bundles of reeds, the capitals like inverted bells. The flanking colonnades were similar but smaller, thus giving clerestory lighting to the central aisles." On the walls were processional scenes and scenes from the private life of the royal family. As if these public purlieus were insufficient, on either side of the halls were yet two more pillared courts each centering (it is thought) on a colossus of the king set on a cement platform in the midst of an ornamental pond. Two further courts with pavilions were planned but never completed.

This central palace, lying north-south, was linked with the Great Bridge running east-west over the Sikket es Sultan, "which was," wrote Pendlebury, "an entirely new feature in Egyptian architecture and one well in keeping with the elaborate parade of the family life of the king." In the center of the bridge, facing both ways down the Royal Road, was the Great Window of Appearance. The king, decked in gold, publicly appearing on his golden dais, had long been a feature of Egyptian life. Akhenaten seems to have improvised a new idea more in keeping with the adoration of the sun viewed in the heavens. And it is possible the king publicly appeared at this window decked in gold, at those late or early moments when the sun shone full on the symbolic Window of heaven bringing the analogy closer to the mind of the onlooker.

On the left of the bridge were the north and south harems.

Some writers have affirmed that Akhenaten, devoted to Nefertiti and his religion, made no use of the harem, but this is no
more than supposition.* It is true that a devotee does not
incline to sexual indulgence. But monastic abstinence was not
considered a virtue in ancient Egypt and a certain priest could
be admonished on his stela with the words:

*Do not refrain from eating and drinking, O Priest of Ptah, from
getting drunk or making love, from spending days in joyous celebrations, or following the dictates of your heart day and night. After
all what are the days we spend on earth, however numerous?*

Far from claiming asceticism, Akhenaten was at pains to
stress the normality of his family life. The reticence in intimate
matters shown by the ancient Egyptians in their art was
abandoned by him. Never before had the king been depicted in
the physical act of kissing his wife and daughters. If it is
accepted that the innovations in art introduced by the king were
for reasons of religious symbolism, then the numerous representations of him embracing his family must come under this
category and can be seen as symbolizing the warm and fecund
kiss of the sun and its generating power in the procreation of
children. But the impression received is that Akhenaten, far
from imitating his solar counterpart, was activated by genuine
passion for his beautiful wife. Are not the titles he gave her
indicative of his love?

She is termed: "The Hereditary Princess, Great of
Favor, Mistress of Happiness, Gay with the two feathers, at
hearing whose voice one rejoices, Soothing the heart of the
king at home, pleased at all that is said, the Great and Beloved Wife of the King, Lady of the Two Lands, Neferu-aten
Nefertiti, living forever."

"Soothed in the heart at home," Akhenaten may not often
have sought the solace of the harem, even though he had only

*The social life at Akhenaten's court should be seen rather in terms of African
tribal life than compared to western mores. The king's plurality of wives reflected
his power and wealth. At least one, other than Nefertiti, is known by name. A
small calcite pot was found bearing the inscription: "The great, beloved wife
of the king . . . who lives in truth . . . the goodly child of the living Aten,
Neferkheprure Waenra [Akhenaten] . . . Kia." Nothing else about this lady is
known.

to cross the bridge over the Royal Road to reach it. Representations of it in the tomb of Ay depict an innocuous-looking establishment like a well-conducted nightclub. The young ladies offer light refreshment. They entertain, dance, and sing, accompanying themselves like modern pop singers with the lute. A number of these lutes are shown and many harps, both Asian and Egyptian, lean against the walls. Wine is not wanting and amphora are stacked in readiness or set out on stands. Outside the harem door a guard relaxes with bent knee.*

The north harem, whose remains were uncovered by the Egyptian Exploration Society, had already been cleared by Petrie. It was here, in a columned hall leading to the garden, that he found the fine painted pavement now in the Cairo museum. The garden itself is similar to the one described in the north palace. It has a stone-lined pool at one end of an enclosed rectangle and a well under a light kiosk at the other with a water conduit running between the two. Rows of pits filled with Nile mud show where trees were planted and the traces of flower beds. The garden was surrounded by a roofed ambulatory supported by brick piers and protected by a low wall. This was gaily painted outside with scenes of life on the banks of the Nile, flowing between banks of black mud. Petrie found the coping stone of the well which bore the name and full titles of Nefertiti.

As in the north palace, a row of small cubicles opened off both sides of the garden colonnade, alike as cattle stalls. They were whitewashed inside and painted with various designs, and seem to us too small for living rooms. They may have been meant for ritual purposes on occasions of state visits, or possibly as bathing boxes when the ladies of the harem refreshed themselves in the pool; or again, as Stevenson-Smith suggests, might they be aviaries for bright-plumaged birds? But it is a fact that even in the private houses of Akhetaton the women's quarters were small and cramped.

*In Ay's tomb the harem was depicted as divided into two noncommunicating suites of rooms, each comprising a small hall with one column and a living room. In the top suite a woman with a flounced dress and a Hittite hairstyle was shown. Could this be a portrait of a Mitannian princess?

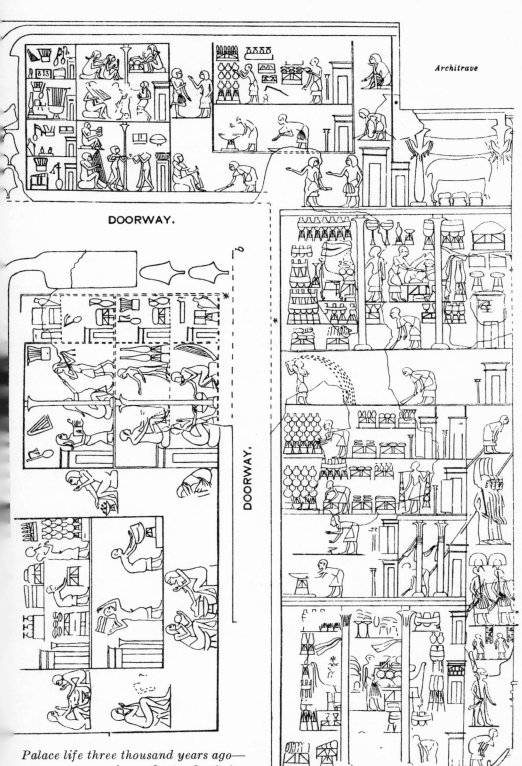

DOORWAY.

DOORWAY.

Architrave

*Palace life three thousand years ago—
from the tomb of Ay.*

A narrow passage, wide enough to patrol, ran round three sides of the harem and the fourth side was the guard-room protecting the only exit to the Royal Road. On the other side of the guard room, abutting on the bridge, was the south harem, a less enclosed unit, which might have been set aside for the queen. Here also was a garden but of a different type. A paved court abutted on it with what seemed like an ornamental pond with a stand for a statue. Nearby was found a pit in which the pet cats and dogs of the harem had been interred.

As the visitor to Tel el Amarna will find, the remains of this labyrinth of pillared courts, sumptuous halls, faience inlays, reliefs, painted walls and pavements, colossal statues, porticoes, and ornamental gardens, are today little more than patterns traced in the dust. The Versailles of ancient Egypt, the magnificently designed palace, which Pendlebury called "the largest secular building in the ancient world" and the only one in Egypt constructed of stone, is indeed a "colossal wreck" reduced to that "decay" mentioned by Shelley.

III

The palace was not the day-to-day residence of the king. This lay immediately beyond the bridge, one of the several buildings on the royal estate. It comprised a garden full of trees, a group of magazines or store chambers, and a private house. Pendlebury suggested as the king's own quarters a little suite of rooms forming a bedroom, bathroom with a bath slab of stone and stone basin, and a latrine. Here was found a private altar set against the wall and the famous painted fresco of two of the little princesses—part of a large group depicting the whole family designed in a color scheme of terracotta, gold, and blue.

Whatever human dramas of love, hate, pride, or tragedy were enacted between these walls, nothing was left behind to assist the biographer. Petrie, who first examined the king's house, expressly stated that he found no objects at all. Pendlebury discovered a mute tribute to the long-dead lovers in a fragment of limestone bracelet carved with the names of

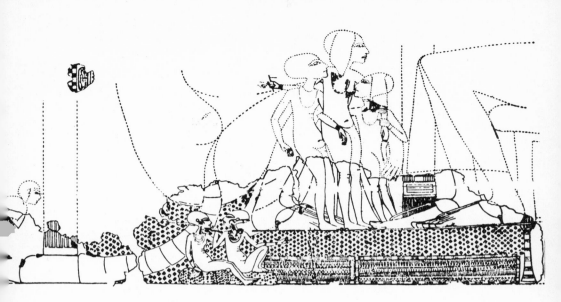

Tel el Amarna mural of the royal family "at home" shows Akhenaten enthroned with Nefertiti sitting opposite. The enlarged detail shows the two youngest princesses. The reconstruction is by W. Stevenson-Smith.

Akhenaten and Nefertiti, and as if thrown into a deserted palace in mockery of the king and his high ideals, a statuette of a monkey was discovered in the debris. More interesting, and one of the few finds of human interest, was a small room in what might have been the quarters allotted to the princesses. "The mud floor," wrote Pendlebury, "and what was left of the mud-plastered walls . . . were covered with streaks of paint, yellow, red, blue, green, black, where people had wiped their brushes. Indeed, the very brushes and other paraphernalia of painting were found here." This included two paintbrushes of fiber, fish-bone pens, and lumps of red, yellow, and blue paint. Because a room in the king's most private apartments would surely not have been allowed to remain a painter's workshop, Pendlebury suggested that this was in fact the playroom of the royal children where they could amuse themselves and daub as much as they pleased.

The rest of the king's house was taken up with magazines and just such a set of store chambers is shown in the tomb of Mery-Ra, with pillared and linteled doorways and trees planted in the two cross corridors. The storerooms in the relief are neatly packed to capacity with sealed wine jars, gold ingots, vases and dishes of alabaster, treasure chests, and rolls of woven material.

Immediately behind the king's house lies the Records Office, its bricks inscribed "Bureau for the Correspondence of Pharaoh." Here were found the famous cuneiform tablets, and the attempts by the local population and others to discover more such valuable assets has led to the almost total disappearance of the foundations. Closely and conveniently situated near to the Records Office was the Foreign Office, and the House of Life. The Foreign Office was entered through a stone-lined doorway that opened into a small pillared audience hall with a dais, two latrines for the convenience of visitors, and a waiting room. The rest of the building was divided into offices. Their arrangement reminded Pendlebury irresistibly of a modern government building with an outer office for the typist, an inner office for the chief clerk, and a more luxurious room allotted to the departmental chief. The House of Life, marked with the sacred sign of the priestly college, adjoined.

It was here that Akhenaten taught the doctrines and formulas of the new Atenism, as indeed he was forced to do as he had largely originated them.

No question relative to Akhenaten has been more discussed than his religious reformation. Was it so different from the Atenism practiced by his father? Was it inspirational, visionary, and saintly? Or was it caused by the eccentricities of a diseased body, a brain suffering from *idées de grandeur?*

The answer must be found in his own "Hymn to Aten" which, using the formula already employed by such men as Suti and Hor in his father's reign, he presumably added to and rewrote. It is a splendid outpouring of praise to the sun, a magnificent poem. Brushing the cobwebs of superstition aside as though they had never been, the author looks to the highest visible point of the solar system, the sun's orb, and sees the sun's rays as the creating factor of all life, plants, fish, animals, human beings. It seems a moment of ultimate truth, an orgasm of spiritual oneness between the king, luminary on earth, and that greater and everlasting luminary in the heavens.

When the "Hymn to the Sun" became known it not only stirred interest in Akhenaten but produced a wave of enthusiasm for the king who was termed by many the first monotheist and the first individualist in history. He was also credited with liberal sentiments, a saintly and harmonious family life, and a belief in the brotherhood of man and universal love. The reaction when it set in came largely from those Egyptologists who considered the enthusiasm exaggerated and many of the virtues attributed to the king misplaced.

In fact the "Hymn to Aten," which can be read at the back of this book, is a paean of praise, not a pattern of the good life. It posed no ethical standards and demanded no moral virtue. It is the outpouring of an ecstatic, and such a man has, as a rule, little interest in the ordinary values of human society.

An illustration of this can be seen in Sufism, which bears a curious resemblance to the Atenism of Akhenaten. Although of much later date, being a form of mysticism within Islam, it retains traces of sun worship. Originating, possibly, from

Indo-Aryan peoples and from that part of the world once in-habited by the Mitannians, the object of Sufism was to make the soul purely spiritual and unite it by love with God from whom it emanated as a ray emanates from the sun. The Sufi devotee by training had to rise through three degrees of holi-ness to the highest—centainty. At this stage the transcendental objective god had become subjective, and the Sufi devotee found that he himself was consciously God. (Sir Richard Burton, who studied the Sufi fanatics proclaiming themselves to be God, decided there was an affinity between mysticism and insanity.)

Is there any evidence for the suggestion that Akhenaten had liberalistic ideas far ahead of his time? Although the rays of the benign sun represented in all the Amarnan set pieces shine exclusively on the king and his family and do not lave with their luster even the courtiers nearest to the throne, the very nature of the universalist doctrine that included all plants, all animals, all human beings, must have influenced him. He raised up men of low degree such as May and Panehesy to be courtiers close to the throne (but so did Amen-hotep III raise the son of Hapu). And surely sincerely, rather than as a political expedient, he mentioned in his hymn to the sun:

> The countries of Syria and Nubia
> The land of Egypt;
> Thou settest every man in his place
> Thou suppliest their necessities.
> Everyone had his possessions
> And his days are reckoned.
> Their tongues are divers in speech,
> Their forms likewise and their skins
> For Thou, divider, hast divided the peoples.

If he did indeed write the "Hymn to the Sun," then he was the first ruler to include all the races, however "divided," under one god. On the other hand he tolerated slavery, and the recent discovery of a carving of Akhenaten in the tradi-tional pose of striking his enemies finally demolishes the argu-ment that he was a pacifist.

It is established what he thought of himself and the Aten. We have no knowledge what he thought of others; he may have been kind to his own people but not to the priests of Amen or, later, to his queen. But if it is accepted that he was a genuine mystic, a true believer in the universality of all living matter under his father, the sun's disk, then the pattern of his life becomes clear and the violence of its impact on the history of his time, natural.

IV

The temple rituals, the Heb-sed festivals, the chanted hymns, and the famous festivals of Opet when Amen-Ra's sacred boat was brought from its sanctuary in Karnak and carried to Luxor on the shoulders of the priests, were derived from much-loved and sacred traditions cherished for hundreds of years. By turning his back on them when he left Thebes, Akhenaten was forced to substitute a different liturgy, ritual, and service, and attempt to create a theme at least as attractive to the Aten worshiper as the dramatic enactions of the passion play of Osiris. It was for this reason he at first assumed the mantle of the high priest and himself taught in the House of Life or priestly college.

Evidence for the nature of the ritual of Aten worship has only gradually been pieced together from the excavation of a site at El Hawatah south of the city. Sir Leonard Woolley, who was in charge of the work, discovered that the complex bore the charming name of Maru-Aten: The Precinct of the Southern Pool. He thought of it at first as a pavilioned garden and pleasure park for the king.

It was certainly a curious structure. A rectangular buttressed *enceinte* wall surrounded a large area principally given over to a lake and a garden. The lake was one hundred and twenty meters long by sixty wide, its sloping gravel sides lightly puddled with Nile mud. It was a meter in depth, "amply deep enough," wrote Woolley, "for the light painted pleasure-craft of the Egyptians." A long stone quay or causeway projected into the water, and at its end was a small building.

This building had been much decorated. Reeded columns with palm-leaf capitals adorned it as well as a palmette frieze on a cavetto cornice and the royal uraeus snakes. It had been painted throughout with reliefs of Aten worship, running soldiers, foreign captives (both possibly from a tribute scene), and boating pictures. From this pavilion steps descended into the water.

All around the lake stretched the garden, the trees, and bushes, which had been embedded in tubs of mud and carefully tended. The several buildings in the complex, although small, were of very great interest. One appeared to be a kind of small audience hall with, as Woolley at first thought, harem quarters above, but what the king wanted with an audience hall and harem so far from the main city was a mystery. In this building a walled corridor led to a two-pillared room with a stepped dais for a throne and baldachin. It was flanked by the usual robing room, or bedroom, and toilets. A side door led to a further most unusual columned court, virtually a Roman peristyle, with central flower beds. Behind this a third court, also pillared, had rows of cellars on each side, two of which had been bricked in.

Nothing was discovered in these two mysteriously bricked-in cellars but the body of an infant, roughly buried there with its toy pots of alabaster, beads, and amulet. Other cellars had contained over two hundred and eighty stacked wine jars. All had been broken open and their fragments and sealings lay scattered over the floor.

Even more interesting perhaps than this palace temple was a group of buildings in the southwest corner of the *enceinte* wall. They were in fact closely and symbolically linked. First came a curious water court, the central feature being a series of interlocked T-shaped water tanks with sloping sides, half sunk below floor level. The lower half had contained water. The upper half had been painted with water plants, lilies and lotus flowers, in bright natural colors.

"The painted plants seemed to grow out of the real water," wrote Woolley, "and the tanks with their many angles formed a sort of maze out of which the pillars sprang to support the roof. The same floral designs were repeated

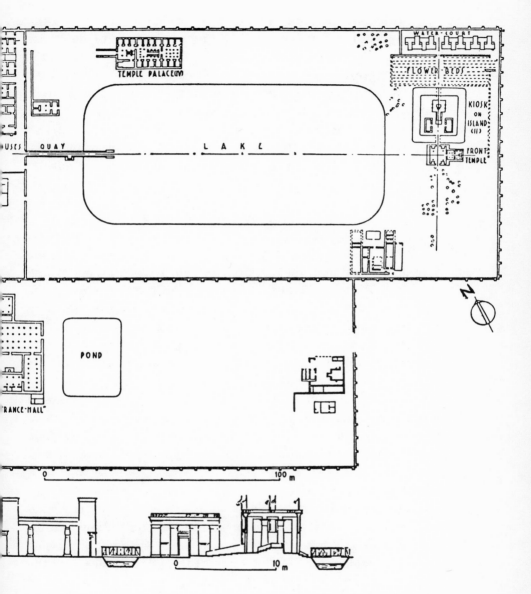

This map and section from A. Badaway's important article in Volume
42 of the JOURNAL OF EGYPTIAN ARCHAEOLOGY shows some of the strange
aspects of the Maru-Aten, a form of sun temple during Akhenaten's
reign.

. . . on the parapet, and the passage was decorated with gaily coloured lotuses, rushes, papyri, and all manner of flowering plants, out of which ducks started in flight or heifers plunged among their foliage.'' This charming little water court resembled nothing so much as the conservatory of a modern botanical gardens. In front of the water court eight flower beds in ordered lines on either side of a path led to a group of interdependent buildings of solid masonry on which had been lavished many rare stones and much rich ornament.

A small temple stood beside a square moat, in Akhenaten's day filled with water. On the island formed by the moat was a raised central kiosk approached by shallow steps, flanked by two pavilions. The best quality of workmanship and the most expenisve materials available in Akhenaten's Egypt had gone to adorn these buildings. Alabaster had paved the floors and lined the doorways, and the incised decoration of many of the pillars and the friezes of uraeus snakes had been inlaid with multicolored semiprecious stones.

One other flimsy building was of particular interest to archaeologists. It lay inside the precincts and abutting on the wall and, when excavated, was found to have contained the royal kennels. At some stage in the history of the town, the sad remnants of the pack of thirty greyhounds, including old dogs and puppies, had been put to death or allowed to die, and their bones were found tumbled together in the boxlike compartments.

After a careful sifting of the facts, Alexander Badawy, another Egyptologist, came to the conclusion that the Maru-Aten site was not a pleasure park but solely a religious center. The word *maru*, of Syrian origin, meant ''seeing'' or ''viewing,'' particularly in connection with the solar deities, and the earliest mention of the word is on a granite stela set up in western Thebes by Amenhotep III, which does in fact hold the key to the meaning of the *maru* and its raison d'etre in Akhenaton. The stela is dedicated to Amen in the ambivalent fashion of the period and the king boasts of ''making for Amen a *maru* as a divine offering in southern Opet, a place of flourishing for my father at his beautiful feast. I erected a great temple in its midst like Ra when he reigns in the horizon. It is planted with all flowers; how beautiful is Nun in his pool every season; more its wine than water, like a full Nile, born of the Lord of Eternity. Many are the gods of the place; the imports of all countries are received. Much tribute is brought here before my father, being the offering of all lands."

The crux of the inscriptions was the information that the *maru* was "a place of flourishing for Amen in his beautiful feast." Substitute the word *Aten* for *Amen* and the sentence describes exactly the complex at El Hawatah.

The ensemble of temple, kiosk, flower garden, and water tanks was, it is thought, "The place to view Aten when he rises in the east."

The disposition of columns suggests that both temple and kiosk were open to the sky. The kiosk is thought to have been one of those sunshades of Ra mentioned on the boundary stela and designated for the royal queens. From Amarnan texts it seems a sunshade was erected for the Queen Mother Tyi, for Nefertiti, Meritaten, and Ankhesenpaaten's little daughter by her father.

H. W. Fairman, who made a special study of the nature of the sunshades, has suggested that they were kiosks. islanded by water, open to the sky, and used as chapels by the royal ladies. There, perhaps, they retired to enact a mystic union with the sun, whose shadow passing over them re-imbued them with fertility and the divinity thought to invest queens as well as the kings with special powers.

The Maru-Aten can then be imagined as a holy place where, with the ancient Egyptian genius for marrying poetry and prose, fact and fancy, a practical demonstration was given of the endless variety of living things created by the sun.

Many symbolic possibilities suggest themselves. Could the moat have represented Nun, the chaos or primeval ocean out of which the sun was born, that sun represented by the living king? And no effort of the imagination is needed to see the flower beds surrounding him as representing the seasons and illustrating in actual scent and flower the lines: "Thy rays nourish every garden. When thou risest they live, they grow by thee." The eleven tanks filled with species of fish

may have played a part in the monthly Aten festival of
Masawat. Each tank, it seems, was painted with different
varieties of water plants, and on the twelfth month the great
annual festival was held, possibly in the month of Tybi (May).
Then Aten was represented not by flowering plants but by the
kiosk, symbol both of generation and regeneration, and there
a great festal gathering was held to worship the Aten "who
had made all seasons." The words "more his wine than
water" and the two hundred and eighty broached jars of wine
suggest a feast prodigal of good-cheer, which there is no reason to believe was puritanical in its nature.

> *All cattle rest upon the herbage,*
> *All trees and plants flourish*
> *The birds flutter in their marshes*
> *Their wings lifted up in adoration to Thee.*
> *The sheep dance upon their feet,*
> *All winged things fly . . .*
> *The fish in the river leap up . . .*

Surely the complex of buildings bounded by the *enceinte*
wall of Maru-Aten held not only fish, plants, flowers, and
trees, but zoological gardens and an aviary.

Badawy suggests the temple palace as the repository for
the "offerings of all lands" mentioned on the stela of Amenhotep III, where wine, meat, ointment, fruit, and wine were
stored. Here the king must have feasted and reenacted in the
upstairs rooms, reached by a stairway (and thought of as a
harem by Woolley), the "creation of man" with Nefertiti.
The Queen's name was at first prominent on all the buildings
of the Maru-Aten—until the time came when clouds covered
the sun and Nefertiti's names and titles were in every case
erased and replaced by those of her eldest daughter, Meritaten.

The solar hymn and the Maru-Aten can be seen together
in a new light. The hymn was not only a poem and a psalm,
but also possibly a liturgy sung and acted at the Maru-Aten.
Then all could participate in the joy of seeing the disk, creator
of all things, daily, monthly, and yearly renewing his bene-
factions to mankind.

8.

YEAR TWELVE

THE RECEPTION OF FOREIGN TRIBUTE

*Year twelve, the second month of winter, the eighth day
. . . The King and the Queen, living for ever and ever,
made a public appearance on the the great palanquin of
gold to receive the tribute of Syria and Ethiopia, and of
the west and the east. All the countries were collected at
one time, and also the islands in the midst of the sea;
bringing offerings to the king when he was on the great
throne of the City of the Horizon of Aten, in order to
receive the imposts of every land and granting them in
return the breath of life.*
INSCRIPTION FROM THE TOMB OF HUYA

I

The reception of foreign tribute was, it is now thought, a
ceremony arranged for each king subsequent upon his coronation. Resembling the medieval swearing of fealty, its intention
was clearly to identify and establish the subservience of the
countries owing allegiance to Egypt; that it was held in the
year 12 of Akhenaten is additional support for belief in the
coregency. For, according to this school of thought to which
the author is a convert, Amenhotep III died sometime between
year 9 and 12 and Akenaten became sole and singular—in
more senses than one—ruler.

If the lives of public men can be divided into parts, then
Akhenaten's reign falls dramatically into three periods. First
came the vital Theban years, the forming of the new ideology
and a struggle to gain acceptance for the revolutionary conception of one god. This struggle—as was inevitable—met
strong resistance. It was a case, perhaps, of the ''irresistible

135

force'' of Akhenaten's Atenism meeting the ''immovable object'' of the traditionalism of the priests of Amen. The conflict of ideas ended in Akhenaten's extraordinary decision to move from Thebes and create the City of the Horizon. The second period terminated with the death of Akhenaten's father. Only the last five years were to prove disastrous to the king, to all that he believed in, to Egypt, and to its empire.

Relatively speaking, the years 6 to 12 at Akhetaton may have passed for the king in prosperity and happiness. If his heart and soul were set on the promotion of his religious ideals, and if the bureaucrats at Thebes largely managed the intricacies of Egypt's foreign and home affairs, there was no reason why matters should not have gone well with him. Within the limited boundaries of his domain dedicated to the worship of the Aten, he was free to act as he chose. His wealth was immense, his subjects subservient, his servants innumerable, his wife beautiful, his daughters many, and, because only the confirmed supporters of Aten followed him into the wilderness, his audience bound to be sympathetic. No dedicated idealist was ever better placed to seek and find an earthly Nirvana.

One of the King's first official acts after settling in Akhetaton was to delegate his duties as high priest to Mery-Ra. This courtier, who was Bearer of the Fan on the Right Hand of the King, Royal Chancellor, and also the pharaoh's ''Sole Companion'' and ''Friend,'' portrayed the ceremony on the wall of his tomb, one of the finest in the metropolis. In the relief, the king, queen, and one of the princesses stand at a window of appearance brightly ornamented with painted garlands of lotus flowers. Flags flutter, the massed courtiers bow and incline long-handled ostrich feather fans. Under the beaming rays of the sun, Akhenaten leans forward with outstretched hand, conferring office on Mery-Ra and saying, ''Behold I make thee high priest of the Aten . . . and I do this for love of thee, and I say unto thee: O my servant who hearkenest to the teaching, my heart is satisfied with everything which thou hast done. I give thee this office, and I say unto thee: thou shalt eat the food of the pharaoh, my lord, in the Temple of Aten.''

The courtiers lift Mery-Ra shoulder-high as he is presented with the insignia of office and various costly gifts are
placed in the charge of servants and attendants. Behind these,
is a chariot to convey the new high priest in triumph to his
villa, with fan bearers to run before and behind, and a band
of women tambourine players leading the procession, while
girls strew flowers in his path. Another and later scene from
the same tomb shows a royal visit to the temple during Mery-
Ra's tenure of office. Aldred suggests that Amenhotep III celebrated three jubilees during the last decade of his existence
and that on each occasion Akhenaten took the opportunity to
organize similar celebrations to the Aten: the first in year
30/2 when Atenism became established; the second in 34/6
when the King Amenhotep IV and his queen changed their
names to the Aten form; and the third in 37/9 when the older
couple could have visited Akhetaton.

This may be the celebration shown in Mery-Ra's tomb. It
is no ordinary affair. Although the temple was only a stone's
throw from the royal residence, a full cortege of chariots,
standard-bearers, and soldiers had been mounted in a parade,
which no doubt passed the length of the town before arriving
in front of the temple pylons.

The king rides ahead, the queen driving her own chariot
in attendance. Then follow four of the princesses and a group
of courtiers, also in chariots. Last come the multiracial soldiers
of the guard, who illustrate the theme of a contented empire.
They include bearded Syrians, befeathered Nubians, the king's
special Mazoi Nubian guard, and Libyans from the west wearing the plaited sidelocks of hair.

In the relief from his tomb Mery-Ra stands before the
temple gateway. Pendlebury found the sockets that held the
bronze pivots of the great gate. It was enormous. Each leaf
of the door (of wood plated with bronze) was three meters
broad—too large to open or shut. But, wrote Pendlebury,
"perhaps to Akhenaten, provided the door was the largest
in the world, it did not matter if it did have to stay perpetually half-open."

In the tomb relief, four priests kneel near Mery-Ra holding plumed fans while others bring out the sacrificial bulls

garlanded with flowers. Altars are piled high with offerings, incense burners smoke, and there is a full orchestra for this special occasion. In addition to women tambourine players, a blind musician plays on a seven-stringed harp while seven other blind men clap and sing an accompaniment.

That Mery-Ra succeeded in pleasing his temporal master is proved by the final relief, where Akhenaten is seen instructing his superintendent of the treasury to hang gold on the neck of the high priest and gold on his feet "because of his obedience to the teaching of pharaoh." His obedience lasted for sixteen years, almost the length of the reign of the master he served.

But the priest who saw to the routine and ritual of the temple—the services and the daily sacrifice—was the southerner Panehesy, the first servitor and superintendent of the cattle of Aten. His official residence, stamped with the royal cartouches, was just beyond the sanctuary wall of the temple and he owned a luxurious private estate in the main town. "Between these two houses," wrote Pendlebury, "the path worn in the desert by the passage of Panehesy and his train can still be seen in the early morning and late evening when long shadows are thrown over the sand." It was in the central room of the offiical residence that the plaster foundations of the famous altar in the form of a miniature chapel were found together with the greater part of the sculptured facade. This has been reerected in the Cairo museum.

The names of Akhenaten's principal followers and the privileged position of each in the court hierarchy are known from the tomb inscriptions. Aahmes, for instance, was not only honored as Fan Bearer on the Right Hand of the King on ceremoinal occasions but was also Keeper of the Storehouses and Steward of the Palace, both onerous tasks. Penthu was court physician; Any, assistant steward; and May, a scribe of recruits. May wrote, "I was a man of humble birth on my father's and my mother's side but the king established me . . . he brought me prosperity when I was a man of no property . . . He gave me food and provisions every day, I who had once begged for bread." In fact he was very well established, bearing many titles including that of Royal Chancel-

lor until, perhaps through pride, he fell from office and met
with sudden disgrace and death. Tutu was Secretary for Foreign Affairs, an unenviable post that became increasingly difficult as the years passed. Panehesy, a young Nubian courtier,
recorded that the king was one "who made princes and formed
the humble." He added, "When I knew not the companionship
of princes, I was made an intimate of the king."

Another Mery-Ra, a different man from the high priest,
held office as overseer of the harem, and Mahu was head of
the police. When excavating the military and police quarters,
Pendlebury found Mahu's house centered between the stables
and the barracks. It was littered with numerous discarded jar
sealings of wine marked "very very good." So Mahu, it seems,
found first-class spiritous consolation during the long dull
hours when crime was in abeyance. But in a relief on the wall
of his tomb, he depicts an occasion of vigilance rewarded. The
scene shows an early morning call from a police runner. A
small fire is lit because the morning air is chilly; his horses
are harnessed to a chariot, and a swift drive to the scene of
disturbance follows, where three culprits are arrested. Two
are foreign; but one significantly is Egyptian.

They are immediately conveyed to the Vizier Nakht, who
exclaims with approval at Mahu's efficiency. "Examine these
men, O princes," says Mahu to the vizier and his staff, "they
are those whom the foreigners have instigated." The words
have a modern ring. Who were the culprits? Were they infiltrators, freedom fighters, would-be assassins? Which for-

eigners are referred to and what exactly were they instigating?

But this is not known, because the Egyptians deliberately avoided immortalizing anything of an unpleasant nature, and the incident recorded by Mahu, like so much else, remains a mystery.

II

If the fortunate few were allowed to prepare rock tombs, lesser courtiers had to be satisfied with tomb chapels set up in the desert. Some of these interments were also found to belong to members of the middle classes, such men as the Mycenaean merchant and Thutmose the sculptor.

Pendlebury was certain that one of the houses in the north suburb had belonged to a foreigner. From a curious and most Mycenaean-looking mask found in the debris, from the shape of the house and the grove of trees planned round it, he deduced that it was the shop of a merchant from Mycenae, the Greek grocer of the day. He appeared to have been a prosperous baker and confectioner, providing cakes and sweet-meats of finely ground flour and honey, delicately flavored with spices. His business was large enough to employ a num-ber of assistants. In addition he operated an agency selling imported oil and Mycenaean pottery. Pendlebury remarked at the rift that seemed to have occurred for several decades between Egypt and Crete. This would fit very well into the new pattern of the dating of the Santorin volcanic explosion. By Akhenaten's day, relations were reestablished and Crete had regained her prosperity under Mycenaean masters.

Even more interesting was the house of Thutmose exca-vated in 1912, not by Pendlebury but by the German expedi-tion under Professor Borchardt. It was conveniently near the great palace at the corner of the south wadi and the Street of the High Priest, a small but genuine estate. The lid of an ivory case recovered from a ditch gave the name of the owner —Thutmose, Chief Sculptor. Thutmose's property included outbuildings, a large yard, well, workmen's cottages, and a second and smaller house which, according to Borchardt, be-longed to the figure sculptor. Exquisite as is some of the

Amarnan art, Akhenaten's chief sculptor was no Epstein. Individuality and self-expression were at a discount and Thutmose ran what was more in the nature of a business—an art factory working overtime to provide for the unending demand for statues and reliefs to adorn palace, temple, shrine, *maru,* and sunshade. Under pressure the atelier of Thutmose used a conveyor-belt system, the sculptor specializing in heads, hands, and feet, a second craftsman carving figures in the round, while a number of apprentices were employed to do the donkeywork and mass produce the uninspired and repetitive reliefs.

In spite of the limitations set on his talents, Thutmose created masterpieces. His studio was in two small rooms adjacent to the hall of his house where, like any modern sculptor, he kept his unfinished works on wooden shelves around the walls. At some moment in time the whole outfit was abandoned. The unfinished royal portrait busts were left stacked in situ as if the sculptor intended to return in a few days, and whatever tragedy struck the king, Thutmose was removed from his eminence as chief sculptor at Amarna.

Did the destroyers of Akhetaton enter his studio and throw the hated effigies to the ground? Or was the house boarded up, leaving the stone-plaster heads to stare blindly through the centuries at the silence while white ants gnawed into the woodwork, until shelf and its contents thudded into the soft sand silting into the empty rooms? The second hypothesis seems to be true, because the portrait heads were found intact, and the destroyers, venting their spleen on palace and temple, had left the insignificant house of Thutmose untouched.

Here in the shifting sand was found the famous bust of Nefertiti. Here were found a whole series of less famous but equally fascinating royal portrait heads cast in plaster from sculptured stone—even possibly from life. Eleonore Bille-De Mot, who has made a study of the masks (now in Berlin), is convinced that many of them were molded on the living faces of the Amarnan royal family. If so, the actuality of these likenesses from a vanished past must enthrall historian and layman alike.

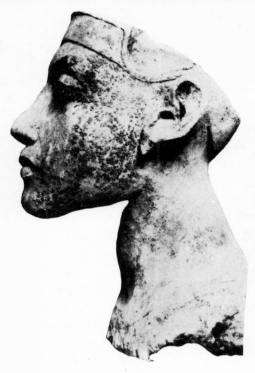

This quartzite head of Nefertiti was found in the studio of Thutmose.

This head of Smenkhare shows his resemblance to Nefertiti. They were almost certainly brother and sister.

Most of the nameless heads are attributable. Smenkhare's expression is sad, supercilious, and noncommitted. It is a face whose exquisite beauty rivals, if not surpasses, the famed loveliness of Nefertiti. Akhenaten's head, uncaricatured, shows a curious combination of strength and weakness. A second likeness of the king, clearly molded to the living flesh, catches a glimpse of the visionary in him in a look of startling and intense fervor. A head of Meketaten in stone, round with the prettiness of youth, can be compared to her tragic death mask, thin and pinched with pain. Ankhesenpaaten looks proud; Ay secretive and diplomatic; Amenhotep assured and regal. An older face, drawn with suffering, is possibly the great king's death mask. Whatever caused Thutmose to abandon the likenesses of the Amarnan royal family, a unique collection of contemporary portraits was preserved.

III

The picture of life in Akhetaton at the peak of its prosperity should be widened to include two of its most influential men, Ay and Horemheb. By the exigencies of fate, both in turn were to become pharaoh after Akhenaten's death. And both made terms with the priests of Amen.

But Horemheb went further than Ay and became, outwardly at all events, a devoted adherent of the Theban god. Under these circumstances his reluctance to mention his close connection with Akhenaten's court was natural. So well did he cover his traces that only in recent years has the part he played in events come to light. The discovery originated through the deciphering of a few lines of hieroglyphic writing on a relief acquired by the Brooklyn Museum. Before his seizure of the throne, Horemheb had built a tomb at Memphis. It was broken up and some carved blocks found their way

Heads of Akhenaten: young and idealistic (left), older, disillusioned (right).

to the museums of Leyden, Berlin, and Vienna. They were recognized as all being part of a large scene in which Horemheb was being honored by the pharaoh. The king's name had been carefully obliterated and the name of the god altered to Amen. But John D. Cooney recognized that the block in the Brooklyn Museum was part of the same scene. It represented a group of officers gathered together to see their commander honored. Above one of the men was written, "Standard-bearer of the 'Love of Aten' Regiment Niakhay." The obliterator of Horemheb's connection with the heretic pharaoh had overlooked this reference and it can now be seen that the unknown pharaoh was Akhenaten and that Horemheb was no humble scribe of recruits at this period but already had risen from the position of Royal Scribe and Great Steward to become Commander of the Army and to take precedence of two viziers.

The nature of his duties must have removed Horemheb often from court. The man closest to the king and who, next to him, wielded the greatest power was Ay.

A study of his chief titles is instructive. He was Father of the God (king), a designation that, even if he were not Nefertiti's father, meant near relationship—physical or governmental—to the pharaoh. He was Master of the King's Horses in Two Lands, which gave him control of the main fighting arm of the Egyptian army; he was Acting King's Scribe, best translated perhaps as Private Royal Secretary, a position at the very center of power; and he was Hereditary Prince. This epithet is interesting, suggesting a family and blood descent from royalty and confirming the supposition that his mother Tuaa may have been of the blood royal. It can be seen he was in excellent position to control affairs during Tutankhamen's minority and on the death of the young king occupy the vacant throne.

Ay's sacerdotal titles were Doer of Right and Priest of Maet. The second has special significance because Maet was a vital force in both Akenaten's religious conceptions and those of his father. Amenhotep III was given the coronation name Nebmaetra as a child, when he was still a firm adherent of Amen, so it is possible one of the seeds of Atenism can be sought for in this goddess, daughter of Ra, who was an emanation of the sun, the upholder of universal law and order.

Most curiously, from some unknown source, Shakespeare derived the essence of the idea of Maet, called by him Degree, and, in the famous speech of Ulysses, wrote:

> *The heavens themselves, the planets, and this centre*
> *Observe Degree, priority, and place . . .*
> *Office, and custom, in all line of order:*
> *And therefore is the glorious planet Sol*
> *In noble eminence enthron'd and spher'd*
> *Amidst the other; whose med'cinable eye*
> *Corrects the ill aspects of planets evil . . .*
> *. . . O when Degree is shak'd,*
> *Which is the ladder to all high designs,*
> *The enterprise is sick! How could communities,*
> *Degrees in schools, and brotherhoods in cities,*
> *Peaceful commerce from dividable shores,*
> *The primogenitive and due of birth,*
> *Prerogative of age, crowns, sceptres, laurels,*
> *But by Degree, stand in authentic place?*
> *Take but Degree away, untune that string,*
> *And, hark, what discord follows!*

Shakespeare seems nearer Akhenaten's age in this passage than to our own time.

Maet not only represented law and order. Toward the end of the eighteenth dynasty it was thought that the gods who nourished themselves on her truth and justice found the offering of a tiny image of Maet the culminating point of the divine service and more agreeable than all the riches in the world. By then Maet had become an important solar deity who, on the lower level, absorbed the attributes of several other female goddesses, Nut and Hathor, both aspects of the sky, and the ancient Neit of Sais from whom they were derived. On the higher level, according to Madame Desroches Noblecourt, she was "the breath of life, the female principle, perhaps even light itself."

Whether Ay was, or was not, Nefertiti's father, Ay's wife Tyi is expressly stated to be, not the mother of, but the Nurse of the Great King's Wife, Nefertiti. She was also

Tutoress of the Goddess and, strangely enough, The King's Concubine. In order to get around the difficulties created by these clearly stated titles, Aldred has postulated that Tyi was the second wife of Ay and therefore, naturally, Nefertiti's wet nurse and tutoress. In the context she could only have been the concubine of one king, Akhenaten. But could the queen's own mother-in-law and foster-mother have been her husband's concubine? It is perhaps impossible to answer this question or to judge with an unjaundiced eye the morality of the Egypt of three thousand years ago, an age before the advent of Greek philosophy, monogamy, Saint Paul, and the Puritans.

IV

An entire book on Nefertiti has been written. This is courageous because not one utterance of hers has survived. Studying the historical Nefertiti is like watching a personage through the thick, soundproof glass of a television studio. Even the movements of this long-departed queen seem automatic and solely dictated by her husband. Akhenaten extends an arm to welcome the rising sun; so does his queen. He offers oblations to Aten, and Nefertiti, like his shadow, copies him. Elsewhere she embodies the female principle so necessary to the worship of Atenism (and the creation of life). With the king she stands at a window of appearance, turns to kiss him as they drive from the temple in the same chariot, pours wine for him at a state banquet, encircles his waist with her arm as the royal pair sit enthroned at the reception of foreign tribute and is even seen seated, like an office girl in a Hollywood comedy, coyly upon his knee. As a producer of princesses to carry on the solar line, she was an unqualified success.

The appearance of the princesses on the tombs and stelae are not certain indications of their birth dates. It is possible Akhenaten and Nefertiti were married as early as year 26 or 27 of Amenhotep III and that Ankhesenpaaten, as well as her two older sisters, Meritaten and Meketaten, were born at Thebes. Three more daughters were later added to the family,

Neferneferuaten Tashery, Neferneferure, and the youngest, Setepenre.

Akhenaten's first stela announced that he intended to marry his eldest daughter Meritaten and include her with Nefertiti in his funerary arrangements, thus continuing the pattern set by his father. But by the time the elder princess had reached puberty, the king altered his plans. Meritaten was married to the young prince designated as heir and co-regent, Smenkhare, and the king transferred to his second daughter, Meketaten, the honor originally intended for her elder sister.

Today when centuries of custom have ingrained in mankind a horror of incestuous relationships, and modern man has lost his age-old belief that "divinity doth hedge a king," Akhenaten will gain no sympathy. Yet to a sun king who cherished as dearly as he the religious myth of his divine solar origin, it was imperative to be mated to a direct descendant of that "mother of the sun" who may have been, two thousand years earlier, queen of Sais.

Meketaten died and the "heartbreaking scenes" of mourning in the royal sepulcher, where the king and queen bend grief-stricken over the corpse of their second daughter, are, as Madame Desroches Noblecourt writes, "unique in the history of Egypt." A nurse, clasping a baby that has just been handed to her bedside the deathbed suggests that Meketaten died in childbirth, and a fragment from her coffin giving the names of Neferkheprure (Akhenaten) and Nebmaetra (Amenhotep III) is yet more evidence for the coregency of the two kings.

Balked by death, Akhenaten persisted in his attempt to recreate the divine pattern and about year 15 married his third daughter, Ankhesenpaaten. It was the first marriage of this princess (later to become Tutankhamen's queen) and resulted in the birth of a daughter, the little Ankhesenpaaten Tashery.

This was the total of the royal nursery. Because only princesses were depicted at this period, it is not known if Nefertiti bore the king sons. The convention not to depict

royal princes at this epoch is an irritation to the student, but
there is one representation of four of the princesses driving
in their chariots each with a companion. These seem to be
male. In the leading chariot the companion has placed his
arm round Princess Meritaten. Would this pair not have been
Meritaten and her young husband Smenkhare?

The queen's sister Mutnedjmet seems to have acted as
first attendant on the royal princesses, judging from some of
the earlier tomb reliefs. Like Nefertiti she lays no claim to a
royal title, a fact that Aldred cites as one of the proofs of
Nefertiti's nonroyal origin. On the other hand she is followed
everywhere by two achondroplastic dwarfs, Pera and Re-
neheh. The artists of Akhetaton delighted in depicting the
little people, and there are several representations of them.
They were nicknamed "The Day" and "The Sun," also with
heavy humor "The Queen's Vizier" and "His Mother's
Vizier." This can only mean that they had come from the

Mutnedjmet and her two dwarfs are seen here at bottom right.

Theban court of Queen Tyi, perhaps with Mutnedjmet, and after the death of Amenhotep III. It follows that if Mutnedjmet inherited the queen's dwarfs, she was brought up by Tyi at Thebes and was more than likely her daughter. An exquisite gold and alabaster centerpiece of a boat with a young

Part of an alabaster centerpiece found in Tutankhamen's tomb shows a young girl (probably Mutnedjmet) in the prow of a boat. The whole fragile piece measures only twenty-seven inches high and twenty-eight long. The boat, a model of those used for the Maru-Aten ceremonies, is steered by a dwarf—perhaps Mutnedjmet's.

girl at the prow (Mutnedjmet) and an achondroplastic dwarf at the stern was found among Tutankhamen's treasures. It may have been an heirloom made at the Theban court of Amenhotep III.

By a twist of fate Mutnedjmet, one of the least important characters of the Amarnan drama, was destined to survive. After the holocaust, when all Akhenaten's family had vanished from the scene, General Horemheb seized power. Mutnedjmet, the younger sister and the children's governess,

was raised to the dignity of the throne and, by marrying the
new pharoah, conformed to the ancient and hallowed practice
of the dynasty and, it is thought, legalized the general's claim
to kingship.

V

The opponents of the theory of the coregency produce as
Exhibit Number 1 a letter (Tablet II of the Longman's edition
of 1892 of the Tel el Amarna tablets) sent by King Tushratta
of Mitanni to the queen of Egypt. In this letter the king
sends greetings to the Lady of Egypt and the wording suggests that the lady's husband, referred to as Nimmuria, is
recently dead. Nimmuria is almost certainly the phonetic
sound and Mitannian translation of Nebmaetra (Amenhotep
III) and most Egyptologists agree that the queen mentioned
in the letter is Akhenaten's mother Tyi.

In paragraph 3, Tushratta refers to the queen's request
that friendship may be maintained between Egypt and Mitanni and hopes that it may be ten times stronger than before.
The queen's son Napkhuria (Neferkheprure, Akhenaten) is
also mentioned and the Princess Tadukhipa, wed to Amenhotep in the last years of his life. Tushratta ends his missive
by saying that he is sending the gift of many measures of
choice oil for anointing. An Egyptian scribe endorsed this
tablet on the reverse in hieratic and recorded the date of
receipt. Alas the writing was "too defaced to be legible" and
the date can be read either as 2, in which case no coregency is
possible, or 12.

Those who do not agree with the theory of a coregency
further point out that even if the illegible number is 12 not 2,
Tushratta would hardly have written to Tyi twelve years
after Akhenaten's succession as if the affairs of Egypt were
still in her own capable hands. But if it is accepted that Amenhotep and, when he became an invalid, Tyi, handled the
affairs of state during the coregency, the letter makes sense.

The younger king's move to Akhetaton then appears in
the context of practical politics as the pious hope of Amen-

hotep and Tyi that at the distant and desolate site of Tel el
Amarna their son would find sufficient scope for the exercise
of his devotions and his royal rights to avoid disturbing the
peace of the status quo. Later, his parents might expect him
to be better equipped to handle affairs of state and the control of a mighty empire. For like most parents they probably
inclined to optimism and refused to recognize the limitations
of their son's character. Amenhotep had a palace in Akhetaton also, called the House of Rejoicing. The relations between the coregents had remained cordial; and whatever the
older couple thought of Akhenaten's lack of political ex-
pediency, they seem to have taken pride in their son's
spiritual qualities.

It is certain that Amenhotep and Tyi paid at least one
visit to Akhetaton. Subsequently, presumably after the death
of her husband, Tyi came again, alone. Is it possible that the
older king died in the City of the Horizon?

Only two of the plaster casts found in Thutmose's studio
were obvious death masks. One was of Meketaten, who is
known to have died in Akhetaton, the other of Amenhotep III.
If the king had died at Thebes would a death mask have been
taken and sent by boat to the City of the Horizon? It is possible but unlikely.

The pattern of events may have been that Queen Tyi,
seeing the state of her husband's health, brought him to
Akhetaton to facilitate the transfer of absolute power to her
son and to make the latter responsible for the royal household—the servants, scribes, harem women, and Amenhotep's
young wife Tadukhipa, the Mitannian queen. Politics and
etiquette required that on Amenhotep's death this young
foreign princess should be remarried to the reigning king,
Akhenaten.

The coregent's visit is likely to have happened in year 9,
and if the supposition is correct, the flotilla that set sail down
the Nile must have been a large one to include not only the
principal members of the Malkata court but a large portion of
the treasury. In the days before currency, wealth was in kind,
but it is interesting to recall that Egypt traded gold with
other eastern powers. The pharaoh himself was the reserve

bank and Tyi must have wished to store the royal reserves of gold in those many magazines attached to the royal palace at Akhetaton. The queen may also have brought with her at this period the state archives and the recent letters to Amenhotep from his eastern allies. These in themselves would have been no light weight to transport. As Maspero wrote, "Imagine tablets of clay varying in thickness and shape between the size of a cuttle-fish and that of a small sponge cake. The messenger who carried many of them ran the risk of literally sinking under the weight of state affairs."

Finally the queen brought the personal members of her household: her own steward Huya, her baby son Tutankamen, and Prince Smenkhare. In year 9 Smenkhare was about twelve years of age. His resemblance to Tutankhamen was very marked. In fact he also bore a resemblance to Nefertiti and to Akhenaten, whose younger brother he undoubtedly was. He was the most beautiful of all Tyi's children. One London neurologist, shown the stela of Smenkhare and his wife Meritaten walking together in a garden, immediately diagnosed the prince as having once suffered from infantile paralysis. Whether he had contracted this malady as a child or not, there was a look of suffering in his face that added a touch of poetic melancholy to the symmetry of his features (see page 142).

A year or two later, whether at Thebes or Akhetaton, Amenhotep died. If at the City of the Horizon his widow and son would have accompanied the corpse and catafalque back to Malkata to see to the proper rites and burial ceremonies. Amenhotep the Magnificent's vast mortuary temple was already completed. In the king's own words it was

a very great monument, an everlasting fortress of sandstone, embellished with gold throughout, its floor shining with silver, and all its doorways with electrum. It is wide and very long, adorned for eternity . . . with royal statues of granite, quartzite and precious stones, fashioned to last for ever . . . Its workshops are filled with male and female slaves, the children of chieftains of all the countries which his Majesty conquered. Its magazines are stored with unaccountable riches. It is surrounded by villages of Syrians . . . ; its cattle are like sands of the shore totalling millions.

Nothing is left of this "everlasting monument" but the two gigantic colossi of the king, nearly seventy feet high, each cut from one block of stone and known as the Memnon statues. The great king was laid to rest with every honor among his ancestors in the Biban el Moluk, the sacred Valley of the Kings.

Akhenaten's coregency ended with the death of his father but according to custom it was likely he would appoint a younger man to share the throne with him. If no son of his own was old enough to fill the vacant double throne, Smenkhare, his eldest surviving brother, would have been a natural choice. And the divinity of the two kings was possibly confirmed by marriage to a solar princess, Smenkhare marrying his niece Meritaten, Akhenaten his second daughter, Meketaten.

This supposition is based on the death of Meketaten, which can be dated with some certainty to year 12, in which case she must have married her father in year 11. Smenkhare was not crowned until year 15, but the choice of the coregent, the substitution of Meketaten for Meritaten, and her marriage surely all belong together.

VI

The reception of foreign tribute in year 12 was the most magnificent spectacle ever witnessed in the City of the Horizon. If the argument advanced in these pages is correct, then it may have been occasion for genuine rejoicing.

The storm of war already gathering in the east had possibly not yet burst; the distant thunder and the danger signals could be ignored, and the Aten sun seemed to shine in a cloudless sky. In the author's opinion, the shrines and names of the gods had not yet been desecrated. Egypt was yet mighty, rich, famed as the greatest nation in the civilized world, and all the tributary countries and the lands within Egypt's "sphere of influence" sent delegates, gifts, and tribute. The nine hundred altars, built perhaps for this very special occasion, promised days and nights of feasting for the foreign delegates.

Pendlebury claimed to have discovered the remains of the Hall of Foreign Tribute built into one side of the temenos wall of the temple. But Fairman disagreed and considered the hall an erection of a temporary nature made for the occasion. The main features of this structure were a low pedestal base approached in the center of each side by a ramp. Twelve columns—four a side—supported the roof of this balustraded pavilion, which, open on every side, formed a frame to the throne.

This was a gorgeous affair of wood, plated with gold, and made as a palanquin with carrying poles. The armrests were carved in the form of sphinxes and two lions sculptured in the round guarded the throne.

Tyi seems to have returned from Malkata for the great occasion. Her steward Huya, with the second Mery-Ra (his counterpart at Akhenaten's court), was one of the principal organizers of the festivities, minutely described by both men on the walls of their tombs.

The crowds wearing their best apparel—new wigs, sandals, jewelry—are out in force; the freshly shaven heads of the priests shine; the high dignitaries, courtiers, and ambassadors are gathered to do homage and the king's guards stand at attention.

The king and queen are seen borne to the pavilion in their gold palanquin on the shoulders of courtiers. Before them, as if heralding a god, walks a priest scattering the pungent perfume of incense from a censer, while professional mummers perform a pantomimic and symbolic dance. Behind the royal couple come all six of the princesses, well attended, and an impressive parade of the officers, servants, and soldiers of the royal entourage.

Akhenaten and Nefertiti enter their pavilion while the princesses cluster around stroking a pet gazelle, creature emblematic both of female grace and the sun. The games begin. Professional wrestlers, boxers, fencers, buffoons, and mummers perform before the assembled foreign dignitaries, while, a second show in itself, the tribute is presented.

Long-robed Asiatics kneel before the throne, their arms uplifted in salutation, as teams of splendid Syrian horses are led past drawing exquisitely decorated chariots. Then comes a large contingent of handcuffed slaves, and after them a parade of objects carried by Syrian servants—bows, spears, shields, daggers, and vases of precious metal filled with spices and unguents. Wild animals, led by their keepers, form part of the procession, which includes a large mountain lion—presumably tame, led by a halter. Finally, perhaps the pièce de résistance, comes a band of women, entirely naked.

From Cyprus and Crete are vases; from Libya ostrich eggs and plumes. Befeathered Nubian emissaries bend low bringing sacks of gold dust, bars and rings of gold, as well as skins, weapons, and elephant tusks. The Nubians, not to be outdone by the lion-taming Asians, have a tame panther, cattle, an antelope and, led on strings, a charming group of little monkeys. The Nubian slaves, male and female, end the procession, carrying their babies in baskets on their backs. The king and queen are borne in triumph back to the palace, and stand at the window of appearance.

And a scene from Horemheb's Memphite tomb can be fitted into this moment of time. It depicts the king and queen leaning forward over a cushioned balcony to listen to the words spoken by Horemheb who, loaded with gold necklets, raises his right arm toward the sovereign while in the other he holds the fan that entitles him to his honor of Fan bearer at the Right of the King. Horemheb speaks:

Words spoken to His Majesty when came the Great Ones of all Foreign Lands to beg life from Him by the Hereditary Prince, Sole Friend, and Royal Scribe, Horemheb justified. He said, making answer to the King . . . foreigners who knew not Egypt are beneath thy feet for ever. Aten [the god's name had been replaced by Amen] has handed them over to thee.

The foreigners lift their arms in adoration to the royal presence. Five of the eight chieftains depicted are Syrian. Underneath them is written: The Great Ones of all Lands who came to beg life of the King. Horemheb's importance is stressed by the fact that it is he who speaks to the king's envoys sent to every foreign land. There are so many lacunae in the text of this speech that it is hard to interpret, but the trouble in Syria is already seen to have begun, although Horemheb claims to have defeated the king's enemies.

The evening feast that followed the day's celebrations (described in the tomb of Huya) contained the usual ingredients of wine, women, and song. There were two orchestras: an Egyptian group of young ladies with lutes and harps, dressed like a school choir in long white linen robes, and a group of Asiatics. The Asiatic male musicians had come, it seems, in the train of Queen Tyi. They wore long flounced robes and pointed caps bound across the brow with fillets and carried hand lyres and trigons. But their principal instrument was an enormous standing lyre played by two performers. It had an octave of strings and was mounted on an ornamental stand in the form of a vase, the keyed frames supported at the top on two spear-shaped rods. The banquet fare was plain but satisfying, and the emissaries eat their way through a mountain of food: beef, mutton, duck, fowls, simply cooked. As a *bon-bouche* they were perhaps served with that great Egyption delicacy—mice in honey.*

Disillusionment is not infrequently the aftermath of festivity. When the last of the visitors had departed and the stewards and seneschals, clearing away the debris, the set decorations, and the garlands, carefully tabled the items of tribute, did they recollect that the Syrian lords had quarreled among themselves? Did Tyi feel apprehensive and sigh for her headstrong and idealistic son; and Smenkhare, with sad drooping mouth and half-closed eyes, sit at Akhenaten's feet and listen to the king talking on and on in his sonorous voice about light, and unity, and joy? Did Nefertiti wait in vain for a visit from her lord and feel a chilling of the heart? And did the Asiatic governors and envoys returning to the far cities of Tyre, Byblos, Beyrut, Tunip, and Damascus murmur secretly among themselves? Were rumors spread that the new king appeared a weaker ruler than his father and that the Khatti—the Hittites from the far north, already infiltrating into northern Syria—paid well for friendly assistance?

---

* The two stewards, Mery-Ra and Huya, are seen ''tasting the viands'' at the banquet with habitual eastern precaution. This was an age-old custom to insure no poison had been added to the royal food.

9.
THE
SYRIAN WAR

The gods of Egypt dwell in Tunip, but we no longer belong to Egypt. For twenty years we have sent messengers. If we mourn then will the king also have to mourn and when the enemy enters the city he will do to us as he pleases and the king will be forced to lament. And now Tunip your city weeps and her tears are running and there is no help for us. For twenty years we have been sending to our lord, the king, the king of Egypt, but there has not come to us a word from our lord, not one . . .
A TABLET FOUND AT TEL EL AMARNA

I

The common people of Tunip (Aleppo), not the governor, addressed this heartrending appeal to Akhenaten. His reply, if any, is not known. But his predicament is more readily understood when the extent of his father's dominions is realized. The largest empire Egypt ever controlled, it extended over the whole of the Euphrates, included the Tigris up to Assyria, the caravan routes across the desert to Palmyra, in fact the whole of Syria, Mesopotamia, Chaldea, and Assyria. Like India at the time of the British Raj, this vast domain of city-states, tribal countries, and friendly kingdoms looked to Egypt and its pharaoh for leadership. It was held together less by arms than by clever diplomacy. The bait was peace that allowed unhindered trade and nurtured prosperity. Backed by the latent striking force embodied in the might and efficiency of the Egyptian army, Amenhotep had kept control of the innumerable kings and petty chiefs throughout his long reign. To many of the governors and peoples of the east, loyalty to Egypt had become a habit, but once the precarious balance of power was upset, trouble was likely to follow.

Two factors led to the rapid disintegration of the empire. The first, the expansion of the Hittites under their able king and general Suppiluliuma, was beyond Akhenaten's control, but the second may have been the king's own obtuse attitude to the realities of government. As Petrie wrote, under Akhenaten the Egyptians "lost interest in Syria, lost the power of sparing troops to manage the country and keep order, and lost heart in foreign matters since they were absorbed in the home polities of religious revolution.

So soon as the strong hand of the power of Egypt ceased to act in all emergencies, to interfere in every squabble and to make capital out of the internal discords of the Syrians, so soon the Syrians began their old life of aggression one on the other . . . Hence the weakening of Egypt threw Syria into a state of internal discord," he said.

It is no coincidence that the trouble started after the death of the son of Hapu and during the last two years of the coregency when the older king had become too ill to govern.

Documents that belong to an earlier period found in Akhenaten's House of Correspondence—those curious squares of burnt clay impressed with cuneiform—reflect the peace Amenhotep's rule brought to the Middle East and the friendly relations existing among the rulers.

In one letter Tudhalyas (father of Suppiluliuma), king of the Hittites, offered a daughter to Amenhotep. In another Tushratta of Mitanni greeted his half sister, Queen Gilukhipa, and sent her ornaments, gold earrings, and jars of perfumed oil. (The gifts were in the nature of conscience money because Tushratta, involved in civil war, had strangled Gilukhipa's full brother as a defensive measure. He was not, wrote Maspero, "without anxiety as to the consequences which might follow this execution should Gilukhipa desire to avenge the victim." Hence the presents. In the event, Gilukhipa made no move against the Mitannian king and his fears were allayed.)

Among the many kings who wrote to Amenhotep was the king of Alashia (Cyprus?) who sent copper and asked for silver in return. Kallimasin, king of Babylon, married an Egyptian princess and in return sent Amenhotep one of his own daughters; and the king of Assyria sought for help against the Khatti, whose inroads were already proving troublesome.

Like the Egyptian pharaoh, Tadhalyas the Hittite was considered divine and called himself the sun. The Hittites also practiced the elongated skull deformation considered so fashionable at Amarna. But king-god though he might be, Tadhalyas and the other royal despots of Mitanni and Babylonia wrote in most human fashion. Their missives were practical and businesslike and dealt with the trading of copper, ivory, oil, horses, slaves, and women for the vaunted gold of Egypt. The letters, which began with the time-honored formula of polite eastern greeting—"May it be well with thee, with thy government, with thy wives, with thy children, with thy horses, with thy chariots . . ." ended invariably with a request for gold, "more gold, and yet more gold." But, as Maspero wrote, "the gifts sent never seemed to realise the expectations of the recipients."

The last years of Amenhotep's reign saw the gradual breakdown of stability and order, a state of affairs reflected in the letters. Reports of caravans being plundered came from Babylon; Syrian princes were called up with their men to the army; Tushratta imprisoned two infiltrators; the king of Alashia complained of Lycian pirates; a king was forced to ask a neighboring chief for a passport to travel to Egypt to condole (probably for the reception of foreign tribute); and Askelon was ordered to supply passing troops with "meat, drink, oil, and oxen."

Possibly, Amenhotep was no sooner buried than the tribes were at each other's throats. It was a pattern that had been repeated at the death of most of the kings of the empire. But this time no valiant young pharaoh rode out at the head of his well-disciplined army to quell the disturbers of peace.

The author, who had dated the outbreak of the Syrian war to the end of Akhenaten's reign, was pleased to find her views largely corroborated by Cyril Aldred.* In an excellent chapter on the Tel el Amarna tablets this eminent Egyptologist concluded that the letters found at Tel el Amarna were those received when the king was in residence there . . .'' In that case serious trouble is unlikely to have occurred until after year 12.

The chronology of the tablets is controversial and, writes Aldred, it remains doubtful . . . whether the Amarna archive will ever be sorted into its proper chronological sequence.''

But one reconstruction of the war that brought Akhenaten's reign to an end was made long ago by Petrie. It makes such good sense and fits in so well into the probable course of events that the author has no hesitation in using it in this chapter.

The seed of discord that led to war was sown in a central Syrian valley and the trouble started with an altercation between three local chiefs. The politics of this internecine affair were complex because all three protagonists were fighting in the long run not for or against Egypt but simply to further their own interests.

Namyawaza (pro-Egyptian) allied himself with Biridashyi (neutral) against Itakama (neutral) for the purposes of loot and to increase his territory. The skirmish took place in a large river valley on the upper part of the Litani. Itakama, seeing himself outnumbered, asked for Hittite support (which was immediately forthcoming) and, so assisted, was successful in repulsing and defeating his enemies. But Biridashyi, warring for gain not politics, followed his inclination, changed sides, and joined the victor. The pro-Egyptian Namyawaza, instigator of the affair, found himself in such straits that he wrote to the king of Egypt complaining that his late ally Biridashyi ''has made the city rebel and delivered it to the Khabiru. Two have joined forces with Biridashyi

* See *Akhenaten* by Cyril Aldred.

and say, 'Come we will kill Namyawaza.' So I have taken refuge in Damascus.''

"I feel as if I were dead, and have no followers!'' he exclaimed in his misery, begging the king to send troops at once to defend Egyptian territory.

Whatever happened to Namyawaza the result of his little war was a disaster for Egypt. The Hittites occupied the whole Litani Valley and, allying themselves with neighboring chiefs, found themselves in an excellent position to invade the fertile plain of Damascus. The most important of these allies were Abdi-Ashirta, king of the Amurru or Amorites, and his son Aziru, the villains of the piece so far as Egypt was concerned.

Ezekiel once apostrophized the children of Israel with the words: "Thy father was an Amorite and thy mother Hittite." It is interesting to find Hittites and Amorites allied in a war against Egypt with a people called Habiru* or Khabiru.

Aziru, the Amorite, proved an able general and a wily politician. While flirting with the Hittite envoys, he kept up a lengthy and specious correspondence with Tutu at Akhet-aton and, as the rebellion spread south, steadily consolidated his position. Finally all Galilee was lost to Egypt. This cut the caravan route to northern Syria and Mesopotamia, so that King Burraburiash of Babylon was forced to complain. Robbers, he wrote to Akhenaten, had killed his merchants and despoiled his caravan on Egyptian ground. He adjured the king to compensate the owners of the stolen goods and subdue the robbers or trade would cease. Further, because the robbers had cut off the feet of one merchant and retained another as a slave, the men must be rescued and returned.

If these reports came to Akhenaten, it must be admitted in fairness that they were confusing. It was difficult for any-

---

* Who were the Habiru? Nathan Ausubel believes that they were neither a race nor a nation but that the Semitic word applied loosely to nomadic tribes, specifically those who came from beyond Jordan or the Euphrates. After the termination of the Syrian war, five kings of the Amorites were reigning in Judea from Jerusalem to Hebron. Their old allies the Habiru may have been settled among them and undoubtedly these people mingled with the Children of Israel at a later date to found the Jewish people.

one so far away to grasp the real state of affairs. If the protagonists were known, the degree of their loyalty to Egypt was not. And as only one of the Tel el Amarna tablets indicates the reply sent by the king or his advisers they show only side of the picture. The repeated requests of Egypt's allies and faithful governors for help convey more dramatically than dispatches the course of the war. And as the danger steadily mounted and threatened to overwhelm the pro-Egyptian cities, their cries for the help that never seemed to materialize became desperate.

But complaints against Aziru reached such proportions that even Akhenaten was forced to act and the Amorite was sent for and traveled to Egypt to plead his own cause.

The interest of the Tel el Amarna tablets to the ordinary reader is that they were written by human beings in moments of stress. Seen through the eyes of those taking part in it, the Syrian war becomes real and the characters of two men in particular emerge from this conflict of long ago—Aziru the Amorite and Ribadda, the loyal Egyptian governor of Byblos, who opposed his advance.

Ribadda, in letter after letter, had urged Egypt to send more troops. He accused Abdi-Ashirta and Aziru of disaffection. But Abdi-Ashirta was not at all ready to be classed as an enemy of Egypt. Protesting his innocence, he counter-accused. His loyalty, he announced to Akhenaten, was so profound that he was in actual danger owing to his great friendship with Egypt. He asked for a new governor to replace Ribadda and tactfully sent "ten women as requested" to the king. And Aziru, returned from Egypt, also wrote a letter full of loyal sentiments and duplicity. "To the great king, my lord, my god, my sun," he began. "I Aziru, thy servant, prostrate myself at the feet of my lord, my god, my sun, seven times and seven times. O my lord, I am thy servant . . . hearken not to wicked men who slander me before the king, my lord, for I am thy servant forever."

Someone in authority, possibly Akhenaten himself, was not taken in by Amorite flattery. He sent a severe reprimand to Abdi-Ashirta for "having received the messenger from the land of the Khatti" and he was asked to convey Aziru back to Egypt as hostage. But Aziru excused himself. He was too engaged with repulsing the invading Hittites to leave the theater of hostilities, he wrote.

Meanwhile the Hittites, aided by Aziru and the Habiru, advanced from their base on the Euphrates and struck across country to the Orontes. Bypassing Tunip (Aleppo) and using a classic military maneuver, they marched inland encircling the well-defended coastal towns of Simyra (Smyrna), Byblos, and Beirut. Cutting to the sea south of these, they took Sidon.

Ribadda suddenly found himself outflanked. All his previous requests for extra forces had been ignored. The Habiru had taken possesion of the hinterland, and one of his messengers, en route for Egypt, was despoiled. Even the sea route was blocked and his ships could no longer get through without incident. The Hittites, who now controlled Sidon, began plundering the inland farms, and in one of his many letters to Akhenaten, Ribadda asked sadly how this could be prevented, "seeing that I am now without forces to protect the country which is all in the hands of the rebels. No, I can do nothing and the king of Egypt will never regain his hold on the land." In another letter he sent a further desperate appeal for help: "I await the arrival of the soldiers by day and by night and if the king my lord does not send help to me, I shall perish and the king will lose a faithful servant." The military situation as he described it was indeed bleak:

"The city of Byblos which from time immemorial had been the faithful handmaiden of the king of Egypt," Ribadda wrote, "is now utterly lost because the king had taken no thought of its safety. Would that he would protect that which belonged to his father's house! . . . The people of the cities which are in the mountains and the frontier have gone over to the enemy and joined the rebels . . . Thus all the countries rebelled and there are no more loyal people left in the land and our sons and our daughters submit to abide under the rule of the rebels. Unless the king takes immediate steps to protect his interests the whole land will be in rebellion against him and what is then to become of Byblos? The rebels have made a league among themselves and I, Ribadda, fear there will be no one to deliver me out of their

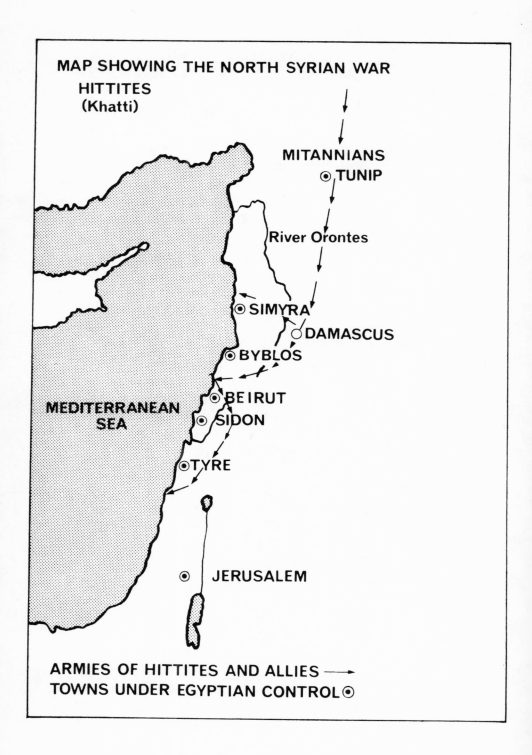

MAP SHOWING THE NORTH SYRIAN WAR

HITTITES
(Khatti)

MITANNIANS
⊙ TUNIP

River Orontes

⊙ SIMYRA

○ DAMASCUS

⊙ BYBLOS

MEDITERRANEAN
SEA

⊙ BEIRUT

⊙ SIDON

⊙ TYRE

⊙   JERUSALEM

ARMIES OF HITTITES AND ALLIES ──→
TOWNS UNDER EGYPTIAN CONTROL ⊙

hands, for being shut up in Byblos I am like a bird shut in a cage. Why does the king continue to be careless about his land? . . . If the king has any doubt about the distress which has fallen on Byblos, let him make inquiries . . . Would that the king would listen to the words of his servant and save my life for then he could protect his loyal city. The king is merciful and I, Ribadda, pray day and night that I may be under his rule for, if I am not, what is then to become of me?''

Even Ribadda's wives and children counseled him to make terms with the enemy and in one missive he went so far in his exasperation with Egypt to exclaim: ''If thou, O king, wilt not send me an answer, I will abandon the city, and I and my friends will cease to be thy subjects.'' But he did not abandon it and stayed on until the end. Tunip, whose people had cried so poignantly that ''there was no help for them,'' had been taken and all over Syria towns were submitting to the invaders ''forced by hard necessity and neglect,'' as Petrie wrote, ''to give up an alliance which had become a real bond of loyalty during the previous generations.'' Cities that dared defy the enemy went up in smoke. The horrors of war were as real then as today and whole communities were effectively wiped out without the aid of steel, iron, gunpowder, or atomic energy. The pattern of destruction was simple. The city was first looted of everything of value, then set on fire. Able-bodied men and nubile women were retained as slaves; all the rest—children, the aged, the halt, and the lame—were thrust into the flames or slain.

This was the tale of horror and destruction that struck the hearts of the inhabitants of Tunip, Simyra, Byblos, and Tyre, as they gazed in fear over the walls of their cities.

The day came when Ribadda wrote, ''Simyra your fortress is now in the power of the Habiru.'' This was the turning point of the war. With the enemy in control north and south of them, the cities of Tyre, Byblos and Beirut were doomed. Ribadda was forced to send his messenger to Egypt by night ''because of that dog, Abdi-Ashirta,'' and added the pathetic cry that if the king distrusted him he would be pleased to resign and leave the king himself the unpleasant, and by this time impossible, task of driving the invaders out of the land.

Tyre was next to fall. The governor, Abimilki, had written several letters asking for wood and water to be sent immediately. He reported that Ugarit and Kadesh were also in enemy hands and that Aziru was collecting a fleet of ships to attack Tyre by sea. The main water supply of Tyre seems to have been inland and in a further letter Abimilki reported that Aziru had seized it "after our soldiers had abandoned it and there is now no water, nor wood, nor burial ground." This was the last letter written to Akhenaten by Abimilki. Placed in a hopeless situation, he defected and went over to the enemy.

Byblos and Beirut remained the only towns loyal to Egypt holding out in northern Syria. While Abdi-Ashirta, still posing as a faithful subject, wrote to Akhenaten that he was guarding "the whole land for the king," Ribadda struggled on hoping against hope for asistance. There was an anti-Amorite party that Ribadda attempted to stir into further activity, and for this or other reasons he journeyed to Beirut. While he was absent the people of Byblos themselves wrote to Akhenaten. "The gatekeeper of the king is killed," they informed him, "and there is no food or grain for the troops . . . They will kill us . . . We are anxious . . . We asked for troops to be sent to us, young men, or old men, or soldiers of any kind whatsoever; but a deaf ear had been turned to us and therefore has happened what has happened. One of our officers himself saw the city of Simyra destroyed, and his eyes fell sick when he saw these things . . ."

Ribadda came back from Beirut a saddened and frightened man. Ammunira, governor of Beirut, had written to Akhenaten during his visit that "the governor of Byblos is with me and I am indeed guarding him until the king shall care for his servant," but shortly after Ribadda's departure, either with or without the connivance of Ammunira, Beirut also fell and Byblos was left alone to face the might of the invader.

Ribadda was an ordinary man with no leanings to play the hero or seek posthumous fame. He constantly likened himself to a "bird caught in a net" and begged the king to send a ship and rescue him alive from the town. Yet he stayed at his post and did his duty. As he wrote with feeling, "Abdi-Ashirta's enmity is bitter." Besieged Byblos was in the grip of famine. "Send provisions," he begged, "for there are none and our sons and daughters and timber are sold for food." In an outburst of rage he exclaimed, "What dogs are the sons of Abdi-Ashirta! Who act according to their hearts' wish and cause the king's cities to go up in smoke!"

Some line of communication must still have been maintained with Egypt by the besieged, for Ribadda received word to abandon Byblos and flee to Egypt. This he felt unable to do. Besides, he added sadly, old age and disease pressed on him. In his place he sent his son.

The last letter found among the Tel el Amarna tablets from Ribadda is short and records only his anguished cry: "Byblos the faithful city will fall; Behold, my city is lost!"

For the loyal commander of Byblos "the rest is silence." Overwhelmed by the flood tide of war it was taken by the enemy. Mitanni, whose king, Akhenaten's own brother-in-law,* had been so friendly to Egypt, joined the Hittites; the area of conflict moved south to the regions of Jerusalem, Gaza, and Lachish, and most of the Egyptian empire, which generations had helped to establish, was lost in the space of a few months.†

II

Causes other than Akhenaten's preoccupation have been sought to account for the disastrous loss of Egypt's eastern empire. The suggestion is that Tutu, the minister who handled Akhenaten's foreign correspondence, was a traitor; that

---

* In fairness to Tushratta, there is no evidence he made terms with the Hittites. He either died in battle or was murdered. But Mitannian soldiers fought side by side with the Hittites in the war. As a result their empire was overrun by their northern cousins and never reestablished its independence.

† This is conjecture but although initial Hittite penetration may have been slow and taken many years, the invasion and seizure of the coastal cities is likely to have been accomplished in one swift-moving campaign.

Aziru on his visit to Akhetaton suborned Tutu with gifts and that thereafter, in Hittite pay, he kept from the king all knowledge of the true state of affairs.

In a letter Abdakhiba, king of Jerusalem, whose city was soon menaced by the rising flood of rebellion was most concerned to inform the king of the serious state of the country and wrote, ''Cities of the king have fallen away. I continually tell the officers that all the dependent princes will be lost. Let troops be sent for the king has no longer any territory.''

This was a repetition of the bad tidings from the north. The lines in his letter that are of particular interest to historians read: ''I am slandered because I reproached the king's officer with favoring the Habiru.'' In addition at the end of the letter he added a superscription repeating what he had said earlier: ''To the scribe of my lord the king—The whole territory of my lord the king is going to ruin.''

Petrie wrote, ''This last injunction to the scribe to impress the facts on the king is curious; it bears such a stamp of sincerity that it seems alive in its earnestness even now.'' In a subsequent letter Abdakhiba wrote again underlining his information, ''To the king's scribe. Abdakhiba your servant. *Bring the message plainly before the king.*''

It is hard to avoid the interpretation that Tutu, the scribe in charge of the king's correspondence, or foreign secretary, was the king's officer who favored the Habiru. In his letters Abdakhiba indeed seems to be attempting to bypass the man in charge (Tutu) and, via a scribe with whom he was personally friendly, to inform the king of the true state of affairs.

Information on the course of events from the Egyptian point of view is meager. If Horemheb was commander of the armies under Akhenaten, he should be our informant because he inscribed an autobiography on his coronation stela. The information he gives is disappointing. Horemheb's concern in hiding his association with Akhenaten coupled with the Egyptian custom of recording triumphs and successes but never disaster or failure is exasperating in this case.

Equally exasperating to the seeker for evidence is Horemheb's reference throughout the inscription to "the king" when he served under at least three—Akhenaten, Tutankhamen, and Ay.

One episode that seems to date from Akhenaten's reign refers to a campaign when "he Horemheb was sent as king's envoy to the regions of the sun disk's uprising returning in triumph, his attack having succeeded. No foreign land stood before him; he despoiled them in the completing of a moment."

This does not sound like a description of the Syrian war. It has been suggested from the context that it was a campaign in Nubia (which made no attempt to break away from Egypt at this time) undertaken prior to the reception of foreign tribute. And a line from Tutankhamen's stela is likely to be a better description of the state of affairs in the east: "If an army was sent to Djahy [Syria] to widen the frontiers of Egypt it met with no success at all."

One paragraph from Horemheb's stela undoubtedly referring to Akhenaten and which has intrigued some historians reads, "He [Horemheb] being summoned before his sovereign when it, the palace, fell in a rage, he opened his mouth and answered the king and appeased him with the utterance of his mouth . . ."

From this some have deduced that toward the end of his reign Akhenaten's mind was disordered and that, as in the story of David and Saul, Horemheb, the mighty man of war, was the only friend who could bring him back to reason.

To the author the above lines will hardly bear out this interpretation. If the king suffered an attack of madness surely the court physician, Penthu, or the priests of Aten would have been sent for, not the general of his armies. The occasion described seems from the context to have happened but once and may well refer to the occasion when Akhenaten at last heard (perhaps from that scribe friendly to Abdakhiba or from Ribadda's son) the true state of affairs in Syria and the loss of his empire. This is a far more logical explanation and Akhenaten had every excuse for falling into a rage at the news. The man who would have been sent for at this moment was, of course, his military commander, Horemheb, who was able to "appease" the king with an account of the steps he had taken to safeguard the country.

But what in fact were Horemheb and the army doing at this low ebb in Egypt's fortunes? In one inscription from a doorpost, now in Cairo, he describes himself as "a henchman at the feet of his lord on the battlefield on this day of slaughtering of the Asiatics."

But which lord? Was it the young Tutankhamen or, contrary to all previous assumptions, could Akhenaten at last have donned the *khepersh,* girded his loins, and gone into battle?

But even if the Egyptian army had become slack after thirty-eight years of peace, even if Tutu kept information from the king, even if Horemheb was occupied (as he may well have been), the question remains, Why was no force mounted and dispatched to Syria? Because every tablet found in the cache at Tel el Amarna emphasizes that troops were not sent, this must be true. Tutu's tablets were not the only means of information at Akhenaten's disposal. What was he himself doing during those five years from the reception of foreign tribute to his disappearance from the scene?

The answer seems to be that at this period two passions engaged Akhenaten to the exclusion of everything else. If the first was the fulfillment of his ideal to establish the worship of the spiritual Aten everywhere in his domains, the second was less edifying and, the author believes, contributed both to the downfall of the religious edifice the king had attempted to build with such passionate sincerity and to his own demise.

10.
LOVE

SACRED AND PROFANE

Love for me
Has the shining, has the beauty
of the Sun . .
SAPPHO

I

Smenkhare was a remote and shadowy figure to the first Egyptologists who explored Akhetaton. Considered a prince of unknown parentage married to Akhenaten's eldest daughter, Meritaten, his role of coregent was barely suspected. That he reigned for a brief year and vanished from history was then the sum total of their information.

But after the discovery of Tutankhamen's tomb, Professor Percy E. Newberry wrote a monograph on Smenkhare. He produced some curious information. There is no doubt today that Smenkhare's burial chambers were despoiled to add to the luster of Tutankhamen's funerary equipment and the gorgeous array of treasures that would, according to Egyptian theology, belong to the young king in the afterlife. Among these was a box on which was written the full titulary of Akhenaten followed by the name Neferneferuaten. This meant "The Beauty of the Beauties of Aten" which, originally borne by Nefertiti, was afterward transferred to the boy king Smenkhare. On the knob of the box was written, "Ankheprure [the coronation name of Smenkhare] beloved of Neferkheprure [Akhenaten]." On a knob on the adjoining side is inscribed "Neferneferuaten beloved of Waenra [Akhenaten]."

Stele of the co-regents Akhenaten and Smenkhare.

Even more remarkable was a stela in the Berlin museum at first thought to be Akhenaten and Nefertiti, until it was realized that the second figure wearing a king's *khepersh* helmet must be Smenkhare. In the stela the king is looking back in profile to Smenkhare, whom he is chucking under the chin, while Smenkhare's arm, encircling him rests on his shoulder. There is no avoiding the fact that in the sacred symbolism of Amarnan art the linking of arms indicated physical marriage. One historian has suggested that Akhenaten in this stela was merely "carrying to an extreme his pursuit of a dream ideal, the double principle of the couple." But if, parted for some unknown reason from Nefertiti, Akhenaten had wished to portray his "double principle of the couple" would he not have pictured Smenkhare with his young wife, the king's daughter Meritaten? Or himself with his sun princess daughter-wife, Ankhesenpaaten?

Newberry was less equivocal on the deductions to be drawn from the stela. "The intimate relations between the Pharaoh and the boy," he wrote, "recall the relationship between the Emperor Hadrian and the youth Antinous. The epithets 'beloved of Waenra' and 'beloved of Neferkheprure' (both titles of Akhenaten) are also remarkable."

In private Pendlebury was even more outspoken. If a man living in apparent happiness with his wife forms an ardent attachment to a young boy and his wife leaves him, then, whether today or three thousand three hundred and twenty years ago, the two events are likely to be linked. Although such an authority as W. Stevenson-Smith has doubted the validity of the assertion that there was a rift between Nefertiti and the king, this was a matter to which the Egyptian Exploration Society devoted much scholarly time and thought.

The evidence was first discovered in the Maru-Aten, where the female principle was idolized. Sir Leonard Woolley wrote:

"Here, as nowhere else, the queen's name Nefertiti, has in nearly every case been carefuly erased and that of her eldest daughter, Meritaten, written in palimpsest upon the stone, her distinctive attributes have been blotted out with cement, her features recut and her head enlarged into the exaggerated skull of the Princess Royal. This alteration is most thorough-going in the case of the little temple and island kiosks—a group of buildings . . . called 'the Shadow of Ra' . . . The ownership or patronage of the precinct was transferred from mother to daughter either during the former's lifetime or on her death. But Nefertiti, if alive, could hardly have agreed to so public an affront, nor would her death have been seized upon by so devoted a husband as an occasion to obliterate her memorials; are we to suppose that things were not so happy as they seemed in the royal household, and that a quarrel so serious as to lose the queen her position put an end to the idyll which had long been the standing theme of the court artists?"

An even more extreme example of the defacement of Nefertiti's name was seen on a limestone block found in the royal palace. It bore the legend "daughter of the king of his body whom he loves, Ankhesenpaaten." The name of the princess had originally been followed by the words "born of the principal wife Queen Nefertiti," but the queen's cartouche had been effaced. This was unprecedented. Only the assumption that the beautiful Nefertiti was in disgrace with the king could possibly account for the effacement of the name of the king's Great Wife from an inscription to her daughter in the place in which she had, until then, been first lady.

Evidence of a different kind was found in the house of an overseer of works called Hatiay. Like all the better-class houses of Akhetaton, it was built of unbaked sun-dried mud brick. The average house of the well-to-do citizen was in shape a rectangle with a symmetrical grouping of rooms around a central hall. The light for this was obtained by carrying the walls of the hall higher than those of the surrounding chambers and inserting small windows in the upper part. The windows themselves consisted of slotted gratings made of stone.

The stables with tethering stones for the horses were outside, as were also the cattle byre and the kitchen, where there was a built-up rack for storing or drying flat loaves of bread and a cement-coated slab for kneading dough. Outside too were the grain bins, filled from a circular staircase and emptied from the base by a trapdoor. Inside the house the women's and children's quarters were considerably restricted. There was an anointing room, a kind of shower bath, and a closet latrine with a pierced stone seat. The doors throughout were of wood and pivoted from top to bottom.

As a general rule all the houses of the well-to-do resembled one another. The entrance doorway was of stone and was invariably carved and painted. The lintel of Hatiay's entrance doorway had fallen into the front hall of his house in the north suburb, where it was found. Ten cartouches on the central portion of the lintel bore the names of Akhenaten, Nefertiti, and the Aten, but in this case the name of Akhenaten had been savagely cut out and Nefertiti's and the Aten carefully retained. This was in the north suburb to which it seems Nefertiti was banished or to which she voluntarily retired.

The coronation of Smenkhare can with certainty be dated to year 15. The coronation hall, an extension of the palace, where several bricks stamped with the young king's name were found, was built for the occasion. Its main feature was a vast hall closely packed with a forest of square brick pillars. The roof of this huge structure was painted sun yellow and decorated with vines and painted plaster grapes which, from their frequent use at Akhetaton as a decorative motif, must have held an esoteric significance for Akhenaten.

Beyond was a small shrine open to the sky, where, beyond the gloom of the hall, the coregent may have stood to be consecrated by the divine rays of the "Living Aten." He was the only king to have been crowned at Akhetaton.

About this time the great gateway in the north palace was also built. It was a precursor to the gateways used so largely later by the Romans with a central entrance flanked by two smaller side gates. In this case the centerpiece of the whole structure was another of those windows of appearance. Pendlebury, who excavated this architectural feature, was disappointed to find few large fragments of painting preserved unbroken. The painting, in falling from the room above the gateway, had largely disintegrated but sufficient was found to establish the main outlines of the subject. Its reconstruction was only made possible, as Pendlebury wrote, "by the careful noting of every fragment of plaster."

"We know from the cartouches," he continued, "that Akhenaten, Smenkhare and Meritaten were present and we found traces of horses and chariots as well as human faces. The panels were framed Victorian-style in imitation grained wood—a method used also in a fresco from Tyrens. The scenes themselves were painted on a yellow background . . . The presence of Smenkhare and Meritaten alone with the king and the complete absence of Nefertiti make it clear that this gateway was decorated after Nefertiti's fall from power. The facts can only be explained if we regard Nefertiti as having gone into dignified retirement and carried on as if nothing had happened.''

The north palace showed a great deal of hurried and slipshod work. It fulfilled the conditions that Akhenaten seemed to require for a sun temple (see diagram, page 15). It had a central pool, window of appearance, zoological section, and possibly an aviary and monthly garden. Yet Whittmore found fragments of furniture and woman's finery in the so-called aviary! It is a puzzle and exactly where the queen retired to is not made clear but it seems to have been some building adjacent to the north palace. Discussing Queen Nefertiti's break with the king, Pendlebury continued, ''It is therefore all the more remarkable that our theory of last year seems to have proved correct and that the palace whose presence we suspected built up against the wall to the west really does seem to be the palace to which she retired.''

Nefertiti's palace was built, it seems, on the terraced slopes of the hills, which at this point plummet into the Nile. It lay mainly under cultivation and was almost impossible to excavate, but Pendlebury traced some really massive walls and piers. Of the clay wine jar sealings found here ''by far the larger proportion bore the name of Nefertiti,'' wrote Pendlebury. ''This very definitely connects Nefertiti with the building and yet the building is later than the wall and gateway which can be dated after her fall from power. I do not see what other theory will fit the facts.''

It is true that the facts can be fitted into a definite pattern. If Madame Desroches Noblecourt is correct in suggesting that the king married Meketaten in year 11, then the likelihood is that some little time before that event (year 9?) Tyi came to Akhetaton bringing the invalid Amenhotep and her two young sons with her. Because Akhenaten was then thirty-six and his younger brother only twelve, it is possible they had never met. The king was a lover of beauty and the delicate and lovely boy, so like Nefertiti in looks, must have made an immediate impression on Akhenaten and his choice of coregent inevitable. That Smenkhare might prove a catalyst to disaster was unlikely to have crossed his mind.

II

Amenhotep and Tyi became dedicated to the Aten toward the end of the king's reign but it is certain that no persecution of the priests of Amen emanated from Malkata. If the period of coregency between the old king and his son is accepted, it surely follows that Akhenaten's attempt to impose Atenism by force on the whole country must be put forward in time until after his father's death. For in spite of Amenhotep III's special claim to be the son of Amen and the apparent good relations that existed between himself and his son, the older king's name was everywhere effaced where it appeared as Amenhotep. Only as Nebmaetra was it respected.

Tyi, the Great Wife, is also unlikely to have stood aside tamely and allowed her husband's name to be desecrated. She died before her son, because the sections of a golden shrine that he dedicated to her were found and she may not long have survived the king whose reign she had shared from the beginning.

With his father and mother dead, Akhenaten was at last able to unleash the fury of his fanaticism and actively enforce the religion of Akhetaton throughout the land.

Those who, reading the Tel el Amarna tablets, hear those heartrending and unanswered cries for help cannot help asking once again, "But where were the armies of Egypt? Why were they not sent?" Could Tutu, one man among the thousand of scribes, messengers, army officers, and courtiers, have been entirely instrumental in preventing the dispatch of troops to Syria?

But the hacking of the time-honored and holy names of the thousand and one gods of Egypt from the temple and tomb walls could hardly have been accomplished without the backing of a considerable military force. (Could it be of this event Manetho wrote, "They [the polluted people] were guilty of sacrilege and destroyed the images of the gods . . . and ejected the priests and prophets naked out of the country.")

If Akhenaten's iconoclasm coincided by ill-fortune with the Syrian war, then the trade recession that must have followed would have been blamed less on happenings in the remote east than on the Atenist innovations and the anger of the gods. Egypt had become rich on loot, but wealth had been maintained for the benefit of the whole empire by peaceful trade. With the east in enemy hands and most of the trade routes cut by land and sea, the whole community must have suffered at every level.

Tutankhamen's stela set up only a few years later gives the gloomy picture of a rich country reduced to conditions of chaos.

"Egypt was in ruins," the stela recorded. "Wrongdoers flourished, the temples . . . had fallen into neglect, their shrines . . . overgrown with plants . . . their halls a trodden path . . . the land in confusion." Saddest of all for the country people who derived so much comfort from their prayers: "If one prayed to a god or a goddess in no wise did she come!"

How was the enforcement of Atenism put into practice? Were the priests prohibited from holding services and is that what is meant by the god or goddess "in no wise coming" when prayed to? Were the temple revenues and its treasure seized by the king in the same way that Henry VIII of England later enriched himself when he despoiled the monasteries? Were all those priests who did not turn to Atenism killed or driven out?

Except for Manetho's confused version of the affair, all the historian has to go on is the savage effacement of the names of the gods from Nubia to the delta, and the inadequate description on Tutankhamen's stela. As has been seen, the Heliopolitan god Atum and his pharaonic counterpart Ra-Harakhte were not proscribed. Neither were Shu and Tefnut (Atmosphere and Dew) but the other gods of the Heliopolitan Ennead, such as Osiris and Isis, were certainly not spared and the most savage attacks of all were directed against Amen and Min, the gods of Thebes.

If, as is stated, the shrines and temples were deserted and overgrown with weeds, then it appears that Akhenaten's reforms had been at least in part successful. But the far-reaching changes he desired to impose could not possibly have been accomplished by a few of the king's men, civil priests armed with no more effective weapons than royal edicts, hammers, and adzes. Only the strategic placing of troops up and down the country could have produced even a token acceptance of monotheism. The answer to ''Where were the armies of Egypt during the North Syrian campaign?'' seems to be found if the above argument is accepted. And because the enemy, Amorites and Hittites, were halted in the region of Hebron, an effectual force must have been spared to guard the boundaries of Egypt. Even if this army in ''attempting to widen the frontiers of Egypt met with no success at all'' (as described by Tutankhamen), it was able to prevent another foreign domination.

These military units were possibly under the command of Horemheb. Had he been in charge of enforcing the religious reforms he would scarcely have been able to avoid the taint of Atenism and be held up later as a true son of Amen-Ra. And his role as ''guardian of the land'' would have carried with it a popularity he made full use of after the king's death.

III

If the prosperity of the country was at a low ebb, conditions at Akhetaton also deteriorated. The workmen engaged in building the tombs received less pay and their standards of living fell. The noblemen had less to spend. Even the king, who had inherited such fabulous wealth, seems to have felt the pinch and several ambitious architectural projects were abandoned. Morale was also low. The aftereffects of the religious reforms may not have been considered in their practical effect by the court. In addition the Atenist society led by the ideal pair, the king and queen, that ''double principle of the couple'' needed by the worshiper of Aten, was at variance. And the courtiers were forced to witness their king's strange behavior as, month by month, Akhenaten, magnetized by Smenkhare and gripped by a passion that was not religious, heaped honor and glory on his coregent and neglected his queen.

Passion is a dangerous element that begets rifts, quarrels, and violence. Those nearest to the king, men and women, must all have been affected by the new situation. There may even have been a moment of revolt by the queen—perhaps the only violent action the gentle beauty took in her life. On the other hand, it may have been the king who took action against the queen and hated her, not for what she had done to him, but for what he was doing to her. The psychological pattern is well-known.

The break seems to have occurred after Smenkhare's coronation in year 15. Nefertiti went to the northern suburb, taking little Tutankhamen with her. This was surely dictated by human, not political, motives, because she had taken responsibility for the child from Queen Tyi and was attached to him. Of greater significance was the presence of Ankhesenpaaten with her mother. Had she not married her father and produced a daughter by him? Yet she was the only adult royal princess not granted a sunshade of Ra, an honor accorded even to her daughter, little Ankhesenpaaten Tashery. The removal of the princess from the palace to her mother's castle of Aten in the northern suburbs is an action that speaks louder than words of the true state of affairs at court.

Meritaten was now first lady in Akhetaton and represented the female principle in the rites at the Maru-Aten. The only stela found depicting her with Smenkhare shows the girl queen hopefully offering her husband the fruits of the mandrake. These were well-known as love apples, believed in the east to have stimulating and aphrodisiac qualities and to produce fecundity in women. There is an inscription on a block from Hermopolis mentioning a baby princess named Meritaten-the-less, so it is possible the love apples had their desired effect. But the infant did not long survive, and no other children were born to the royal pair.

Equally the rift in the royal family must have profoundly

affected the courtiers. When Hatiay savagely hacked Akhenaten's name from the lintel of his door, he demonstrated
that sides had been taken and parties formed. And it is not
difficult to guess that the divine prestige of the king, posing as
embodiment of the Aten, was seriously diminished by the
latest developments.

Preeminent at court was Ay, the father of the god and the
power behind the throne. What were his reactions?

Ay, bound to the king by ties of friendship, faith, and consanguinity, had been from the first an enthusiastic follower
of Akhenaten and Atenism. But he was also, if not the queen's
father, her foster-father and her uncle. Nefertiti was his
wife's foster-child and beloved pupil. His loyalties were to
both king and queen. When the parting of the ways came, it
seems possible that, whether Ay remained in person by the
king's side or not, he transferred his allegiance to Prince
Tutankhamen and the queen. It is also possible that he conceived a hatred of Smenkhare that pursued the young king
beyond life into the shadows.

And it is in the shadows with the lights turned off that
the last scenes in the drama of Akhenaten's life are acted.
Some have suggested that the child Tutankhamen was a candidate of the priests of Thebes, who had elected him king in the
first place and supported him against Smenkhare and Akhenaten. This does not seem to tally with the known facts.
Tutankhamen was brought to Akhetaton too young to have
seemed a likely candidate to the throne to anyone. And he remained on in the City of the Horizon as an Atenist for years
after his accession and Akhenaten's death. This rules him
out as a tool of the Theban priests. In addition there is the
fact that his great restoration stela was cut not in Thebes
but in Heliopolis. The line on the stela reading, "for whom
the souls of Heliopolis assembled in order that he might be
fashioned to act as king" points to the fact that Tutankhamen
first went to Heliopolis to be crowned and accepted by the
people.

Another theory is that the queen remained pro-Atenist
and that the king began to veer back to Amen. This is surely

nonsense. Whatever Akhenaten's character, he was strong in his views, a true mystic and religious enthusiast. To have given up the ideals that were so ingrained in him would have been to invoke in himself the madness he is sometimes accused of. Yet how then is it possible to account for Smenkhare's actions? At the end of this extremely confused period, he is found in Thebes with Meritaten (renamed Meritamen) building a temple to Amen. Of the many strange events in Akhenaten's reign this must be accounted one of the most extraordinary.*

Some Egyptologists have taken for granted that Akhenaten, attempting to restore his popularity with the south, sent his coregent to treat with the priest of Amen at Thebes. On the analysis of the king's character the author cannot accept this. At no time in his life did Akhenaten seek popularity. As the embodiment of the Aten, he moved in a higher sphere. Did the king, who believed himself a god, change entirely, abandon his ideas, the very ideas that had created Akhetaton and its worship of the sun's disk and seek to treat diplomatically with the priests of the deity whose sanctuaries he had recently defaced?

Some other reason must be found for the presence of Smenkhare in Thebes. The young man had been brought up in the permissive religious atmosphere of Malkata. His worship of the Aten may have been little more than a necessity to gain a crown, and his departure to Thebes looks in this light like a dramatic break with his brother, coregent, and lover.

What dictated it? Whether Smenkhare sickened of life at Akhetaton and Meritaten won back her husband, or whether the young man sensed which way the wind was blowing and abandoned Akhenaten, are questions that cannot be answered. It is even possible that Akhenaten, although alive, had lost his reason, but all these theories belong to the realms of fiction. That the youthful royal pair were welcomed in Thebes and for a brief time set up a regime worshiping Amen-Ra is certain. But the regime was overtaken by the tide of events

* See Chapter 13, for possible explanation.

and ended either shortly before or after the death of Akhenaten.

This happened with startling suddenness in year 17. Although in the City of the Horizon the stage is in shadow, the
actors can still be perceived. Akhenaten, pharaoh of Egypt,
is alive; Nefertiti withdrawn to her palace compressed between the river and the rock and so much on the verge of the
town that it seems to be trying to escape from it, and
Tutankhamen and four of the queen's remaining daughters
are with her. Suddenly, before the play seems ended, the
curtain falls. The spectator is left robbed of the grand finale,
with nothing to guide him as to the fate of these great ones of
Egypt. Nothing at all. Gone are the king, the queen, and three
of the princesses. Smenkhare in the first flush of youth has
died at Thebes.

When the curtain again rises, it discloses what appears
to be a different play, acted with different characters. The
child king, Tutankhamen, holds the center of the stage, married to Queen Ankhesenpaaten. The clouds have lifted. The
sun (a Theban sun) beams on them, reflecting their youthful
innocence, charm, and happiness. In control in the wing are
Ay, now regent, and Horemheb, generalissimo of the armies
and vice-regent. These two at least must have known the fate
of Akhenaten, Nefertiti, and Smenkhare, but left no records.

A silence so profound, an obliteration so complete, hints
at a tragedy of classical proportions. Only a discovery made
in Thebes at the beginning of the present century holds some
clue that might help to elucidate this enigmatic end to an
epoch.

11.
THE LAND OF
SILENCE

Behold the dwelling of the dead!
Their walls fall down, their place is no more,
They are as though they never existed.
That which has come into being must pass away again
The young men and maidens go to their places;
The sun riseth at dawn and setteth again in the
western hills.
Men beget; women conceive,
And the children too go to the places appointed
for them.
Oh then be happy . . .
Set behind thee all cares . . .
Until the day cometh when thou too shalt go down
to the Land of Silence.
ANCIENT EGYPTIAN POEM

Many years ago a strange set of relics, a defaced coffin and decayed mummy, were found in a small and obscure tomb in the Theban hills. And for sixty years a violent controversy has been waged among the experts over this long deceased corpse. Whose was the body stowed away with such scant ceremony in Tomb 55 in the Biban el Moluk? Was it or was it not the remians of the famous Akhenaten? The drama of the story intensifies as it unfolds.

Early in January, 1907, Theodore M. Davis was still financing excavations in the Valley of Kings and had chosen the site for the season's work to the left of the path worn smooth by the annual influx of pilgrims visiting the tombs of the Ramessides higher up the valley. Had Davis chosen the right side of the path then he, and not Lord Carnarvon, would have discovered the treasure of Tutankhamen. As it was, although he found a lesser treasure, its interest for students of the Amarnan period was immense.

Workmen clearing the apex of a hill covered with limestone chippings thrown out from the tomb of Ramses IX had sunk pits through the rubbish. During this operation steps and a walled-up doorway—sure prelude to discovery—were unearthed, and as it was already late in the afternoon the opening of the door was postponed until the following morning. Weigall was now inspector of antiquities for Upper Egypt. A small group consisting of Weigall, Maspero, Howard Carter (later to achieve such fame), Lindon Smith, and his wife, all assembled early. Although Edward Ayrton, in charge of the actual excavations, had not yet arrived it was decided to start operations without him. The eight foot high by six foot wide doorway at the bottom of the steps was blocked with a roughly built wall of limestone fragments sealed with the royal necropolis seal of the jackal and nine captives, the identical seal found intact on the tomb of Tutankhamen. In this case too the seal had never been broken and hopes ran high that here again might be that longed-for discovery, an unrifled tomb.

Those who have followed closely every detail of the account of the opening of Tutankhamen's tomb know the formula: the steps, sealed doorway, the passageway blocked with rubble, the second doorway also blocked and sealed, and, beyond, the mystery of the tomb. But this strange tomb, Number 55, was to be unlike any other discovered either before or since.

To begin with, after the intact seals had been photographed and removed and the wall taken down, it was found that the passageway descending into the bowels of the earth had not been blocked entirely. There was a three-foot clearance, upon which lay one side of a shrine of wood overlaid with gesso and gold foil. It had been abandoned in who knows what moment of panic or disaster. Weigall succeeded in laying a plank over the rubble beside the shrine door and, because it was impossible to photograph, Joseph Lindon Smith was asked to draw what he could see of its inscriptions. He was an American artist whose forte was to reproduce ancient Egyptian art both accurately and tastefully. Lying at full length on the plank, with his head pressed on the limestone ceiling of the passage and his nose "almost on the door" and with the bad air from the tomb stifling him, Lindon Smith set to work. He wrote, "I manipulated a torch so as to get most of a cartouche which was partly concealed by a stone that had fallen on top of it." Extricating himself from his cramped position, he showed the drawing to Maspero, and the assembled company were delighted to learn that the cartouche contained the name and titles of the Great Queen Tyi. Theodore Davis, certain that he had succeeded in discovering the tomb of the queen, was "almost inarticulate with joy." Even Maspero was excited, and Lindon Smith, the lightest and most agile man present, was asked to penetrate the tomb chamber.

After negotiating the narrow passage, he stood for a moment motionless on the threshold, trying to interpret the disordered scene and the objects caught in the arc of light thrown by his torch. His presence produced a change of atmosphere in the airless tomb and, even as he peered, the gilt and gesso parted from the face of one of the shrines and slid in fragments to the ground. "There was a loud ominous crash," wrote Lindon Smith, "which was heard at the mouth of the tomb. At this point Maspero shouted, 'Hey! What are you doing down there, Mr. Smith? Touch nothing!'"

At this opportune moment Edward Ayrton arrived and promised to clear the passage of its filling of rubble at once, so that all the enthusiasts—Maspero, Weigall, Davis, and Carter—might enter. He also arranged to shore up the golden shrine—a difficult task, but at last this was accomplished and the passage to the tomb opened.

It proved to be roughly carved from the living rock of the mountainside. When first penetrated, it presented a scene of the utmost disorder, further confused by a fall of rock that had flaked from the ceiling. Debris lay over everything. Apart from the dismembered shrine and a set of four canopic jars in a recess, the principal object in the chamber was a battered but once magnificent coffin. It was of cedarwood with carnelian red, blue, and turquoise glass and white crystal inlaid in gold in a kind of "imbricated shawl" or *rishi* design. A solid bronze uraeus snake with a gilded head—proof positive that the mummy was royal—was still on the brow and the regal false beard, worn only by the pharaoh, depended from the chin. But the gold mask had been roughly torn from the face and the identity of the deceased everywhere obliterated.

The coffin had once rested on a four-legged wooden bier, but water from a rock fissure had decayed most of the woodwork in the tomb, and the coffin had been precipitated onto the ground with such force that it had split, half spilling its contents. Golddust lay everywhere. Mrs. Emma B. Andrews, staying with Theodore Davis as his guest, visited the tomb. She wrote in her diary, "All the woodwork of the shrine, doors, etc., is heavily overlaid with gold foil and I seemed to be walking on gold . . . even the Arab working inside had some of it sticking to his hair . . ." And she recorded the layout of the tomb as she remembered it.

The coffin was not in the center of the chamber but at an angle, rudely pushed against the wall, while the four sides of the shrine lay in haphazard fashion half in, half out, of the tomb chamber. The contents posed a number of questions. If the tomb had been robbed in antiquity, why was a solid gold pectoral still loosely covering the disfigured face of the mummy? Above all, what was the identity of the tomb's solitary occupant?

Maspero was pressed by Weigall and Davis to pronounce his opinion. He had read the hieroglyphs on one of the faces of the shrine, which announced unequivocally that King Akhenaten had this shrine made for the king's mother, Great Wife of the king, Tyi. Beside the inscription was engraved the portrait of the queen, clad in a flowing dress of linen, Amarna style, wearing the Aten crown—a disk surmounted by two tall plumes—and caressed by the rays of the sun. Opposite her the figure of her son had been carefully erased. But even with this evidence Maspero refused to commit himself. He was emphatic that this was a reburial and that "therefore an archaeologist should avoid deductions that might prove to have been made without due consideration of all the relevant facts.'' He added, with remarkable prescience, ''I believe in the end the identity of the owner of the coffin may prove a surprise.''

A few days later, after the coffin lid had been carefully removed on a padded tray, the royal mummy was examined. It was covered from head to foot with heavy sheets of gold, the size of foolscap, which had fallen from the inner lining of the coffin and which in themselves represented a fortune. The sheets of pure and glittering gold were piled on the floor and beneath them was revealed the outlines of a body of mediocre size. It lay with the left arm bent across the breast and the right arm straight down the side—the usual pose of a queen— and had been carefully wrapped with fine linen bandages held in place by ribbons of gold foil circling the thighs, knees, and ankles. These were joined to a strip that ran the entire length of the mummy, front and back. It was in poor condition. The feet were exposed and the head was entirely separated from the body. When touched, the linen decomposed and the mummified flesh crumbled in a few seconds to dust, leaving for examination nothing but the ribbons of gold, a skull, and the skeleton. Later the gold ribbons also disappeared without trace.

The remains were first examined by an obstetrician who was passing through Luxor and who pronounced the pelvis to be that of a woman—much to the delight of Davis, firm in his certainty of having discovered Queen Tyi's tomb. But his elation was shortlived. The bones, placed in a sealed basket, were forwarded to the Cairo museum and in due course given a routine inspection by Sir Grafton Elliot-Smith, professor of anatomy at the Cairo School of Medicine. Not even knowing in which tomb they had been discovered, his anatomical report stated that the skeleton was that of a young man not more than twenty-five years of age and the cranium ''exhibited in a remarkable manner the distortion characteristic of hydrocephalus.''

It was Weigall's turn to be overjoyed. He was writing a life of Akhenaten and was convinced the mysterious remains were those of the heretic king. Nor was he deterred by the thought that, because Akhenaten reigned at least seventeen years (including the period of the coregency), if indeed the mummy was his, he must have married Nefertiti and inaugurated his famous religion reform at the very tender age of eight. Weigall's explanation, widely accepted at the time, was that Akhenaten had died and was buried at Tel el Amarna. But that when the court moved back to Thebes the royal coffin was transferred for safety to the protection of his mother's tomb. Later, under Horemheb, the tomb had been again entered, Tyi's coffin removed, and the pharaoh's mummy defaced by the usurper's orders. It was a well-reasoned and convincing explanation. Its weakness lay in the impossibility of reconciling the age the mummy was said to be at death—twenty-five—with the known facts of the heretic pharaoh's life.

There the matter rested for nearly twenty years, but the curious features of the burial in Tomb 55 continued to intrigue the minds of archaeologists. For although the skeleton remains were those of a king, the sides of two of Queen Tyi's shrines had been abandoned in the tomb. Why? And if the tomb was Akhenaten's, why had the clinical report on the bones insisted that they were those of a youth. If, on the other hand, the royal corpse was not the king's, the four amuletic bricks found in place at the four cardinal points, bearing Akhenaten's name and magically guarding the tomb from intruders, were hard to explain.

As more became known about Akhenaten, Nefertiti, and their history, the interest, far from diminishing, mounted. And after the find of Tutankhamen's treasure in 1922, Dr. Donald Derry, professor of anatomy at the University of Cairo, was asked to reexamine the bones of the unknown occupant of Tomb 55.

The skull had been smashed by the rockfall but Derry was able to make a better restoration than Elliot-Smith twenty years earlier. In consequence he established that the skull was not hydrocephalic* in character as Elliot-Smith had sur-

---

* Hydrocephalus—an abnormal accumulation of cerebrospinal fluid within the skull resulting in the enlarged deformation of the head, noticeable in many of the representations of Akhenaten. The author has suggested earlier that these exaggerations in the representations of Akhenaten were of esoteric and religious rather than medical significance.

mised, but was broad-headed and markedly resembled the skull of Tutankhamen. Furthermore, far from advancing the age of the tomb's occupant, Derry was convinced that the deceased king, whoever he had been, was not more than twenty-three at death.

Dining with Derry in 1949, Joseph Lindon Smith found in the course of conversation that of all those who had entered Tomb 55 on its discovery in 1907 he and his wife were the only two still alive. He recalled that he himself had been the first to enter the sepulchral chamber. Later, as one of the group led by Maspero to investigate the contents of the coffin, he was astounded to hear Maspero say, "Mr. Smith, you have the delicate hands of an artist, please dismember the body." Lindon Smith gave Derry an eyewitness account of how he had carefully lifted the golden sheets, one by one, from the mummy, Davis staring in fascinated amazement as the pure and heavy bullion piled up. Only one sheet was inscribed. This Lindon Smith had extricated from the back of the mummy wrappings. Even here the defacers had been at work, for a cartouche had been cut from it, and there were traces of a name that Maspero considered to have been Akhenaten's. But the famous Egyptologist had still refused to commit himself on the identity of the tomb's occupant.

Over the dinner table Derry was able to bring Lindon Smith up to date. In his reexamination of the unknown occupant of Tomb 55, Derry had noticed the great similarity between the skull and that of Tutankhamen. He was convinced the two were brothers, but if the unknown was not Akhenaten then who could he have been?

In his dilemma he had approached the curator of the Cairo museum, Mr. Rex Engelbach, who in his turn decided to reexamine the archaeological remains discovered with the body, the inscriptions on the coffin in particular. Studying them with care, he found that not only had the name of the occupant been carefully erased, but that previous to this alterations had been made in gold foil and patched on. Another point of interest was that the portrait heads of alabaster on the canopic jars found in the niche bore the simple courtier's wig not the royal headdress. The royal uraeus had been added later. This discovery and a careful reconstruction of the coffin texts indicated that jars and coffin had been intended for a member of Akhenaten's family who afterward came to the throne. Only one king, thought Engelbach, seemed to fit the context—Smenkhare—and he concluded that the coffin and jars had been made for Smenkhare when he was "Favorite of Akhenaten" before his coronation, and at his untimely death had been altered to include his royal status. But Engelbach, like others before him, could not account satisfactorily for the funerary furniture belonging to Tyi, for the magic bricks bearing the name of Akhenaten, or for the savage ravishment of the names and titles of the young king from his coffin.

Engelbach's views on the identity of the tomb's occupant did not remain unchallenged. Two famous specialists of hieroglyphs now entered the field: the late Sir Alan Gardiner, who believed from the inscriptions on the coffin that it had contained the mummy of Akhenaten, and H. W. Fairman, who thought the coffin had been made for Smenkhare's wife, Princess Meritaten, and adapted later for Smenkhare.

The longest inscription from the foot of the coffin was transcribed by Gardiner as "Recitation by . . . [name erased] . . . I shall breathe the sweet breath that comes forth from thy mouth and shall behold thy beauty daily. My prayer is that I may hear thy sweet voices of the north wind, that my flesh may grow young with life through thy love and that thou mayest give me thy hands bearing thy spirit and I receive it and live by it. And that thou mayest call upon my name eternally, and it shall not fall from thy mouth my beloved brother . . . [erasure] . . . thou being with me to all eternity, living like the living Aten."

This passage reads so like a poem of love that it was natural for Gardiner to think of it as spoken by Nefertiti before her disgrace. And he imagined her as acting in lieu of the guardian goddess Isis, symbolizing love and protection at the foot of her husband-brother's catafalque.

C. E. Aldred was another expert who now joined in the

controversy. Siding with Gardiner, he believed the coffin to be Akhenaten's and suggested, as a possible reason for the youthful age attributed to the unknown, that Akhenaten suffered from endocrine disease—a complaint where "cases have been recorded in which the bones at 36 years of age reveal the condition which in the normal individual they show at 22 or 23." He accompanied his monograph with a supporting treatise from a doctor based on the curious anatomy of Akhenaten's Karnak colossi.

So many different opinions by such eminent men seemed to make imperative a further examination of the skeletal remains. For although the bones had been carefully studied in 1907 and 1922, a reexamination with all the advantages of modern science and medical technique would be certain to establish a definite answer to the question that had vexed Egyptologists for so long.

The task was undertaken by R. G. Harrison, Derby professor of anatomy at Liverpool University, with the collaboration of the late Dr. A. Batrawi, professor of anatomy at the University of Cairo, and the assistance of Dr. Mahmoud el Sayed Mahmoud, professor of radiology at the Qasrel-Aini Hospital at Cairo.

At the outset Dr. Harrison commented that before medical interpretations could be deduced from Akhenaten's grotesque statuary, it was necessary to establish that these were in fact a true likeness of the king.* And he stressed that the examination of the skeletal remains, to be of value, must be entirely impartial.

In this dedicated spirit Dr. Harrison began his investigations. They were exact and painstaking. The results so eagerly awaited were at last published and the scientific verdict was that "The remains are undoubtedly from a man, less than 25 years of age and about 5 ft. 7 ins. in height at the time of death. If certain valuable anatomical criteria . . . are to be utilised, it is possible to be more definite that the age of

---

* Surely no man who widely publicized his family life with his wife and daughters would have also depicted himself without genitals if he had, in reality, been so deformed?

death occurred in the *20th year* . . . There is no evidence of hydrocephalus in the skull . . . no abnormality . . . the bodily physique and proportions are within normal limits . . . [There is] evidence in certain parts of the skeleton of a trend towards femininity (for instance, the angle of the neck of the femur, the lack of robustness in certain of the long bones which are nevertheless undoubtedly male, slender metacarpal bones and feminine traits in certain of the measurements of the pelvis which is also undoubtedly male) . . ."

Dr. Harrison stressed that no endocrine abnormalities were present. The inference to be drawn from the medical report was obvious, and at least one part of the mystery was solved, one argument silenced. The body in Tomb 55 was proved finally and conclusively to be Akhenaten's coregent and young brother, Smenkhare.

12.
THE MYSTERY OF TOMB 55 SOLVED?

Ages to come shall know no male of him . . .

And his name shall be
Blotted from the earth.
JOHN FLETCHER

I love a dire revenge!
IBID.

What was the end of Akhenaten and Smenkhare? How did they die? Maspero was doubtful if the king's tomb had ever been occupied and Pendlebury established that his canopic jars had never been used. (His canopic chest dating from the earliest years of his reign bore the Ra-Harakhte symbol.) But he had sworn on his boundary stela to seek his everlasting rest in the City of the Horizon and nowhere else. Could Ay have brought his body to Thebes for reburial?

If neither the king's tomb nor his canopic jars were used the question can be asked whether his body *was* embalmed and interred according to the ancient rites. For Akhenaten had repudiated Osiris, god of the dead and of the resurrection in whose name the deceased preserved his mortal remains to be reborn into eternal life.

The dynastic Egyptians were the first people to evolve the doctrine of resurrection. But with that curious mixture of the practical and the spiritual so characteristic of them, they imagined a risen soul with the physical body he had inhabited in life; his "mansions of eternity," solid buildings; his meat, weapons, furniture, and tools, mundane. Hence the practice of embalming and the whole elaborate ritual of royal burial.

Yet the Egyptians, of all civilized peoples, had the keenest perception of time and eternity. Their realization of the briefness of life compared to the unnumbered aeons of cosmic time led to the extraordinary efforts made by their rulers and great ones to outlast the earthly span allotted them.

For millenniums the Egyptians carried a double burden, and a large proportion of the population—masons, artists, goldsmiths, sculptors, priests and embalmers—were engaged perpetually in the fruitless attempt to bypass death.

For a strong consciousness of "the everlasting" impelled this ancient race to make the same provision for the dead as for the living. And the pharaoh ordered the cutting of his tomb at the same time as the building of his palace and the construction of two sets of furniture, one for this world, one for the hereafter, while to maintain the royal dignity in the afterlife, each king's relic was buried with a vast quantity of wealth in gold and precious stones. Ironically, the repeated depredations of the tomb robbers served a useful purpose by bringing back into circulation this accumulation of treasure for which the dead had no need.

It is difficult to say what provision Akhenaten had made for his eternal rest. His ushabti figures recovered from Tel el Amarna, the shrine he made for his mother Queen Tyi, his canopic chest, tomb, and sarcophagus indicate a traditional attitude to the funerary rites. But what remains of the king's funerary equipment may date to the earlier period of his reign. When he repudiated Osiris, he may have given instructions that his body was not to be embalmed, or thinking himself immortal, even have made no provision at all for his own demise. The absence of any sign of the king's burial, the inexplicable disappearance of Nefertiti, and the death a few months earlier of Smenkhare at Thebes leave the field of surmise wide open to the Egyptologists as to the earnest student of history. All that can be positively deduced from the dockets and ostraca recovered from Tel el Amarna is that year 17 was the last year of Akhenaten. His successor

Tutankhamen remained in the City of the Horizon. The child king and his advisers retained the worship of the Aten—not for a few months—but for nearly four years. It was an interim period of uncertainty with those in charge of affairs debating the wisest course of action.

Thereafter the practice and doctrine of Atenism declined. As it had evolved from Ra-Harakhte of Heliopolis, so it re-entered the Egyptian pantheon by the same route, and was again embraced by the established sun worship. Tutankhamen was taken first to Memphis and then Thebes to be crowned and, like a hive deserted by its queen, the City of the Sun began to empty of life. The citizens packed their household goods and moved away, leaving many of the houses boarded up as if the owners were uncertain whether they might not one day return. At last Akhetaton was left to silence and to the desert. Without daily watering, the flowers, trees, and bushes withered. The houses were pillaged of stone and wood. Later* came the iconoclasts, when the temples and palaces were ruthlessly destroyed and all mention of the name of Akhenaten and his god erased.

Because this is almost the sum total of information† to be derived from Tel el Amarna, the discovery at Thebes of the tombs of the two young royal brothers of Akhenaten is of outstanding importance to his biographer. It is surely the most curious freak of fate that of all the scores of royal tombs in the Biban el Moluk only these two escaped complete despoliation. But where Tutankhamen had been interred with all the care, pomp, and circumstance that love and wealth could bestow, his brother, no less royal, was meanly housed with a poor minimum of funerary equipment. Later even this

---

* In 1939 twelve hundred limestone blocks were uncovered at Hermopolis in the foundations of a construction of Ramses II. They were sculptured with reliefs of the Amarnan period. This seems to indicate that the abandoned city of Akhenaton was not destroyed until the reign of Ramses II (1304-1237 B.C.). In this haul were found the reliefs of both Akhenaten and Nefertiti in the pose of smiting their enemies, thus disproving the contention that the royal couple were pacifists.

† The stories of Akhenaten's heart scarab being sold to an American and of Nefertiti's golden coffin being borne down swiftly in the twilight from the hills by a band of Amarnans must be considered legendary until some positive evidence of the existence of these relics is established. The discovery of several of Akhenaten's ushabti is not proof that he was officially interred, because they would have been made for him before death. See final chapter for an alternative suggestion.

Painting from Tutankhamen's tomb shows Tutankhamen in the figure of the Sempriest (RIGHT) and Smenkhare as the dead king entering the hereafter (LEFT).

miserly interment had been desecrated. The wonder of Tutankhamen's treasure has resounded throughout the world and given his name that immortality craved by the Egyptian hierarchy. Smenkhare's sepulcher has done little more than provide a conundrum for historians.

It presents a problem that has baffled the experts but because the identity of the mummy has now been established as Smenkhare's an effort should be made to solve it.

In the first place it is recognized by several that not all Tutankhamen's glorious treasure had originally been made for him. As Madame Desroches Noblecourt writes: "Some of Smenkhare's burial furnishings found their way into Tutankhamen's tomb. The little golden sarcophagi containing the royal viscera for instance and certain inscribed bands found on the mummy show that Smenkhare's name had been scratched out. Several experts agree that Smenkhare's tomb was partly stripped of its contents by Ay . . . to the benefit of Tutankhamen.''

It follows that the treasures of Tutankhamen should more precisely be renamed the treasures of Tutankhamen and Smenkhare. A reconstruction of the face made from the skull of Smenkhare and published with Dr. Harrison's article seems to confirm one of Professor Engelbach's suggestions. This was that Tutankhamen's magnificent second coffin had belonged to Smenkhare and was ravished from his burial furnishings. Carter described in detail his first view of this coffin: "I was then able to roll back the covering shroud [in Tutankhamen's tomb]. It was one more exciting moment. We could now gaze, with admiring eyes, upon the finest example of the coffin-maker's art ever yet seen . . . representing a wonderful picture of Majesty lying in state. This second coffin . . . sumptuously inlaid on thick gold-foil with cut and engraved opaque glass, simulating red jasper, lapis lazuli, and turquoise respectively, symbolises Osiris. It is *Rishi* in ornament [this also applied to the coffin in Tomb 55 and the coffins containing the visceral] . . . In this case the king wears the *Nemes* head dress, and is . . . embraced with the wings of the vulture *Nekhebet* and the serpent Buto . . . *"It fitted the outer shell so closely that it was not possible to pass one's little finger between the two."*

If the gold mask on the coffin portrays Smenkhare at the time of his death, as must now surely be allowed, certain interesting deductions can be made. The face seems much swollen compared to the sculptures of the young king found at Tel el Amarna, and the sclera of the eyes are deliberately depicted as yellowed. Too much cannot be made of this. The inlay may have become discolored over the centuries but swelling of the face and jaundice can be symptomatic of certain poisons. And that he was the victim of power politics and deliberately removed from the scene is at least possible. (Many years ago Howard Carter commented that Smenkhare might have met his death at the hands of a rival faction.)

The most realistic interpretation of Smenkhare's extraordinary return to Thebes is to imagine that Akhenaten was not fully in control of himself or affairs in the last years of his life. An inscription in the tomb of Mery-Ra (the administrator) dating from this late period shows so much haste and roughness of detail that it seems to reflect the course of events. The centerpiece depicts Akhenaten and Smenkhare (in lieu of Nefertiti) with his arm around the king. That the attributes of the pharaoh and his partner had never been affixed is significant, and the whole inscription gives a sense of hesitancy. There is an etiolation of impetus that contrasts strongly with the certainty of purpose with which the City of the Horizon had been founded thirteen years earlier.

If Akhenaten *was* still alive,* then it was surely without his entire knowledge or consent that the young coregent traveled south. Whether a strong nucleus of the priests of Amen had remained on undaunted at Thebes, or whether they crept from their hiding places to welcome back the king is not known. But to suggest that they one and all switched their allegiance from Amen to Aten at the pharaoh's word and back again is to oversimplify human relationships and to ignore Tutankhamen's stela. Set up for all to see it is unlikely to

---

* The possibility that Smenkhare outlived him is discussed in the final chapter.

Engelbach postulated that this second anthropoid coffin found in Tutankhamen's tomb had been made for Smenkhare. Note the swollen face and the expression of suffering. This magnificent coffin and the smaller anthropoid coffins for the viscera (definitely Smenkhare's) were all similarly designed.

The miniature gold coffin was one of four containing the king's viscera. It is agreed that Tutankhamen's canopic chest was taken from Smenkhare's funerary furniture.

Seen here is the reconstruction by Professor R. G. Harrison of the frontal view of the skull face found in Tomb 55.

have falsified the state of affairs that must have preceded Akhenaten's end. The description of neglected and deserted temples overgrown by grass and weeds, of "a country in ruins" and "wrongdoers unpunished" suggests a serious breakdown of law and order.

A country torn by faction and ineffectually controlled is ripe for violence. Although Smenkhare settled in Thebes with his wife and built a temple to Amen as if no religious revolution had occurred—no temple walls had been defaced and no priests deprived of their offices—his reign as a Theban king was brief, his end untimely. Epidemics and disease were rife in Egypt, but the death of Akhenaten so soon afterward and the disappearance from the scene of so many of his court does suggest treachery and bloodshed. Can any clue to the pattern of events and clash of personalities be found in Tomb 55?

The meager information derived by the excavators was published by Theodore M. Davis in 1910. An important point is that the doorway to the tomb bore the necropolis seal of the jackal and nine captives, untouched. Any further cartouche giving the name of the king in whose reign the tomb had last been penetrated was either absent or unnoticed. But the floor of the tomb chamber was scattered with many lead and clay seals bearing the cartouches of Tutankhamen. Nor was there any evidence whatever that the tomb had been reopened at a later date.

A pit was found by Davis a few yards from both Tomb 55 and Tutankhamen's as yet covered tomb containing cups, jars, and relics from a royal funeral ceremonial. Cartouches associated the relics with Tutankhamen, and one piece of cloth was marked in hieroglyphics: "Good god, lord of Egypt, loved by Min, Amen year 6th." It has always been considered that these remains were buried after Tutankhamen's death and funeral rites. But if the cloth was contemporary with the year the objects were interred, they could not have been used on this occasion because he died in the ninth year of his reign. Year 6 would however fit very well the probable date of the ceremonies that marked the reburial of Tyi and Smenkhare. And the rolls of mummy wrappings found in the pit would in that case also be explained. These were not cut from the cloth but woven specially for the purpose with selvaged edges, and would, if the above supposition is correct, have come from the rewrapped mummy of Smenkhare.

It is now supposed that after his departure from Akhetaton, Tutankhamen spent a year in the older Memphite capital and established his position with the priests of Heliopolis before traveling south.

It was no doubt on this occasion that the royal flotilla stopped at Akhetaton en route for Thebes and brought with it the catafalque, furniture, and golden shrine of Queen Tyi. For Akhenaten's attachment for his mother was such that he must have intended her to be buried in the royal tomb at Tel el Amarna. Either she died, or her coffin was brought back there, for sarcophagus fragments have been recovered bearing the cartouches of Akhenaten and Tyi, and the king supplied the "golden shrine of pharaonic burial to his mother's equipment in order to do her special honor."

Why, after being brought to Thebes, Tyi's remains were not immediately placed in her husband's tomb higher up the valley is not known. For religious reasons it may have been difficult to break the seal on a royal tomb once placed under the protection of the gods. Or with the Theban Amen so recently reinstalled, the priests may have demurred at placing the queen, buried as an Atenist, beside her husband.

Ay, who controlled affairs of state for his nephew, the young king, possessed a small rock tomb at the foot of the sacred necropolis. And nearby was a larger tomb that held the remains of Smenkhare. For when this prince had died in Thebes—of natural or unnatural causes—his wife and the priests of Amen saw that he was given as splendid a funeral as the resources of the royal treasury permitted. Repudiating his association with Akhenaten, he had been buried as a king and a man, and in his burial the priests had emphasized his worship of Osiris, god of resurrection.

It was natural that Ay, looking for a ready-made tomb in which to place Queen Tyi's catafalque and funerary equipment, should think of using his own "mansion of the dead" for the purpose. But that he should despoil Smenkhare's last resting place is so extraordinary that it requires an explanation.

But it is easier to ask questions than to answer them. Was Tutankhamen at fifteen showing signs of ill health? Had Ay any reason to suppose or suspect that the king would die so young? Or was Ay, desiring a suitably splendid collection of funerary furniture for the royal burial, faced with a depleted treasury and a shortage of gold?

And in providing so generously for one nephew did Ay have no scruples in robbing the other? If Tutankhamen was his beloved young protégé, was Smenkhare for some reason anathema to him?

It is certain that no inhibitions prevented Ay from breaking the sealed entrance of his older nephew's tomb. He tore the mummy from its magnificent *rishi* coffin and, for reasons that can be conjectured, rewrapped it in the posture of a queen. That it would have been buried so by Meritaten and the priests of Amen is inconceivable and the rewrapping explains why such personal ornaments as Smenkhare's gold mummy bands, reinscribed, found their way into Tutankhamen's coffin.

The mummy of the king was then placed in a nonroyal coffin that had been made either for Meritaten when a princess or for Smenkhare himself as a youth. Fairman and Aldred have both made out an excellent case for the coffin having belonged to Meritaten. But all their arguments would apply equally well to Smenkhare before his coronation when he was enacting "the double principle of the couple" with his elder brother. In either case the coffin, designed for a person only five feet two inches in height (possibly the size of Smenkhare as a youth), was too small for the five feet seven inches tall mummy. Whether the coffin had belonged to Meritaten or not, the canopic jars were hers. For Ay filched Smenkhare's magnificent canopic shrine—one of the most beautiful objects in Tutankhamen's tomb—and alternative containers had to be found for the viscera of the dead king. The feminine inscriptions on the coffin were altered to fit a king; a royal beard, bronze uraeus, and gold mask (perhaps from some other part of his burial equipment) were added; and new longitudinal and lateral gold bands inscribed with his name and titles were placed on the mummy. This was found to be too large for the small coffin and the lid had to be replaced as a loose-fitting cover. The inscriptions on the alabaster canopic jars were ground away and glass royal uraei fitted.

How much more of Tutankhamen's fabulous treasure was taken from Smenkhare's equipment? It is impossible to say what part of the magnificent alabaster unguent jars, the gorgeous jewelry, the inlaid furniture, or the elaborate embroidered vestments, had once belonged to the older prince. Certainly a case can be made out that the justly famed and magnificent gold and polychrome throne was his. For would this costly article, Atenist in design and conception and made at Akhetaton, have been commissioned during the first four years of Tutankhamen's reign while Ay and Horemheb debated anxiously the necessity to leave the religion and its center and return to the more broadly based worship of Ra-Harakhte? Because the brothers were so alike and both married daughters of Akhenaten, the charming crowned king tended by his queen and blessed by the Aten shown on the back of the throne can represent equally Tutankhamen and Ankhesenpaaten or Smenkhare and Meritaten. So that Ay can be imagined striding through the tomb chambers with his minions, stripping them of every object of value and beauty, until finally only a coffin, a lion-headed bier, and four canopic jars (and these not his own) were set aside for the royal remains.

This minimal amount of funerary equipment was, together with four magic amuletic bricks, all that Ay was prepared to allow to the dead Smenkhare in his long journey through eternity. One brick bearing Osiris symbols and Akhenaten's name came from the first year of his reign before his departure from Thebes. The others had been hastily molded to match and inscribed with a hieratic text in ink.

One such magic brick with its torch intact was found at the entrance of the burial chamber containing Tutankhamen's (Smenkhare's) canopic chest. The magical formula read: "It is I who hinder the sand from choking the secret chamber. I am for the protection of the Osiris [the dead

king]." The bricks in Tomb 55 have been cited as proving that Akhenaten's body also once rested in this chamber but W. H. Fairman disagreed. He affirmed that only one brick bore Akhenaten's name in its early form, that the hieroglyphs on the others were too badly worn to be recognizable and that each brick bore the word *Osiris,* which Akhenaten would not have countenanced. "The conclusion is inescapable that the bricks cannot have been part of the actual burial equipment of Akhenaten."

It can be established with some degree of certainty that the rape of Smenkhare's funerary equipment and his reburial and his mother's were contemporary and date to year 6 of Tutankhamen. Smenkhare's coffin must first have been brought into the rock-cut tomb and placed on a lion-headed bier a little to one side of the burial chamber. Next the queen's catafalque was carried in and enclosed by a pall studded with gold marguerites and placed over supports. Lastly the shrine was erected, the furniture piled up, and the canopic jars placed in a niche. There also seems some evidence that a chariot was part of the queen's equipment and she was certainly provided with the oils and unguents considered by the Egyptians so necessary in afterlife, as in life.

Signs that all these had once been stored in the chamber were found by Ayrton and Weigall. There was the fragment of a chair with the names of Tyi and Amenhotep III, two marguerites of gold that had fallen from the pall, the socle of a statue, a woman's toilet jar, and, among other remnants, a casket of cedarwood framed with ebony veneer inscribed "That which is in gold of the household vases." Unfortunately it was empty. There seems no doubt that Queen Tyi's shrines, her furniture, and by inference her coffin had once stood in Tomb 55. The side of the shrine noticed by Lindon Smith showed Akhenaten, his figure obliterated, making an offering to the Aten. Behind him Queen Tyi poured incense on the flames of a second altar. The Aten sun shed its rays on both altars and royal officiants, while above was written: "[Right] The King of Upper and Lower Egypt living in truth [Maet]; what he made for the king's mother the Great King's wife Tyi. [Left] The King of Upper and Lower Egypt,

The portraits on Tutankhamen's throne:
Are they Smenkhare and Meritaten?

the Lord of Two Lands Nebmaetra [Amenhotep III] the king's mother the Great King's wife, Tyi, may she live eternally.''

In ruthlessly despoiling Smenkhare's tomb, Ay appeared to have been activated by personal animus. Was there need to take all? For the furnishings found in Tutankhamen's sepulcher were sufficient to equip not only one but several princes for a luxurious afterlife. And that Smenkhare was left with even a semblance of a royal burial was no doubt due to the influence of those priests of Amen who had supported him and to the fact that his younger brother was king.

But if Ay, under Tutankhamen, was responsible for the reburial of Tyi and Smenkhare, who was the antagonist who later reentered the tomb and desecrated the mummy. Could this also have been Ay?

No tomb robber could have resisted stealing the solid gold lining of the coffin or the golden pectoral lying loosely over the ravished mask. If it was not the necropolis ghouls, could it have been the iconoclasts? Although Akhenaten's figure had been erased from the side of his mother's shrine, the rayed sun's disk was untouched. Neither a Nineteenth-dynasty pharaoh nor Horemheb, who reverted to the worship of Amen-Ra with apparent fervor, would have left unscathed such a blatant example of the heresy.

It seems as if the desecrater must have been Ay, and if the desecration of the tomb was not religious iconoclasm, then it could only have been activated by hatred and the desire for revenge. Ay had been Akhenaten's right-hand man during the Amarnan years. That he might have been ousted from his close and privileged position as the king's confidant by a youth with a charming countenance would account perhaps for his virulent dislike of that youth. And on a deeper level Ay might have felt that the religious revolution he believed in had been brought to nothing through the king's unfortunate passion for his young brother. For (he might have argued) was not the destruction of the king's image as the male ''principle of the couple'' a contributory cause in the decay of Atenism? Each age has its own set of moral values. The ancient Egyptians were no Puritans in regard to sex but they may have regarded homosexuality with distaste, as we view incest today.

If, as seems most probable, Ay was the tomb wrecker, it is not difficult to place the opening of the tomb to immediately after Tutankhamen's death. Ay, in charge, had assumed the role of king. His love for one of his nephews and his deep grief at the youth's untimely end would have done nothing to assuage his hatred of the other. As dictator, no scruples prevented him from doing as he chose. The time had come to wreak his revenge and, pursuing Smenkhare into the shadows, destroy his chance of immortality and happiness in the "fields of Yaru" (heaven).

First his sister, Queen Tyi, must be removed from the contaminating presence of her son. Possibly it was at this stage that Ay opened Amenhotep III's magnificent tomb to include the reburial of his Great Wife. The tomb was looted and wrecked in the time of the Ramessides and little remained of either the Great King or the Great Queen in the tomb chambers, but Arthur Weigall claimed to have found evidence that Tyi's last resting-place was beside her husband.

The last visitation to Tomb 55 before its rediscovery in 1907 can be envisaged. The priests, no desperate robbers but devout and superstitious men, worked, fearing as they desecrated the dead one that he might curse them from the land of shadows. This would account for the evidence that their orders were carried out in a hasty and slipshod fashion. First they had to break down the sealing of the door and remove enough of the filling of the corridor to enable the queen's burial equpiment to be removed. The shrine with its pall was the largest object in the burial chamber. This was dismantled, some of the marguerites from the pall falling onto the floor where they were discovered so many centuires later. Queen Tyi's catafalque was reverentially carried out. With this space clear, the priests could turn their attention to the desecration of Smenkhare's burial. The amuletic bricks were rendered ineffectual by wrenching off their amulets. Akhenaten's name was not everywhere erased. But Ay's wrath does not seem to have been concentrated on his erstwhile friend and master because several objects bearing Akhenaten's

The gold pectoral found on the chest of Smenkhare's mummy.

name were found untouched in Tutankhamen's tomb. Neither at this stage was the Aten disk singled out for destruction. For Ay, ardent Atenist, most likely remained a private worshiper to the end of his life. Only Smenkhare's identity was utterly obliterated, and the young man was doomed to walk nameless in the shadows through eternity, bereft "for ever and ever" of power and kingly dignity, the boon of an identity denied him.

The obliteration of Smenkhare's titles from the coffin was thoroughly done. Even the cartouches behind the mummy were excised. The gold mask, evidently a portrait, was torn off. And if the canopic jars, which bore the likeness of Meritaten, were not defaced, only the royal glass uraei being snapped off, nothing else was left to tell the gods whose remains lay in the tomb.

Was Ay present, slaking the thirst of his hatred and supervising the priests as they worked in feverish haste and apprehension by the feeble light of the flickering oil lamps? And was it he who made that last violent gesture of antagonism? For somebody, it seems, seized the solid gold pectoral from the chest of the mummy and "twisting the figure into a battening vulture" slammed it down onto the face of the corpse. Aldred writes, "It is difficult to see how otherwise it got bent into such a small arc embracing the head so closely and what it was doing in so unsuitable a location."

The work of tampering with the abodes of the dead and the haunts of the spirits was considered dangerous. Falls of rock often occurred when sealed rock tombs were reopened, and perhaps some distant rumbling in the mountainside disturbed the workers on this special occasion. Queen Tyi's catafalque and furniture had already been removed, the coffin of Smenkhare effectively defaced, and the desecraters had just coaxed the roof and door of a shrine out of the narrow entrance when work was suddenly abandoned. The heavy sides were dropped, a new wall to the door hastily built and sealed, and Tomb 55 was left in disorder to guard its secrets through the long centuries.

13.
THE PROPRIETY
OF TIME

*If a man will begin with certainties he shall end in doubts;
but if he will be content to begin with doubts he may end
in certainties.*
FRANCIS BACON, *Advancement of Learning*

*The inseparable propriety of time is even more and more to
disclose truth.*
IBID.

*They that deny a God destroy men's ability, for certainly
man is of kin to the beasts by his body and if he be not kin
to God by his spirit he is a base and ignoble creature.*
IBID.

I

The author's opinion that disaster overtook Akhenaten, that his reign ended in strife and intrigue, and that he left a legacy of bitterness and irreconcilable hatred has recently been strengthened. Fresh evidence has come from Professor Ronald Harrison, who in 1966 examined the remains of Smenkhare. Three years later he led an expedition to the Valley of the Kings with the object of subjecting the mummy of Tutankhamen to a "postmortem" conducted with all the aids of modern scientific knowledge.

In whatever fashion Akhenaten and Smenkhare met their deaths, it has always been supposed that Tutankhamen, whose funeral obsequies were conducted with such lavish care, died of natural causes. But after studying X-rays of his mummy and microscopically examining parts of the skin tissue for nine months, Professor Harrison came to a startling conclusion. He diagnosed the cause of death as a blow on the skull, which produced a brain hemorrhage, unconsciousness, and finally extinction. An irregular gaping wound was found at the exact spot where Howard Carter had noticed a scab. Carter also commented on the fact that Tutankhamen's head was closely shaven. To shave the scalp may have been a practice at the City of the Horizon continued by Tutankhamen after his move to Thebes, but there is the possibility that he was so shaven by the court physicians in their efforts to dress the wound.

If the round-cheeked, doe-eyed youth, Tutankhamen, was a victim of violence, what Nemesis might not have overtaken his predecessors? For with Ay as regent and Horemheb as vice-regent the king had endeavored to set in order the affairs of state. And he had attempted to heal the breach created by Akhenaten in the conservative religious structure of Egyptian life. Granted that the fatal blow that killed Tutankhamen was inflicted by an assassin and not caused by an accidental fall, who was behind the attack? Who was the enemy possibly referred to by Tutankhamen on the left wall of his third shrine, when he begged the gods to save him from "the hand of the evildoer . . . the butchers who make short work in Heliopolis . . ."? The Atenists? The Amenists? An adherent of Horemheb? Or was Ay again the villain of the piece, the classic wicked uncle?

The floral wreaths and tributes that decked the coffins and the fabulous wealth of furniture that surrounded the corpse seem to show less the remorse of a secret murderer than the genuine affection lavished by grieving relatives. So splendid a funeral, so great a treasure heaped round the dead king, above all the ostensible figure of Ay named as chief mourner on the wall of the tomb, seem to exonerate him from any part in the untimely death of his younger nephew. But if Smenkhare was murdered to make way for Tutankhamen, as the author suspects, some of the elder prince's supporters might have sought revenge and killed the young king, who was possibly innocent of all knowledge of the intrigues of his close advisers. Ay's intense grief at his death would then be understandable and he would have had the strongest motive for violating Smenkhare's tomb. Unable to wreak his hatred on the living, he may have found satisfaction in depriving Smenkhare (as he thought) of resurrection through Osiris and condemning him to everlasting limbo.

Further evidence of the uncertainty of the times, of palace intrigues, plot, and counterplot, was found far from Egypt. By an extraordinary chance the gist of a letter from one of the Amarnan royal family has survived. It was written by Tutankhamen's queen, Ankhesenpaaten, and the record of it was discovered in the Hittite capital of Bogazköy in Asia Minor. "My husband is dead," wrote Ankhesenpaaten to the Hittite king, "and I have no son. People say that you have many sons. If you send me one of your sons, he will become my husband for it is repugnant to me take one of my servants [subjects] to husband."

(This is final proof, if proof is needed, that the Eighteenth-dynasty kings of Egypt only inherited the throne legitimately through marrying the heiress princess.) The Hittite king, amazed and suspicious at the queen's letter, sent a courier posthaste to Egypt for first-hand information on the state of affairs. Ankhesenpaaten, renamed Ankhesenamen on the return to Thebes, sent back a second missive to the Hittite king: "Why do you say, 'They are trying to deceive me?' If I had a son, should I write to a foreign country in a manner humiliating to me and to my country? You do not believe me and you say so to me! He who was my husband is dead and I have no son. Should I then perhaps take one of my servants and make of him my husband? I have written to no other country, I have written only to you. They say that you have many sons. Give me one of your sons and he will be my husband and lord of the land of Egypt."

Seen in the light of later events this human letter is

pathetic as well as foolish; for would an enemy* prince have been so calmly accepted by the Egyptian hierarchy even if married to the heiress? This strange missive sounds like the romantic attempt of an indulged and haughty royal lady to impose her own pattern on a difficult situation. Can she have realized the ruthlessness of ambitious seekers for supreme power? Surely the astute Ay (who was hand in glove with Horemheb) could never have advised or known of such a scheme.

But Egypt was a rich prize and the Hittite king, whatever his misgivings, decided to risk the venture. One of his younger sons, Prince Zennanza, equipped as a royal bridegroom and suitably escorted set out for Egypt. But his enemies overwhelmed him even before he reached the Egyptian frontier. Somewhere between Asia Minor and the delta he was set upon and murdered by "the men and horses of Egypt." Because the Hittite king had elsewhere written "the general of the Egyptian army does not promote my son to the kingship," it seems most probable that Horemheb, who guarded Egypt's frontiers, was responsible for the elmination of a foreigner and rival to the throne.

Whatever her feeling, Ankhesenamen married her great-uncle Ay. It was no doubt a token marriage only to enable Ay to ascend the throne legitimately and he may not have been in her mind when she wrote to the Hittite king. Was Horemheb the servant to whom she referred with such hauteur?

Ay reigned briefly four years and one month and in the tomb he constructed for himself in the western branch of the Biban el Moluk he is seen in wall paintings in company with

---

* The queen's letter is the more extraordinary seen against the background of Hittite-Egyptian relations. The Hittite crown prince described conditions and his brother's murder in a letter: "Now my father sent men and horses and they attacked the borderland of Egypt . . . and then he sent more and they attacked them again. Thereupon the Egyptians were terrified; they came and asked my father to send his son as their king. Accordingly thereupon my father gave them his son; thereupon they conducted him to Egypt. Then they murdered him. And he was buried there. He, my father, marched into Egypt. The land he smote and destroyed the men and horses . . ." The Egypt mentioned was some part of Syria still under Egyptian control.

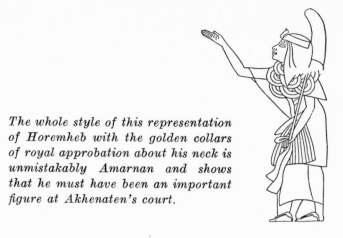

The whole style of this representation of Horemheb with the golden collars of royal approbation about his neck is unmistakably Amarnan and shows that he must have been an important figure at Akhenaten's court.

Tyi, Nefertiti's nurse, the wife of his Amarnan years! He was succeeded by Horemheb, the last king of the eighteenth dynasty, who conformed to the time-honored pattern and married Nefertiti's sister Mutnedjmet. The inference is that she was by then the last of the Amarnan royal ladies. The troop of lively little princesses depicted charmingly grouped about their parents the sun king and queen at Amarna must one and all have been dead. Ankhesenamen, so scornful of the servant she could not bring herself to marry, may have shared the fate of Prince Zennanza.

Horemheb had been vice-regent during Ay's regency. Because he called himself son of the Horus, he was probably nominated as coregent with Ay at some period during his four years' reign.

In the Egypt of today and particularly among the supporters of Communism, Horemheb is regarded as a good king. He was, what all rulers must be to be "good," strong and active and he attempted to reform some of the abuses that had become rife in the administration. For instance, he ordered that tax gatherers and members of the police force found robbing the poor man were to be given no quarter. A stern sentence of exile in the mines and their noses cut off was to be imposed on such malefactors. And to carry out his reforms Horemheb appointed two judges "perfect in speech, excellent in good qualities, knowing how to judge the heart." Although some have tried to build up the image of Horemheb as "representative of the workers" the evidence for this is slight. He stressed his claim to be hereditary prince and showed his conservatism by marrying Mutnedjmet. He had probably been an ardent Atenist with the name of Pa-aten-em-heb but as the candidate of the Theban priesthood he renounced his former doctrines and strongly supported Amen-Ra. Whether, as some have thought, he initiated the widespread and vicious attacks against the heresy is very doubtful, but had he been the last to enter Smenkhare's sepulcher before the door was sealed, he would surely not have left unscathed the representation of the Atenist sun and its rays.

His was yet another tomb discovered by Theodore Davis in the Biban el Moluk. On one of the door posts was found an inscription in black ink disclosing that it had last been entered in 1100 B.C. But tomb robbery in the Valley of the Kings is as ancient as the first tomb tunneled in the rocky mountainside. This one had been thoroughly cleared of its contents. Besides litter discarded by the robbers, only a huge pink granite sarcophagus remained, its lid tilted off. It was cut in Amarnan style, with a guardian goddess at each corner spreading her wings protectively around the now vanished contents. When Davis found it, a skull and the bones of more than one skeleton were lying at the bottom. Further exploration of the tomb revealed additional skulls and bones, some of which appeared to be female. The tomb robbers in their hasty search for the rich jewels and amulets hidden in every layer of the mummy wrappings had evidently torn them to bits and left bones scattered about the tomb. The government inspector of 1100 B.C. had done what he could for these poor anonymous remains. Finding the skeletons strewn in all directions, he had replaced one skull in the sarcophagus, two in one ante chamber, and one in another dividing the bones in haphazard fashion between the four. "It will now never be known with certainty whether one of these four heads wore the crown of the pharaohs," wrote Arthur Weigall.

II

There is therefore little evidence in the tomb of Horem-heb that can contribute toward the history of Akhenaten's last years, and whatever the royal tombs at Tel el Amarna contained would have been removed when the site was abandoned.* Smenkhare's sepulcher has been well searched for clues. There remains, however, the rich treasury of Tutankhamen and the chambers in which it was found.

In spite of three separate attempts to rifle the tomb in antiquity, a bewildering wealth of objects lay stacked in the four small rooms. If the public were dazzled by the treasure, the archaeologists found it a mine of information. For here for the first time the elaborate ritual of Egyptian royal burial could be studied in detail—and of a king who began his reign as an adherent of the Aten and returned to the worship of Amen-Ra of Thebes. Surely in the burial of the supposed youngest brother of Akhenaten something might be found to elucidate the mystery of the final years of the heretic king's life?

Several objects among the treasures have already been mentioned. The box with Akhenaten's touching tribute to the young Smenkhare, the gorgeous golden-plated Atenist throne that may have been Smenkhare's, his glittering Osirian coffin and his canopic chest—one of the most beautiful of the many objects discovered—were all found in Tutankhamen's tomb. The realization of how much of Smenkhare's funerary furniture was ravished to equip his younger brother is of comparatively recent date. A question remains. Did Ay when appropriating the furniture also appropriate the tomb itself for Tutankhamen? And if so, were the paintings now to be seen on the walls of the sepulchral chamber already in situ before the boy king's death?

The scene most often reproduced from the chamber walls depicts the ceremony of Opening the Mouth.

It was the culminating moment of the funeral rites when the dead king was imagined as being brought to life in the

---

* A small cache of jewelry is alleged to have been found in 1882 near the royal tomb at Tel el Amarna. It included a gold ring of Nefertiti, gold earplugs, and a carnelian, glass, and faience necklace. It is suggested that they are relics abandoned after the transfer of the royal burials to Thebes. The objects are too few and too fragmentary to answer the question of whether Nefertiti was buried at Amarna; one ring and half a ushabti figure are insufficient evidence. But Meketaten, Akhenaten's second daughter, was undoubtedly buried in the royal tomb.

hereafter. With a special sacred implement, the Sem-priest touched the lips of the mummy reciting:

Opened is thy mouth . . . Horus adjusts for thee thy mouth, and opens for thee thy eyes and ears, thy flesh and bones being perfect in all that appertains to thee . . . thy own true heart being with thee, thy breast which thou didst have on earth. Thou comest in thy former shape even as on the day wherein thou wast born. There is brought to thee the son thou lovest [the king's successor] the courtiers making obeisance. Thou enterest into the land given to the king, into the sepulcher of the West . . .

The ceremony was traditionally performed by the succeeding king. In this case the cartouches above the Sem-priest announce the figure as being that of Ay. But is it?

Ay was no longer young when he came to the throne. Although it was natural for the court artist to flatter his subjects, would he have delineated Ay at Tutankhamen's death as so very immature, more of a boy than a youth, younger in fact than the dead king? The argument depends on the eye of

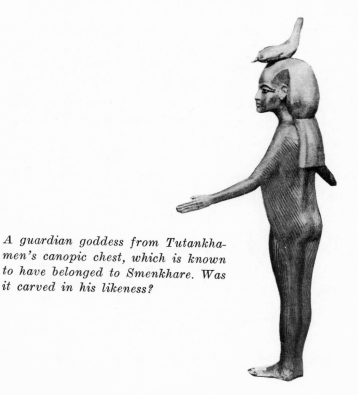

A guardian goddess from Tutankhamen's canopic chest, which is known to have belonged to Smenkhare. Was it carved in his likeness?

the reader. He is asked to study the portrait head of the ten-year-old Tutankhamen, of Ay as the Nile god, and the precise, aloof, and classical profile of Smenkhare. Returning his gaze to a reproduction of the wall painting, he may ask: "But is not the figure of the Sem-priest a representation of Tutankhamen? And is not the Osiris figure of the young king intended for Smenkhare?"

Allowing this to be so for the sake of argument, it is worthwhile examining the new pattern of events that emerges. The consensus of opinion has been that Smenkhare and Akhenaten died within a year of one another, but that the older coregent outlived the younger. There is no absolute proof of this. If the reverse was the case and Smenkhare became supreme king at the age of eighteen, on Akhenaten's death, he might have made the decision to nominate Tutankhamen as his succesor and coregent in Akhetaton while he himself reverted to the worship of Amen-Ra. This rereading of events would solve the awkward question of Smenkhare's move south to Thebes, which is simple to understand when seen as happening not before, but after Akhenaten's end. Smenkhare was crowned as an Atenist at Amarna but after the coregent's death he might have thought it expedient to be recrowned at Thebes; the temple he dedicated to Amen-Ra may date to this occasion. Once in the southern capital he may have had to play his hand his own way and establish an authority that did not include the close assistance of his astute Uncle Ay or his seasoned general Horemheb. It would have been a decision his supporters had occasion to regret on his untimely death.

The complicated ritual of Egyptian royal burial had evolved over the centuries and every detail of the ritual was invested with the aura of divine sanction.

From the moment of death when the women of the court gathered kneeling and beating their breasts until the final Opening of the Mouth ceremony each step was ordained. First the body was taken to the embalmers. Herodotus described their mode of operating: "They take first a crooked piece of iron and with it draw out the brain through the nostrils . . . while the skull is cleared of the rest by rinsing with drugs; next they make a cut along the flank with a sharp Ethiopian stone, and taking out the whole contents of the abdomen which they cleanse, wash it thoroughly with palm wine . . . After this they fill the cavity with the purest bruised myrrh, with cassia, and every other sort of spicery . . . and sew up the opening. Then the body is placed in natron for seventy days which must not be exceeded . . . It is then wrapped round with bandages of fine linen smeared over with gum . . .''

The embalmed corpse placed in its coffin was drawn to the river Nile by ''bulls without blemish.'' And once across to the western bank the sledge containing the catafalque was conveyed to its last resting place in the Valley of the Dead. It was pulled, at least part of the way, by the nobles of the court, and the funeral ceremonies were long and elaborate and included drinking, dancing, and sacrifice.

''There is a procession to be made for thee on the day thou art reunited with the earth: thy mummy case of gold with head of lapis lazuli . . . while thou art placed in the hearse and oxen drag thee. Then shall musicians await thy coming and the dance of the *Muu* be performed at the door of thy tomb. The words of offering shall be pronounced on thy behalf, and victims slaughtered at the door of thy stela.''

Not only the ceremony but every part of the burial itself had esoteric significance. Of the four burial chambers the eastern one represented rebirth; the southern eternal royalty; the western funeral destinies; and the northern resurrection. Even the four shrines that canopied the sarcophagus were shaped differently, one in semblance of a prehistoric palace of the north, another of the south, and a third of a pavilion of the Heb-sed festival. And each aspect of the tomb, the objects in it, the placing of them, the three coffins, sepulcher, four shrines, and pall had meaning. In attempting to sweep away with a regal wave of the hand two thousand years of superstition what, one wonders, had Akhenaten substituted for such ornate and elaborate obsequies?

At Amarna all the gods were banished and replaced with the faceless globe of the disk, the human figures reduced to the size of midgets, and the king alone (with the attendant figures of the queen and their daughters) dominated the scene. The conception, if egocentric, was cosmic, immense,

simple. To understand how revolutionary Akhenaten must
have appeared to his contemporaries and the gulf between his
ideas and Theban theology, compare the Amarnan set pieces
with the reliefs on the shrines enclosing Tutankhamen's
coffins. On these the Aten has not been circumscribed. The
winged disk appears above the doors of two and on the ceiling
of a third shrine, which bears the words: "The rays of the
disk are a protection over thee, their hands carry health and
life, they are health for thy members." But the floodgates
that Akhenaten had shut so firmly on the unruly hosts of the
Egyptian heaven have been lifted. The gods are back in force,
the Aten is overwhelmed. Jostling with such great ones as
Osiris, Isis, Nut, and Nephthys are the "thousand and one
gods"—such strange enigmatic deities as The Upreared One;
Cat; Terrible One; Fat Face; Turned Face; The One belonging
to the Cobra; He in the Netherworld; The Mysterious One. Yet
together with so much that savors of magic, with the liturgical
repetitions, incantations, and symbolism, the inscriptions
show an essence of the sincere and the devout. And the dead
king's prayer for everlasting life seems to echo the cry of
humanity through the ages.

WORDS SPOKEN BY THE KING'S OSIRIS:

> *O Mother Nut [the sky] the Great, I am thy son . . .*
> *may I be protected in thy embrace, may I not die*
> *a second time, may I live for ever!*

AND NUT ANSWERS:

> *Thou wilt be in heaven like Ra. . . Thou art with him in the sky*
> *forever . . . Thou art his son living on*
> *truth . . . I encircle thee with my arms, thou are not*
> *weary, thy members are not tired . . . I have spread*
> *over thee my arms to protect thee forever . . .*

WORDS SPOKEN BY NEPHTHYS [THE COUNTERPART OF ISIS]:

> *I salute thee, arise! Thou livest, thou shalt not*
> *decay, thy body shall not perish! Thy soul is for*
> *the sky before Ra, thy body is for the earth before*
> *Osiris . . . thou hast been called by name, thou has been found . . .*

TUTANKHAMEN REACHES THE GATES OF HEAVEN:

The majesty of this God pauses as he rests at the
gate Orders to those gods who are in it: Open
your doors for me, open your gates, guide me . . .
Open your gates! Osiris, King, Lord of the Two
Lands Nebkeprure, bodily Son of the Sun, Lord
of Diadems Tutankhamen, ruler of Heliopolis of
the South is justified!

Perhaps those who ordered the obsequies of the poor young king, hurried from life on the threshold of his manhood, hoped he would find redress in the hereafter. And that there, learning "the names of the two great gods: Everlastingness and Eternity," he would find the "life, stability, and prosperity" that had been denied to him in this world.

III

For a few brief years Akhenaten had dared to ape god and to throw down his gauntlet before the vastness of the unknown. But he, the fanatical Atenist, far more than the emissaries of Ramses II who broke up his temples and city, was the destroyer of Atenism. In attempting to direct the worship of the god toward his own mortal and ephemeral self, he doomed Atenism to extinction.

The reasons for his failure as a king and as a religious leader are not far to seek. On the mundane level he neglected foreign affairs. Because of the Syrian war, which should have been prevented, Egypt lost most of her empire and the prosperity it had nurtured. Seeking to impose by force a creed in advance of his time and which was actively or passively opposed by most of the people and half the priesthood, he divided the country. Finally, on establishing himself as the living godhead, emblem of the rising sun, he failed in the eyes of his supporters. Through his relationship with Smenkhare he betrayed the "principle of the couple," the generative power of the sun, while his self-deification made it impossible for any other to fill his place on his death.

Akhenaten's religious revolution can now be seen as a schism not only from the worship of Amen-Ra but from the universalist ideas of his father. The theological implications of Amenhotep III's Atenism can be explained as the worship of the unknown god whose visible manifestation, the sun, dispensed life and warmth to all living creatures. The disk was not the deity. It was the window in heaven through which the hidden creator of all poured his radiance on the world. Although the word *Aten* can be traced back to the Middle Kingdom, it came into prōminence at the beginning of the Eighteenth dynasty. The second king of the dynasty, Amenhotep I, was described on death as being "united to the disk," and his successor, Thutmose I, claimed among his titles to be "One who comes out of the disk."

If the Santorin date for the Exodus is conceded, Moses could have been the fount of the new theological thought that, stemming from Heliopolis, gradually filtered through into the first circles of power. Moses, revered in Egypt as well as by his own people, may have inspired the universalist ideas that had their apogee in the reign of Amenhotep III and that were brought to a tragic conclusion by Akhenaten.

Again one wonders whether the damaged manuscripts relating to Akhenaten and Moses, Manetho's source material, were kept in one file and if so under what heading? The ancient Egyptians were a literate people. Their records were meticulously kept and docketed by the scribes on rolls of papyrus. Although they had their own methods of office procedure, matters relating to the Atenist heresy would have surely been placed together. In Manetho's account, what he omitted is as interesting as what is noted down. Evidently the documents he used relating to Akhenaten gave neither the king's name, nor that of his city, nor that of his special god. Perhaps, significantly, the manner in which he died was also obliterated, although not the length of his reign in Akhetaton. On the other hand, the name Moses, had not been scored from the records; the Egyptians also regarded him as a great man and prophet. But, it seems, all mention of his early life and upbringing as a prince at the court of an Egyptian Hyksos king was suppressed. If both men were recorded as leaders of a heretical sect, and in both cases the name and nature of the heresy were carefully concealed, Manetho's mistaken assumption that they were one and the same is understandable.

But the beliefs that Moses took with him into the wilderness, which we know from the Bible, differed greatly from the Atenism of Amenhotep III. The rulers of Egypt were priest-kings believing as a canon of faith in their descent from the sun and any religion they adopted, filtered through their ancient creeds, was bound to become tinged with the golden aura of sun worship.

But although each son of Horus claimed to be divine— Amenhotep III was worshiped as a god in his own lifetime —Akhenaten's predecessors were also practical men of affairs, not unaware of the limitations of human existence. If they claimed to be gods, their immortality was beyond the grave in the fields of Yaru or in the sun boat with Ra. Here, it seems, Akhenaten parted company with them.

For Akhenaten's Atenism was imbued with more than a touch of Vedic mystery. Vedism was a worship of the nature gods who were invoked by the chanting of hymns and the sacrifice of animals—horses and cattle in particular. But the highest element in the religion sought to penetrate into the mysteries of creation and believed in one god—The Absolute— of which the soul of man was an actual part, coming from and returning to its divine source. It is easy to see how Akhenaten, by creed a sun worshiper, by birth a royal prince who believed that he partook of the sun's godhead, might imagine himself truly divine. And that in his city of Akhetaton he sought to enact the god's part, driving his gold-plated chariot like Ra before the admiring populace, shining in solar splendor from his window of appearance, and building his vast palace of stone as for a living god.

If much of Akhenaten's creed was inherited from his father (much also derived from the fusing of Indo-Aryan beliefs with the ancient nature worship of the ithyphallic god Min at Coptos), his was a unique personality. He forged from these diverse elements a new and powerful monotheism. Discarding the shabby superstitions of the shaman, he held steadfastly to the supreme light in the heavens as his sole god and to that answering "something" in himself that he held to be immortal.

His failure as a leader, religious and secular, lay, perhaps, in the peculiarities of his nature. Unlike the world's greatest mystics his religious impulse was turned, not outward toward humanity but inward upon himself. He may represent a typical psychological case, one suffering from who knows what sense of inadequacy, fear, lack of love in childhood, who rejects the normal life to seek mystical experience.

He offered his followers the joy of worship of a single supreme god, the sun, whose embodiment he imagined himself to be. At the same time, unlike Moses, he laid down for them no ethical code of conduct, so far as is known. And the "Hymn to the Sun" is as remarkable in its total absence of moral attitudes as for the universality of its paean of praise.

Akhenaten can be termed, perhaps, the orginal flower child who believed as the hippies of today in the trance and the love-in, spiritual and physical ecstasy. He saw man not superior to, but part of, the natural universe in his true ecological background among plants, birds, and animals. So that these exquisite manifestations of the sun—the "smooth-plumed bird in its emerald shade," flowers, the "pearled Arcturi of the earth," and the graceful-limbed gazelle—were part of the trappings of his sacred ceremonies, the arcana of his religion.

It is unlikely that the uncertainties surrounding the end of Akhenaten's reign will ever be resolved. To the author it seems equally unlikely that his end was orderly or his death natural. Was he destroyed by his antagonists? Or when the time came and he believed his health to be failing did he choose to seek his father, the Sun, in the solitude of the desert? And walking on and on and on across the soft yielding sand did he fix his eyes on that glowing disk until blinded, he fell and felt himself faint and dissolve into its strength, absorbed in its brilliance forever, and at last at peace.

APPENDIX

A NEW DATE FOR THE EXODUS: MANETHO'S ACCOUNT OF MOSES AND AKHENATEN

(THE QUOTATIONS ARE MAINLY FROM JOSEPHUS: BOOKS AGAINST APION I AND II)

> *When he was but three years old . . . there was nobody so unpolite as, when they saw Moses, they were not greatly surprised at the beauty of his countenance: nay, it happened frequently, that those that met him as he was carried along the road were obliged to turn again . . . left what they were about, and stood still a great while to look on him . . .*
> JOSEPHUS

> *Listen then, Socrates, to a tale which, though passing strange, is wholly true . . . there have been many and divers destructions of mankind of which the greatest are by fire and water . . . For in truth the story is told how once upon a time Phaeton yoked his father's chariot, and burnt up all that was upon earth and himself perished by a thunderbolt— a story that has the fashion of a legend but the truth of it lies in . . . the destruction of the things on the earth by fierce fire. The Gods purge the earth with a flood of waters and those in the coastal cities are swept into the sea . . . So at a later time there occurred portentous earthquakes and floods, and one grievous day and night befell them, when a whole body of . . . warriors was swallowed up by the earth and the island of Atlantis in the like manner was swallowed up by the sea and vanished!*
> PLATO'S *Timaeus*

The recent reappraisal of the date of the Exodus comes, not from an historian, but a seismologist. It has been firmly established that the most violent natural cataclysm of historic times occurred in the eastern Mediterranean in the middle of the second millennium B.C. A volcano on the island of Santorin (Thera) became active, erupted, and ended by collapsing into the sea.

The seismic waves or tsunamis occasioned by the final disaster may have reached heights of six hundred and ninety feet and the cataclysm, by fall of ash and force of water, destroyed the ancient Minoan civilization of Crete. Could it not also have caused the phenomena described in Exodus?

The opinion of the renowned seismologist Professor Galanopoulos suggests that this could have been so. He considers that the crossing of the Red Sea may be explained by a tsunamis resulting from the Santorin eruption.*

For the peculiarity of a tsunamis is that at first the water retreats, leaving a portion of the seabed dry. Then a gigantic and terrifying wall of water rears out of the sea and overwhelms the land.

The Red Sea would have been unaffected by the disaster. But many have considered that the Hebrew words *Jam Suf* should be translated "Sea of Reeds," not "Red Sea." Professor Galanopoulos suggests that this Sea of Reeds may be the Sirbonis Lake, a lagoon to the east of the Nile delta, and he mentions an inscription found at El 'Arîsh close to the lake, referring to a great Egyptian disaster that took place nearby.

A careful reading of the text of the Bible seems to bear out the professor's interpretation. When Moses and the Children of Israel fled, they journeyed from Raamses to Succoth and then encamped before Pihahiroth between Migdol and the sea. This means they must have been heading north, for Migdol is close to the Mediterranean and between the right branch of the Nile and the Sirbonis Lake.

The text continues: "And the Lord went before them by day in a pillar of cloud, to lead them the way and by night in a pillar of fire to give them light . . . He took not away the pillar of cloud by day nor the pillar of fire by night." The effect of the volcanic explosion on Santorin would produce exactly this effect of an overcast sky and a lurid glow in the

---

* See *Atlantis* by A. G. Galanopoulos and Edward Bacon for a more detailed account of the theory that the Santorin disaster and the Exodus phenomena were related, also that the numerals recorded by the Egyptian and Hebrew scribes have been misinterpreted and that the number of adults following Moses was not six-hundred-thousand but as few as six-hundred families.

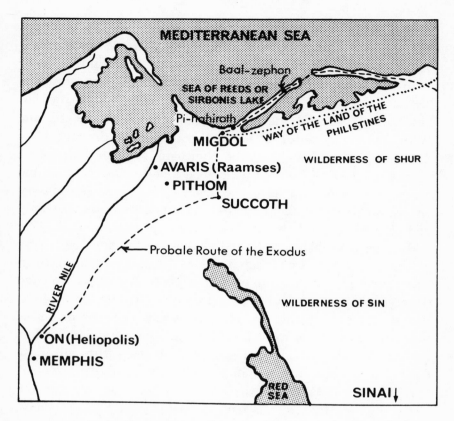

NOTE ON MAP: *It is interesting that a prominent school of modern Jewish thought places the route of the Exodus along the Mediterranean coast, since the names of two places mentioned in the Bible are found in other records. Migdol (tower) was one of a chain of forts guarding ''The Way of the Land of the Philistines'' and Baal-zephon was a sailor's shrine situated on the land strip north of the Serbonis Sea.*

darkness. The Bible says that God led the people, "not through the way of the Land of the Philistines although that was near . . . but through the way of the wilderness of the Red [Reed?] Sea." The way of the Philistines bordered the landward side of the Sirbonis Lake and was the main road from Egypt to Syria. The Biblical text suggests that they turned off this road. The word *near* cannot mean that they were sixty miles to the south on the Red Sea. And if they had fled from the armies of Egypt along the narrow isthmus of the Sirbonis Lake and crossed the gap in the land at the very moment that the waters of the sea recoiled they would indeed have had "a wall of waters on their left." After the miracle* of the crossing, Moses led his people into the Wilderness of Shur, south of the Sirbonis Lake. The Biblical text seems to bear out the theory that the drama of the Exodus, a story that has moved the imagination of millions, took place on the Mediterranean littoral. If it is valid to assume that the Exodus and the explosion of the Santorin volcano took place simultaneously, we should at last be able to date this unique event with some degree of accuracy. The first eruption occurred on Santorin about 1500 B.C. It was a local disaster only and the Minoan inhabitants of the island were able to flee, taking most of their goods and chattels with them. A period of quiescence followed, then a further eruption. The pattern was repeated. For twenty or thirty years the active volcano deposited layer upon layer of volcanic pumice and ash on the island and during this period unusual natural disturbances must also have been experienced by all the countries bordering the eastern Mediterranean. Could some record of these disturbances be contained in the account of the plagues of Egypt? For J. C. Bennett, director of the Institute for the Comparative Study of History, Philosophy, and the Sciences, has independently also reached the conclusion that the prodigious eruption on Santorin was responsible for the Biblical plagues.

An appalling explosion about 1480 B.C. blocked the sea routes with floating pumice and ended the civilization of Minoan Crete. The Bible tells us Moses was eighty years old at the time of the Exodus. If this was the case and the Exodus took place circa 1480, then Moses would have been born in 1560. Both this date and the date of the Santorin explosion are approximate but an attempt should be made to fit the great prophet's life into a new context in Egyptian history.

King Amosis, founder of the Eighteenth dynasty, began

* "For those that believe that the plagues and the crossing of the waters were miracles of Divine Providence alone, the miracle lies in the timing of the occurrences, the synchronising of events. Moses is divinely guided to take advantage of the mechanism of occurrences whose manifestation obeys natural laws which are themselves the work of God." From *Atlantis* by Galanopoulos and Bacon

his reign in 1559. He was the warrior king who claimed to have driven the Hyksos from Egypt. But recent evidence seems to indicate that the Hyksos wars lasted longer than was supposed. He was still besieging the Hyksos stronghold of Avaris in the eleventh year of his twenty-five year reign. And it is significant that the last pocket of Hyksos resistance was at Heliopolis, and the first Theban king to build a palace at Memphis was Amosis's grandson, Thutmose I.

Flavius Josephus, the great Jewish historian, wrote in the first century A.D. and recounted the youth of Moses at the Egyptian court. After praising his unusual beauty, strength, and understanding, he writes that the Egyptian Princess Thermuthis "perceiving him to be so remarkable a child, adopted him for her son having no child of her own. And when one time she had carried Moses to her father to show him the child and said she thought to make him her father's successor . . . she put the infant into her father's hands: so he took him and hugged him close to his breast: and on his daughter's account in a pleasant way, put his diadem upon his head; but Moses threw it down to the ground."

Both the "sacred scribe" who was present and the king were shocked at this evil omen and wished to kill Moses but Thermuthis prevented them, snatching the child away.

"And the king was not hasty to slay him, God himself whose providence protected Moses, inclining the king to spare him. He was therefore educated with great care. So the Hebrews depended on him and were of good hopes that great things would be done by him; but the Egyptians were suspicious of what would follow such his education. *Yet because, if Moses had been slain, there was no one either akin or adopted, that had any oracle on his side for pretending to the crown of Egypt, and likely to be of greater advantage to them, they abstained from killing him* [author's italics]."

From what we know of the ancient Egyptian laws of succession it would have been virtually impossible for Moses, an adopted child and a foreigner, to have been heir presumptive to the throne of the Memphite kings. Only if he was the son of either the sun king or the solar princess would his claims have been valid. Was the picturesque story quoted above a fabrication?

Josephus stated not once but twice that the Exodus took place in the reign of Thutmose and the scientists seem to have proved that this was indeed the case. So it is unwise to ignore the written records. But Moses was first and foremost an Israelite. How then can he have been considered heir to the Horus god-king?

If the early date of Moses's birth, 1560, is accepted, a revolutionary new theory can be advanced. For it is now considered that Amosis conquered the Hyksos only toward the end of his twenty-five-year reign. Manetho stated that the king who finally expelled the foreigners was "Thummosis" (Amosis?) and that the expelled people settled in Judea and founded the city of Jerusalem. The question is problematical and is bound to create controversy, but the volcanic explosion on Santorin and its approximate date has been proved. If the Exodus took place at the same time, the childhood of Moses can be studied in a new light. He is seen to be no longer a pseudo-royal changeling, placed at court in a false position among the enemies of his people, but a prince among princes allied, surely, by blood as well as race to the royal family of the Semitic Hyksos. To Manetho the Hyksos and the Israelites were one and the same people. "This nation called Shepherds [Hyksos] were also called captives in their sacred books," he wrote.

The main reasons heretofore for dating Moses's birth to the Nineteenth dynasty have been that in the first place it was the prelude to not only a change of kings but also of dynasties. This is made clear by Josephus and in the Book of Exodus. In the second place both sources give the length of time spent by the Israelites in Egypt as four hundred years. But in two separate instances Josephus shows that he or his translators confused the word *generation* with *century* and that when he wrote four hundred years he meant four generations.*

* The ancestry of Moses as given by Josephus is that Levi (founder of the priestly caste and brother of Jacob) begat Caath, who begat Amram, who begat Moses. This genealogy does not imply a period of four hundred years. Joseph was the brother of Moses's grandfather Caath.

In foreign policy Horemheb, last king of the Eighteenth dynasty, and the first Ramses saw alike and actively engaged in Syrian wars. But for the Israelites the change from a Hyksos ruler to a Theban pharaoh must have been the change from warmth to cold, peace to war, plenty to virtual slavery. No wonder the Children of Israel wrote of "a king who knew not Joseph" and remembered the bitterness of their sufferings under the enemy.

This is not the occasion to develop the theory that the Hyksos royal family were exterminated and their followers driven out of Egypt during Moses's exile, or that Moses returned to face the Theban king as prince as well as prophet. That Moses came at God's instance to do God's will is the message of the Bible. Could his leadership have been readily accepted by the Israelites because he was the last of their royal line?

Whatever the truth of these suppositions, the concern of Akhenaten's biographer is in the religious beliefs that led one man to found a nation and become one of the great prophets of mankind and another to impose a state monotheism that ended in disaster.

The confused tale recounted by Manetho forms a pattern only if Moses's early date is accepted and it is recognized that the historian is combining the lives of two very different men in one narrative.

Manetho wrote, "King Amenophis [Amenhotep] was desirous to become a spectator of the gods, as had Orus, one of his predecessors in that kingdom, desired the same before him; he also communicated his desire to his namesake who was the son of *Papis,* and one that seemed to partake of a divine nature both as to wisdom and the knowledge of futurities."

The king referred to above was Akhenaten's father. There were four King Amenhoteps but only one whose namesake, the son of Hapu, was renowned as a sage. But what does "becoming a spectator of the gods" mean? Did Amenhotep seek spiritual enlightenment from his prophet, who was perhaps a disciple of Moses? Did his predecessor Orus (or

Horus) refer to Thutmose IV in whose reign the worship of the sun's disk was first established; or the god-king Menes of the first dynasty?

Manetho then relates how Amenhotep the son of Hapu told the king "that he might see the gods, if he would clear the whole country of the lepers and of the other impure people; that the king was pleased with his injunction, and got together all that had any defect in their bodies out of Egypt, and that their number was eighty thousand whom he sent to those quarries which were on the east side of the Nile, that they might work in them and be separated from the rest of the Egyptians."

Lysimachus, the Greek historian, has an alternative version of this account: "The king of Egypt sent some to consult the oracle of Hammon [Amen] . . . the god's answer was this, that he must purge his temples of impure and impious men by expelling them out of those temples . . . the sun having an indignation at these men being suffered to live."

Here Lysimachus establishes without doubt that the people to be expelled suffered in the eyes of the "establishment" from spiritual not physical defects. And Manetho also made this clear in his next passage: "There were some of the learned priests that were polluted with the leprosy; but that still this Amenophis, the wise man and prophet, was afraid that the gods would be angry at him and at the king, if there should appear to have been violence offered to them; who also added this further (out of his sagacity about futurities), that certain people would come to the assistance of these polluted wretches, and would conquer Egypt, and would keep it in their possession thirteen years . . ."

It is evident that Akhenaten's name was deleted from Manetho's source material but not the length of his reign (twelve years, five months), and it can be guessed that at this point Manetho found his source manuscript so confused that he could make neither head nor tail of it. He therefore grafted onto it another story bearing some relation to the first and seeming to supply the missing half.

"After, the king was desired he would set apart (for the

polluted) the city of Avaris which was left desolate of the shepherds. When these men were gotten into it . . . they appointed themselves a ruler out of the priests of Heliopolis, whose name was Osarsiph, and they took their oaths that they would be obedient to him in all things. He then, in the first place, made this law for them, that they should neither worship the Egyptian gods, nor should abstain from any one of those sacred animals which they have in the highest esteem but kill and destroy them all; that they should join themselves to no body but to those that were of this confederacy. He made such laws as these and many more such as were plainly opposed to the customs of the Egyptians . . ."

The manuscript then branches into a dramatic description of war between north and south, which can have nothing to do with Akhenaten but perhaps a great deal to do with Moses.

Only the spiritual side of Moses's life is shown in the Bible. Manetho's narrative suggests that he was also a great general, led his people, fortified Avaris, sent to his Hyksos connections in Jerusalem for reinforcements, and for a short period drove the Thebans south into Nubia.

Seen in the new context of Moses as a prophet and a Hyksos general, Manetho's narrative is enthralling but cannot be elaborated upon here. Manetho ends his story: "The priest who ordained their polity and their laws was by birth of Heliopolis; and his name Osarsiph from Osiris who was the god of Heliopolis; but that when he was gone over to these people (the polluted people) his name was changed, and he was called Moses."

For Akhenaten's biographer the interest lies in what made Manetho equate the heretic pharaoh's life with that of Moses? The argument in this book has been that Atenism originated in the north at Heliopolis. Could Moses, the priest of Heliopolis, have inspired some of his fellows with his breadth of vision and spiritual insight? And could these have originated the cult of the Aten? Moses, according to Manetho, was attached to the shrine of Osiris, god of resurrection, most spiritual of all the Egyptian gods. But some memory of the god Moses worshiped in spirit and truth could, after his departure from Egypt, have given rise to the cult of Aten, the "faceless disk." Is there any significance in the fact that the first mention of "the disk" is found in the reign of Amenhotep I, son of Amosis?

The age of Moses at the time of the Exodus (eighty years) and of the Santorin explosion 1480 are approximate. But granted that the volcanic disaster and the Exodus happened at the same time, then Moses was brought up at the Memphite court before the expulsion of the Hyksos. He returned from his exile in the reign of Thutmose I and led his people out of Egypt under Thutmose II. Sixty years later Thutmose IV, a Memphite prince, openly embraced the cult of the Aten. Several could have been still alive who retained personal recollections of the great Israelite leader and prophet.

It can now be seen that the culmination of true Atenism in Egypt may not have been brought about by Akhenaten but by Amenhotep, the son of Hapu, that renowned sage whose wisdom led to succeeding generations worshiping him as a godlike being. Akhenaten's Atenism with its insistence on worship of his own person and its fanaticism may have been, as Manetho suggests, a schism from a new and truer understanding of a spiritual god. Manetho's account relating to Amenhotep III and his age would not have been effaced by the iconoclasts and there is no reason to doubt that it reflects the actual state of affairs between the older king, his counselor, and the headstrong young idealist with his own band of devoted followers. What more natural than that the king and the son of Hapu were "afraid that the gods would be angry if there should appear to have been violence offered" to the new regime? And that the eventual solution to an awkward problem was the establishment of the City of the Horizon and a modus vivendi that enabled the two royal families to live in amity for the remaining years of Amenhotep III's life.

AKHENATEN'S HYMN TO THE SUN

(AFTER JAMES BREASTED)

THE SPLENDOR OF ATEN

Thy dawning is beautiful in the horizon of heaven,
O living Aten, Beginning of life!
When thou risest in the eastern horizon of heaven,
Thou fillest every land with thy beauty;
For thou are beautiful, great, glittering, high over the earth;
Thy rays, they encompass the lands, even all thou hast made.
Thou art Ra, and thou hast carried them all away captive;
Thou bindest them by thy love.
Though thou art afar, thy rays are on earth;
Though thou art on high, thy footprints are the day.

NIGHT

When thou settest in the
western horizon of heaven,
The world is in darkness
like the dead.
They sleep in their chambers,
Their heads are wrapt up,
Their nostrils stopped, and
none seeth the other
Stolen are all their things,
that are under their heads,
While they know it not.
Every lion cometh forth from
his den,
All serpents, they sting.
Darkness reigns(?),
The World is in silence,
He that made them has gone to
rest in his horizon.
Thou makest darkness and it is
Night,
Wherein all the beasts of the
forest do creep forth.

*The young lions roar after their
    prey;
They seek their meat from God.*
(PSALM 104, 20-21)

DAY AND MAN
*Bright is the earth,
When thou risest in the horizon,
When thou shinest as Aten by
    day,
The darkness is banished,
When thou sendest forth thy
    rays,
The Two Lands (Egypt) are
    in daily festivity,
Awake and standing upon their
    feet,
For thou hast raised them up.
Their limbs bathed, they take
    their clothing;
Their arms uplifted in adoration
    to thy dawning.
Then in all the world, they do
    their work.
The sun ariseth, they get them
    away
And lay them down in their
    dens.
Man goeth forth unto his work,
And to his labour until the evening.*
(PSALM 104, 22-23)

DAY AND THE ANIMALS AND PLANTS
*All cattle rest upon their herbage,
All trees and plants flourish,
The birds flutter in their marches,
Their wings uplifted in adoration to thee.
All the sheep dance upon their feet.
All winged things fly,
They live when thou hast shone upon them.*

DAY AND THE WATERS
*The barques sail up-stream and
    down-stream alike.*

*Every highway is open because
    thou hast dawned.
The fish in the river leap up
    before thee,
And thy rays are in the midst
    of the great sea.
Yonder is the sea, great
    and wide,
Wherein are things creeping
    innumerable
Both small and great beasts.
    There go the ships;
There is leviathan, whom thou
    hast formed to sport with him.*
(PSALM 104, 25-26)

CREATION OF MAN
*Thou art he who createst the man-child in woman,
Who makest seed in man,
Who giveth life to the son in the body of his mother,
Who soothest him that he may not weep,
A nurse (even) in the womb.
Who giveth breath to animate every one that he maketh.
When he cometh forth from the body,
. . . on the day of his birth,
Thou openest his mouth in speech,
Thou suppliest his necessities.*

CREATION OF ANIMALS
*When the chicklet crieth in the egg-shell,
Thou givest him breath therein, to preserve him alive.
When thou hast perfected him
That he may pierce the egg,
He cometh forth from the egg,
To chirp with all his might;
He runneth about upon his two feet,
When he hath come forth therefrom.*

THE WHOLE CREATION
*How manifold are all thy works!
They are hidden from before us,
O thou sole god, whose powers no
    other possesseth.**

* The other hymns frequently say, "O thou sole god, beside whom there is no other."

Thou didst create the earth according
to thy desire.
While thou wast alone:
Men, all cattle large and small,
All that are upon the earth,
That go about upon their feet;
All that are on high,
That fly with their wings.
The countries of Syria and
Nubia,
The land of Egypt;
Thou settest every man in his
place,
Thou suppliest their necessities.
Every one has his possessions,
And his days are reckoned.
Their tongues are divers in
speech,
Their forms likewise and their
skins,
For thou divider has divided
the peoples.
O lord, how manifold are they
works!
In wisdom hast thou made them all;
The earth is full of thy creatures.
(PSALM 104, 24)

WATERING THE EARTH

Thou makest the Nile in the Nether World,
Thou bringest it at thy desire, to preserve the people alive.
O lord of them all, when feebleness is in them,
O lord of every house, who risest for them,
O sun of day, the fear of every distant land,
Thou makest (also) their life.
Thou hast set a Nile in heaven,
That it may fall for them,
Making floods upon the mountains, like the great sea;
And watering their field among their towns.

How excellent are thy designs, O lord of eternity!
The Nile in heaven is for the strangers,
And for the cattle of every land, that go upon their feet;
But the Nile, it cometh from the nether world for Egypt.

Thus thy rays nourish every garden,
When thou risest they live, and grow by thee.

THE SEASONS

Thou makest the seasons, in order to create all thy works:
Winter bringing them coolness,
And the heat (of summer likewise).
Thou hast made the distant heaven to rise therein,
In order to behold all that thou didst make,
While thou wast alone,
Rising in thy form as living Aten,
Dawning, shining afar off and returning.

BEAUTY DUE TO LIGHT

Thou makest the beauty of form, through thyself alone.
Cities, towns and settlements,
On highway or on river,
All eyes see thee before them,
For thou art Aten of the day over the earth.

REVELATION TO THE KING

Thou art in my heart,
There is no other that knoweth thee,
Save thy son Akhenaten.
Thou hast made him wise in thy designs
And in thy might.
The world is in thy hand,
Even as thou hast made them.
When thou hast risen, they live;
When thou settest, they die.
For thou art duration, beyond thy mere limbs,
By thee man liveth,
And their eyes look upon thy beauty,
Until thou settest.
All labour is laid aside,
When thou settest in the west;
When thou risest, they are made to grow
. . . for the king.
Since thou didst establish the earth,
Thou hast raised them up for thy son,
Who came forth from thy limbs,
The king, living in truth,
The lord of the Two Lands Neferkheprure, Wanenre,
The son of Ra, living in truth, lord of diadems,
Akhenaten, whose life is long;
(And for) the great royal wife, his beloved,
Mistress of the Two Lands, Nefernefruaten, Nefertiti,
Living and flourishing for ever and ever.

GENEALOGY OF THE 18TH DYNASTY KINGS

KING	MARRIAGE
Amosis, first king of the dynasty, 1559–1531 B.C. Reigned 25 years, 4 months.	Married his full sister Ahmose.
Amenhotep I became with his mother Ahmose the patron of the Theban necropolis. Son of Amosis. 1534–1504 B.C. Reigned 20 years, 7 months.	Married his full sister Ahhotep.
Thutmose I. His mother was Sensenb. He may have come from a collateral branch of the royal family. Reigned 1514–1502 B.C., 13 years.	Married the Solar Princess Ahmose, daughter of Amenhotep and Ahhotep.
Thutmose II, son of Thutmose I, suffered from a skin complaint that was noted on his mummy (leprosy?). Perhaps for this reason he was overshadowed by his wife who held the reins of government and became regent on his death. 1504–1489 B.C., 12 years, 9 months.	Married his half sister the famous Queen Hatshepsut who governed alone for many years and built herself the beautiful mortuary temple at Deir el-Bahri. She was a solar princess through her mother.
Thutmose III, son of either Thutmose I or II by a concubine Isis. He was chosen to succeed by the Theban priests when still a child, and nominally was coregent with Hatshepsut. Her reign and his coregency lasted 25 years, 10 months. He then reigned a further 21 years, 9 months, 1490–1436 B.C.	Married as a child to Hatshepsut's daughter Nefrure Hatshepsut, the solar princess.
Amenhotep II was the son, it is supposed, of Thutmose III and Nefrure Hatshepsut. Reigned 1444–1412.	Married his full sister but no male heir survived infancy. He had two daughters by his wife, Yaret and Mutemwaya? (see text).
Thutmose IV was the son of Amenhotep II by a Queen Tia. He seems to have been chosen to succeed, as was Thutmose III, at the age of eight and died of a wasting disease at the age of twenty-five. Reigned 1414–1405, 9 years, 8 months.	Married Mutemwaya who was most likely but not certainly the surviving solar princess.
Amenhotep III, son of Thutmose IV and Mutemwaya. His reign saw the climacteric of the eighteenth dynasty. 1405–1367. See discussion on the coregency with Akhenaten.	Married Tyi whose provenance is discussed in Chapter II. She was not a solar princess and Amenhotep III thought it necessary to marry his own daughter, Sitamen. Tyi brought fresh blood to the effete royal line and had many children. Was Nefertiti one of them?
Amenhotep IV (Akhenaten) 1378–1362.	Married Nefertiti.

CONQUESTS

Amosis claimed to have driven the Hyksos out of Egypt but the war continued during much of his reign.

Amenhotep I made war against the Nubians of the south and established his frontier at least as far south as Semna. He waged a successful campaign against Libya and against the princes of Syria.

Thutmose I made war in Nubia and reached the first cataract. He also campaigned in Syria and was the first king of the dynasty to reach the Euphrates where he set up a victory stela. He was the first king of the eighteenth dynasty to establish a palace at Memphis. This may indicate that the north was not wholly dominated until his reign.

Thutmose II campaigned in Libya and Syria. He made war against the rebellious kingdom of Kush (in the south).
His queen, Hatshepsut, made an expedition, now famous, to the land of Punt.

Thutmose III was the great conqueror and "Napoleon" of ancient Egypt. Nubia and the south were pacified but he led seventeen victorious armies into Asia until the overlordship of Egypt was acknowledged throughout the civilized world of the "fertile crescent."

The captive peoples revolted on the death of Thutmose III and Amenhotep II was forced to wage war in both Nubia and Syria. He reached the Euphrates and parleyed with the chiefs of the Mitanni. He seems to have been almost as much of a warrior-king as his father.

The south, which had been pacified, revolted again in the reign of Thutmose IV. He crushed the revolt in year 8 of his reign and brought back numerous captives of Kush to Thebes.

Amenhotep III's activities in the south were mainly confined to erecting numerous buildings although he put down a small uprising in year 5. Egypt's subject nations remained quiescent until the reign of Akhenaten.

* There are many gaps in our knowledge of the eighteenth dynasty kings and queens. Was Thutmose I the son of Amenhotep I? Was Thutmose III the son of Thutmose I or II? Was Mutemwaya as well as Yaret a full solar princess? We can ask, we can conjecture, but we cannot answer as yet with any certainty. The dates given conform to the revised dating suggested by Professor Cyril Aldred.

ADDITIONAL NOTE

Mention should be made of a recent attempt to fit together some of the thousands of blocks that remain of Akhenaten's Theban temple to the sun's disk. Ray Winfield Smith determined to piece together, with the help of a computer, some of these myriads of stones. And in the *National Geographic Magazine* for November 1970 he describes how this was done and his startling conclusions. That Akhenaten built a temple at Thebes to the Aten (or added to or altered an existing one established by his father Amenhotep III) has long been known—but not that it appears to have been nearly a mile in length.. Nor was it realized that in this complex stood a large precinct built, it seems, for the glorification of Nefertiti alone. Winfield Smith reconstructed a "unique ceremonial enclosure," open to the sky, where stood seven square pillars six feet a side broad and twelve feet high. Each surface was decorated with scenes of Nefertiti "facing herself across an offering table, endlessly repeated," under the Aten rays and flanked by one or two princesses. Winfield Smith stresses that these pillars "bore not a single mention of Akhenaten nor even any inscriptional mention of him."

In this book special effort has been made to stress the importance of the queen and the sun princess in the eighteenth dynasty. The queen as well as the king was held to be divine, but of course only the royal queen through whom the king inherited the throne, There is, therefore, nothing unusual in finding that Nefertiti was deified. The interest for the historian is that it seems to prove that she *was* of pure royal descent, and Akhenaten's sister, as concluded by the author. The absence of any inscription to Akhenaten is most interesting. The new Aten worship extoling the reproductive powers of the sun tended to underline the esoteric worship of the female principal. It is suggested that the "ceremonial enclosure" reconstructed by Winfield Smith was a Theban example of a "Sunshade of Ra." The inscriptions at Tel el Amarna mention several of these "sunshades" built not only to Nefertiti but also to the Queen Mother Tyi and several of the princesses. They also were open to the sky and are thought to have been temples where the divine female could enter into mystical communion with the sun's disk.

The depiction of one or two princesses on the pillars reconstructed by Winfield Smith and his team is significant, and the author suggests that the Theban temple may have been dedicated to Nefertiti on her fulfilling her divine mission and giving birth to a new heiress, a new sun princess. Certainly at Tel el Amarna Akhenaten's precedence over his queen is everywhere stressed. In addition there is erasure of the queen's name from the Maru Aten.

Strangely enough, Winfield Smith found also that the Theban representations of Nefertiti had been mutilated in antiquity by "having their facial features, bodies, and limbs hacked away." Since the mutilated blocks were found in the pylon built by Horemheb, Winfield Smith naturally assumes that it was he who had desecrated Nefertiti's images. But at Tel el Amarna the erasure of Nefertiti's name and its replacement by Smenkhare's queen (Nefertiti's daughter Meritaten) preceded Horemheb's reign. It is almost certain that these defacements were made at Akhenaten's orders. Since it was at his instigation also that the names of all the gods except Aten were removed from the walls of the Theban temples, is it not likely to have been he who so savagely mutilated the many representations of the queen? The rays bringing her benison from the Aten disk were also cut through but not the disk itself or the name. Would such an anti-Atenist as Horemheb professed to be have left these last untouched? It is at least a strong possibility that evidence of Akhenaten's antagonism to his queen during the last years of his reign has been found at Thebes.

Finally Winfield Smith's fascinating new discoveries do suggest another motive for Akhenaten's *volteface* with regard to Nefertiti— jealousy of her equally divine status in the Aten cult. In the author's opinion the extraordinary representations of Akhenaten that were made at the beginning of his reign and show hermaphroditic characteristics were of esoteric significance. When Akhenaten forced his artists to represent him half-female was he trying to override the matriarchal image vital to Egyptian religion? Was this the impulse that drove him finally to repudiate Nefertiti and "marry" his brother Smenkhare?

(NOTE: The quotations are all from Ray Winfield Smith's article in the *National Geographic Magazine* for November, 1970.)

INDEX

The index includes the gods of the Egyptian pantheon, members of the Egyptian royal family and their courtiers, the main Egyptian sites mentioned in the book, and writers, explorers and authorities.

This book may be kept

FOURTEEN DAYS

A fine will be charged for each day the book is kept overtime.

FEB 28			
MAR 14			
SEP 29			
APR 05			
GAYLORD 142			PRINTED IN U.S.A.